SUPERFANDOM

SUPERFANDOM

HOW OUR OBSESSIONS ARE CHANGING
WHAT WE BUY AND WHO WE ARE

ZOE FRAADE-BLANAR
&
AARON M. GLAZER

W. W. NORTON & COMPANY
Independent Publishers Since 1923
NEW YORK | LONDON

For information about permission to reproduce selections from this book,
write to Permissions, W. W. Norton & Company, Inc.,
500 Fifth Avenue, New York, NY 10110

For information about special discounts for bulk purchases, please contact
W. W. Norton Special Sales at specialsales@wwnorton.com or 800-233-4830

Manufacturing by Berryville Graphics
Book design by Fearn Cutler de Vicq
Production manager: Julia Druskin

ISBN 978-0-393-24995-8

W. W. Norton & Company, Inc.
500 Fifth Avenue, New York, N.Y. 10110
www.wwnorton.com

W. W. Norton & Company Ltd.
15 Carlisle Street, London W1D 3BS

1 2 3 4 5 6 7 8 9 0

CONTENTS

PREFACE

October 29, 2012, New York City

The Weather Channel had warned us a hurricane was coming, but we weren't too worried about it. Irene had passed through the year before with barely a downed tree, and anyway it was too late to change our plans.

Two nights before Halloween, the staff of Squishable.com, Inc. was getting ready for a party. A virtual Halloween party. Twice before, our fans had surprised us by throwing secret parties on our Facebook page, flooding our timeline with hand-drawn pictures and photos of themselves and their stuffed animals decked out in party regalia, baking cookies, playing games, and generally having a good time. This time we were hosting the party ourselves. The invites had been posted days earlier on numerous social-media platforms, and hundreds of Squishable fans around the globe had already RSVP'd to say that they would (virtually) be there.

New York had preemptively declared a state of emergency, shutting down the subways, so our team was working from various locations around the city. On Facebook, a superfan like Dani would post, "We're watching the weather channel, worrying about all our friends on the coast. Please stay safe!!! On a different subject—will the Halloween party be postponed?" For days, we'd been looking at each other and whispering, "What should we say?" Even with only hours to go, every so often one of us would chime in on our internal chat client with some version of "So . . . maybe this isn't the night for this?" and we'd all Google the weather yet again.*

We didn't want to disappoint anyone, and anyway preparations had already taken up three prime workdays when we should have been designing new products or approving fur samples. None of us had the traditional business background that might have warned about the dangers of the sunk-cost fallacy. The storm's name hardly sounded threatening. Sandy? Really?

Squishable is a technology company with a toy habit, so the internal joke goes. We create stuffed animals. Big ones, little ones, quirky stuffed animals. As a rule the entire team has always been made up of refugees from other industries—software design, law, finance, government, media—and early on it allowed us to bypass a lot of pitfalls. Most toy companies sold largely wholesale; we sold more than half our stock directly off our website. Most toy companies released six to twelve new items per line a year; we released hundreds. Most toy companies targeted kids; we had plenty of kid fans, but our most active audience was teens and young adults. Most toy companies used a design team to come up with new ideas; we used our fans—their concepts, their design input, and, eventually, their drawings. We may have been the first company to ever release a plush Shrimp, Cthulhu, Grim Reaper, and Slice of Toast.

Earlier that year, we'd decided to try a Kickstarter campaign

---

* Please note that here and throughout the book we reproduce all social-media posts in their original, unedited form.

for a Squishable Shiba Inu, a design we hadn't originally planned to make. It had come in second in a contest to determine the next dog breed to be prototyped, ranking just behind the Corgi (which had gone on to become a bestseller.) The Kickstarter launched with the concept art: a red dog with circular eye patches. The answer had been a resounding yes, yes, yes: the fans loved our red Shiba design concept and would gladly wait for the product to be manufactured, shipped, and released.

In early October, the Kickstarter was long over. The prototype pictures had just been posted when we received an unexpected fan comment: now that she saw the actual photo, she thought it should be colored gold, with different eye patches. Suddenly, angry comments filled our Kickstarter, Facebook, and inbox. We had ruined the design. We were evil. We had betrayed them. They were reporting us to Kickstarter. They would never buy another Squishable again.

We felt terrible. How had it all gone so wrong? I bit my fingernails bloody every night agonizing over what to do. We wanted to stay on the fans' good side, but we hadn't budgeted for a second variation. There were tears. Had we torpedoed the whole company by trying something innovative? Ahhh...

By late October, the office was tense. It was the right time for a feel-good event, a way to remind everyone that we were bigger than the color of a Shiba Inu. We wouldn't get a chance like this for another year. In fact, once the holiday rush started in another couple of weeks, it would be all we could do to update social media at all. And besides, we really liked our fans.

At the time, there were only three of us on the creative team to run the party: designers Melissa and Kendra, and myself. Scott, our office manager, was prepping the content and materials. Everyone in the company planned to make at least one virtual appearance—even Charles, our general counsel, would join in.

Because everyone else lived in Brooklyn or Queens, the photography props had been dragged from our Union Square office over to the thirteenth-floor one-bedroom Aaron and I shared by the East River in Manhattan, just barely outside the mandatory evacuation zone. We knew there might be a power outage, so we had brought over half a dozen fully charged laptops. Between a Verizon Fios line, two different cell phone hot spots, and, if all else failed, a battered old Sprint cell modem from 2010, which we'd forgotten to cancel, there were plenty of paths to the Internet in case of emergency.

The fans had been posting their defiance for hours:

"Dear Sandy: do NOT knock out mine or anyone else's power! We have a very squishy holiday party to attend! If you do, you will have to answer to MY wrath!! WRATH!! HELL HATH NO FURY LIKE A SQUISHER SCORNED!!!" wrote Mel.

"I am prepared for Frankenstorm. If we need to evacuate, I am demanding everyone take one full size squishable and one mini. The micros we be hanging on my mom's bag. COME AT MEH BRO!" wrote Samantha.

"Be safe during Frankenstorm everyone! . . . Hopefully your house/apartment won't flood and your Squishables won't get wet!" posted Oceanus, the mini Squishable Narwhal, presumably by way of its owner.

With two hours to go, superfan Sara posted, "Is everyone ready for the Halloween Party?!?!?!?!? I can't wait!! I have costumes ready for some of my squishy friends and I have to make some refreshments when I get home from work today. We carved pumpkins last night so I have to roast the seeds, make pumpkin muffins, popcorn and hot cocoa! I also have some candy and caramel apples too! So excited for a fun and delicious night!!"

Canceling was not an option. We were Squishable! We could weather a stinking superhurricane!

As the wind began to blow like it really meant it, Aaron and I ventured outdoors one more time, passing boarded-up windows and piles of sandbags by the subway entrances. We tried, and failed, to pick up extra batteries for the flashlights, and succeeded in buying the very last available bag of dog food for Oyster, our Yorkie-poodle puppy. Then we went home, filled the bathtub and sinks with water, opened some beers, and waited for seven p.m.

"I'm out—stay safe and dry guys!" wrote Beth, head of the customer-service team, from her home out in Michigan.

As 7:00 hit the Eastern seaboard, pictures started flowing into the Facebook page from early arrivals. "ok! here we go!" typed Melissa into our internal chat client. We posted our welcome to Facebook, and hundreds of fans wrote back variations of:

"WHOOOOO PARTY PARTY!!!"

"Party Time HERE!!!!!!!!!!!! Hoo WAH!!!!!!!"

"Beware! It is a guest arriving in the middle of gale force winds."

"YAYYY! PARTY! :D ME AND MY 13 SQUISHIES ARE HERE!"

"TRICK OR SQUISH!!!!"

. . . and flooded the page with pictures of stuffed animals decked out like ghosts and pirates.

It started to rain at seven-thirty p.m. as we posted the rules for the limerick contest. At 7:45 it *really* started to rain as we posted the first photo of Squishables partying. From Sunset Park in south Brooklyn, Melissa posted a video of Michael Jackson's "Thriller." To the east, in Bedford-Stuyvesant, Kendra posted black-and-white line art for fans to color. Melissa posted a call for drawing ideas. I put up photos of a Squishable Narwhal in a bowl of candy corn and a Squishable Horse bobbing for apples. We used personal Facebook accounts so the fans would know it was really us, and our posts mixed with hundreds of pictures from across the country: Squishable Gryphons dressed as Harry Potter characters, axolotls dressed like Sailor Moon, a bride-and-groom cow and bull, and a raccoon TV announcer.

"Can somebody draw me a narwhal?"

"I am making Zoe & Cthulhu cookies!!!!"

"Do any of you people know how difficult it is to come up costumes for 96 squishables?!"

"There was once a Squish from Nantucket . . ."

"This FB party is totally cheering me up :)"

The windows on the thirteenth floor were rattling in their frames. Down below, a family coming home from a hurricane party was tackled to the ground by a bunch of quick-thinking college kids just before mom, dad, and baby stepped into a wind tunnel between two buildings. They were all right, but their dog had to be reeled in from the flow by his leash.

We stuck to the timeline, tensely submitting each post on schedule. Costume contest at 8:00. Coloring-book page at 8:15. Photo of pumpkin decorating at 8:20. Melissa became overwhelmed by fan drawing requests and Kendra took over. Cell coverage turned spotty, and none of the drawings were posting from phones as planned.

"hahaha omg none of them are coming through. Omg. and there are more requests haha. halp," wrote Melissa.[*]

"We laugh because otherwise we'd cry," wrote Kendra. "I am gonna have grey hair by the end of tonight."

During a lull, we opened one of the backup computers and brought up Twitter and CNN. Battery Park City to the south was underwater. Avenue C a couple blocks to the east was underwater. Hoboken was underwater. The subways were underwater. Through

---

[*]   Using the unedited text of social-media posts in this books saves us from correcting our own transcribed spelling and grammar mistakes too.

the windows, we could see the East River, a whole lot closer than it was before. We found out later that even as we typed, the massive NYU Langone Medical Center ten blocks north had lost its backup generators, its staff scrambling to evacuate patients and babies down its darkened stairwells.

"how are you guys fairing the hurricaine!?!? hope you're okay!" posted fan Rachel.

We forwarded updates of pending power outages to each other. "#ConEd has begun the process of shutting off electrical service to a part of Brooklyn, to protect both company and customer equipment," we warned our Brooklynites. In return, they posted photos from Twitter showing cars floating by, blocks from our apartment.

"Zoe, no offense, this FB party is a beautiful and terrible thing, and our reach is going to explode, but let's never ever ever do this again," Melissa wrote.

"I'm okay for now, just getting a little freaked!" wrote Kendra as the lights blinked on and off like mad.

"You don't have to stay on if you don't want—this is NOT your top priority."

"It's cool!" insisted Kendra. She later admitted she had been typing while huddled on the floor of her hallway, the only place in her apartment without windows, listening to the wind as it tore chunks of metal from her roof.

We posted and posted and posted, and the windows shook and the wind hooooowled, and the streets below turned into rivers. When we looked outside, the buildings around us had become dark, hulking islands rising up from the wet, with rain streaming down their sides. Could that possibly be *water*, pouring through below the FDR Drive? Oyster did not get his evening walk that night. I couldn't have pried him out from under the bed anyway.

At around eight-thirty p.m., just after we posted a picture of a jellyfish trick-or-treating, there was a huge flash of light and a boom from the southeast, and seconds later the lights flickered out for the final time. We would later learn that the big Con Ed transformer over on 14th Street had exploded and plunged the southern half of Manhattan into blackness. Outside the rain poured on and on and on.

We broke out the backup laptops and tried the Internet. It was down. We tried the cell phones. They were down. We tried the old Sprint cell modem. It was working—there was just enough bandwidth to send a final SOS across the river to Brooklyn, where we could still see the lights glowing faintly through the storm. *Tell Facebook we're offline but not to worry, tell them to keep partying without us.* Then those bars too went to zero.

So we sat in the dark and drank beers from the slowly warming fridge and laughed at how weird our lives had become.

The next morning we carried Oyster down thirteen flights of pitch-black stairs to survey the wreckage outside our door. The cars on 20th Street had floated inland and washed up everywhere, scattered across the sidewalk like LEGOs. Each was choked with debris up to the steering wheel. A huge railroad tie had been ripped out of the seawall and hurled on top of a Ford Mustang. The streets were clogged with dirt and sand and broken glass, with streams of brackish river water still cutting channels through the mess as it poured off the island. The bottom floor of the building next door had been torn apart, its crumpled door wedged half open in a deep pool of water like the remains of some kind of swampy apocalypse.

What seemed like the entire population of the East Village was standing on the beleaguered banks of the river, bundled in sweatshirts and blankets against the cold, their arms outstretched over their heads, cell phones held high in the wind to attract a signal off the distant towers in Brooklyn.

The first to contact us was Charles—he'd found working

Wi-Fi somewhere underneath the Brooklyn Bridge where he was sharing space with a dozen bedraggled financiers. Slowly, one by one, the Squishable staff checked in by text and email and chat to say they were damp but safe.

Scott volunteered to cover "the socials" and tell the world we were still here. He checked back in a few minutes later to say that after we had disappeared, a couple of superfans had taken over the party to answer questions about the costume contest, post music, draw pictures, and keep it going until long after midnight. At one point, they had sponsored a countrywide game of "Two Truths and a Lie."

"So happy to hear that everyone in NY is safe and squishy!" fan Cat had posted immediately. It was a perfect moment. Even spread across the city as we were, we all got a little choked up about it.

"That was a very high-octane social media thing we just did," commented Melissa.

As we prepared for the hike uptown, with its promise of working outlets, warm hotel rooms, and steaming, life-giving bowls of noodle soup, my phone chimed one more time. I checked my email. It was a superfan. She wanted to let us know that she was really really really pissed about the color of the Shiba Inu.

Zoe Fraade-Blanar

SUPERFANDOM

WELCOME TO THE FANDOM SINGULARITY

"I Never Tho't I Would Do That!"

In the summer of 1896, Alice Drake left her home in Colorado and boarded a transatlantic liner for Europe. She was young, moneyed, and attractive enough to provoke the occasional ribald comment from the locals. She was also a serviceable pianist.

The Grand Tour was a rite of passage for many an upper-class American during the nineteenth century. Young aristocrats (and their entourage of cooks, servants, tutors, and hangers-on) would travel a careful itinerary of European historical and cultural sites, journeying for months, or sometimes years. In many countries the tradition endures to this day as the "gap year," the "year abroad," or, in some cases, "She's still backpacking around Europe without a job? It's been, like, a year!"

Most parents steered their progeny toward the museums of the Netherlands and the churches and ruins of Italy. Perhaps there would be a stay in Paris for dancing or fencing lessons, or studying at the local art academies. But Alice's destination was not the ruins of Rome or the antiquities of Pisa. With her friend Gertrude by her side, she breezed through Belgium and on to Germany. Pausing only long enough to be homesick in Berlin, she made straight for the distant city of Weimar. There she located the home of composer Franz Liszt, who had died a decade earlier, and talked her way in.

It took two attempts. On the first try, Drake and some of her new friends arrived too late in the afternoon and were forced to content themselves with gawking at Liszt's conservatory. Undaunted, they started again early the next morning. Drake tracked down the surprised caretaker, a "dear old man," and slipped him three pfennigs to persuade him to unlock the door.

She played on Liszt's pianos! She ogled his collection of gifts from the crowned heads of Europe! She prevailed upon the caretaker to autograph the back of a postcard for her (he'd lived with Liszt for twenty-seven years!).

In fact, she spent so long frolicking through the hallowed rooms that her happy little group almost missed their train, rushing from the house and catching it with only minutes to spare. They crowded into the compartment as it chugged out of the station, laughing and breathless, amazed that the caretaker had demanded such a small amount of money for access to such a treasure.

"I never tho't I would do that!" Drake wrote that night in her diary.

Gaining access to home of Wolfgang Amadeus Mozart was less satisfying. Although it had been her top priority upon arrival in Salzburg, the neighborhood was of dubious repute, with narrow, crooked streets and badly worn stone stairs. At one point, she had already pushed her way through the front door and made it all the way upstairs before discovering she was in the wrong house. Unconcerned, she tried again, but the small third-floor apartment filled with Mozart's birth cradle and family portraits failed to meet her expectations. Later she wrote, "I don't enthuse over his music so naturally all this didn't interest me as much. . . ."

At the house of the composer Wilhelm Richard Wagner, things were more difficult still. For the first time, the housekeeper proved reluctant to accept a bribe, and Drake was only allowed as far as the front yard. Later she fumed at how infuriating it was that this would be the one place in Germany where servants seemed immune to tipping.

"It is great fun to sit right next to some great artist and watch them," she wrote in December. When not trespassing, Alice Drake spent her time in Germany seeking out musical performances. Her operas of choice were all Wagner, but when his music wasn't available at the local Philharmonic, she was happy to settle for whatever was playing.

She carefully glued the remains of each concert into a scrapbook: playbills, tickets, and snippets of music. Also into the scrapbook went critiques of each production ("Sucha sang. Her voice is gone so she doesn't charm me in any way whatever."); gossip about the performers ("I think it is so strange we never heard of Alexander Petchnikoff in America. . . . He has recently married an American girl."); opinions about the players ("This is the autograph of the director of the orchestra. He isn't great."); and descriptions of each opera house, diagrams of orchestral positioning, and a catalog of her mental state leading up to and following each production. The state of her handwriting makes it likely that the notes were meant for her own eyes only.

For a performance of Wagner's *Der Ring des Nibelungen*, she wrote: "The Nibelungen Ring commenced this morning. We have tickets for every night. I'm positively holding my breath to see who sings Brunhild. Later: Of all the things in this world, Frauline Revil is on for Brunhild. Well that makes me ill. And raised prices at that. Anyway, Reno and Libau are always fine and it is a treat to hear the orchestra so I guess I can stand it. It is a terrible ordeal though really. . . ."

While in Berlin, Drake was granted an audition with renowned teacher Karl Heinrich Barth. Though the maid was hesitant to admit her, Drake prevailed, and she soon found herself in Barth's music room, hands trembling, gazing in awe at his two Bechstein grand pianos. The man himself arrived ("Golly! But he looked big!"). After playing a few movements ("Very musical," he told her), she was informed she'd managed to secure a coveted spot as one of his students. She marched away from the house grinning, in her words, "from ear to ear."

Yet when the time came for her first lesson a month later, she blew it off to see a performance of her favorite Wagner opera, *Siegfried*. The Kaiser himself was expected to attend.

A Musical Diagnosis

Musicomania, an excessive and uncontrollable love of music, was a real and serious pathological diagnosis for late-nineteenth- and early-twentieth-century Americans. Young Alice Drake was not alone in her obsession; for everyone from clerks to society debutantes, industrialization brought a new approach to experiencing and enjoying what had previously been a relatively small-scale phenomenon. As the post–Civil War economy took hold, the country experienced massive social and cultural change. Urbanization! Railroads! A wage economy where people might spend their money on *anything they wanted*!

At the beginning of the century, music lovers might have contented themselves with gathering family around a piano after dinner, but now the growth of cities meant vast new concert halls. Whereas before they might attend their local church services, new transportation options such as streetcars and railways meant they could attend every church service in town. Preindustrialization, the only option for entertainment would have been local troupes of neighborhood players, provincial and familiar. But now a vast network of traveling virtuosos had become household names, introducing audiences to an entire planet's supply of talent, exotic compositions, and the drama of celebrity culture.

It was a good time to listen to some Wagner! But many enthusiasts felt, why stop there? "They said, well that's great, but we want more. We want the experience to last. So they start to do things on their own, outside of that established 'one ticket for that performance' framework," says cultural historian Daniel Cavicchi. Listening to a concert was enjoyable, but why not collect its sheet music and programs, carefully mounted in scrapbooks? Or stand for hours below a soloist's hotel balcony to catch a glimpse of her face? Or attend every performance of a show, returning again and again to critique how the music sounded from each part of the concert hall? Or travel to Weimar, Germany, to break into Liszt's house?

Young ladies forsook their gentlemen callers for the opera. Office workers bankrupted themselves for just one more performance. Music teachers rushed the stage and hugged the musicians. Middle-aged women stood in their seats and screamed with delight. Obviously, something had to be done.

The close of the American Civil War also fomented a wave of social reformers intent on doing good. The crusade opposing musicomania, while never reaching the fervor of the temperance or abstinence movements, was still a force. Not enough, these activists felt, that a new wave of immigrant culture had already imperiled the purity of truly American music; this new breed of music lover also had no idea how to enjoy it properly. Music should be experienced with self-restraint and a carefully moderated intellectual response, if any at all.

"The concert room was crowded with people clinging to each

other like bees," complained one scandalized Victorian concert attendee. "We saw bonnets torn off," gasped another. For the average Victorian, corseted into a tortuous letter B shape, then swathed in up to five layers of clothing, the unseemliness of the concert hall was abominable. It wasn't that Mozart or Wagner was necessarily a bad influence, but the unbridled emotions they inspired were contrary to every dictate of propriety. In respectable society, where even the most chaste skin-on-skin contact was practically an offer of engagement, a crowd of sweaty musicomaniacs trampling their neighbors in their enthusiasm would have been horrifying.

As Cavicchi notes, by 1833 the term "musicomania" had appeared in the *New Dictionary of Medical Science and Literature*. In those afflicted, "the passion for music is carried to such an extent as to derange the intellectual faculties."

And yet this excitement, this visceral freedom, may be a reason why so many Victorians found musical excess an effective outlet for their repressed longings. Music was rebellious. Music was pure, and good, and beautiful, even if (or perhaps explicitly because) outsiders didn't understand it. Music gave fellow devotees something to discuss and a reason to congregate. Music was something interesting to do.

And in a culture that barely tolerated the concept, music—and the people who made it, and the activities surrounding it, and the audience who liked it—was "fun."

To Fan Is Human

Humans have always experienced an urge to connect, with each other and with ourselves. It's an instinct buried so deep in our brains that we do it naturally, scanning our surroundings, always on the alert for bits of culture that might help us become a "better" us. From an evolutionary standpoint, a group of protohuman hunters who could find something external to bond over were more likely to eat dinner that night, whether it was a shared love of the moon goddess or a shared disdain of those weird sun-goddess worshippers on the other side of the hill.

Fandom refers to the structures and practices that form around pieces of popular culture. It's a very old, very human phenomenon; acting in fanlike ways is probably as ancient as culture itself. History is filled with tales of pilgrimages—traveling to a place, not for its aesthetic or economic value, but simply to feel close to something important. Chaucer's fourteenth-century Canterbury-bound knight, cook, friar, physician, and other companions are traveling to the shrine of Saint Thomas Becket. On the other side of the world, the Kii Peninsula of Japan is still crisscrossed with trails worn by pilgrims from a thousand years ago headed to the shrines of Kumano.

Margery Kempe is known today as the author of a large body of dramatic fiction: stories about family troubles, intrigue, trauma, and healing. Though generally described as autobiographical, her adventures weren't entirely of her own making. Kempe's writing was based on characters from the Bible—the best-known literary work of her time. By the time she died in 1438, she had amassed a novel-length tome of what today would be considered fan fiction, derivative writing that details the further adventures of Mary, Jesus, and other New Testament figures.

Sometimes she produced missing scenes to fill in time periods not present in the official text. Sometimes she imagined entirely original incidents. She pictures herself as a handmaiden to the Virgin Mary; she carries Joseph and Mary's bags when they go to visit family; and she brings a cocktail of wine, egg, and gruel to Mary's bedside to comfort her while she mourns Jesus. In other works Kempe incorporates her own pilgrimages into her stories; she imagines herself asking Mary for a swaddling cloth in which to wrap the

baby Jesus, based on a trip Kempe took to Assisi, where she viewed
a similar relic.

The late-medieval world was saturated with religious imagery.
Church songs, food taboos, spiritual art and architecture, special
clothing, festivals, and complicated rituals, all were rich fodder for
a creative mind. Modern scholars interpret these stories as a way to
bring Kempe closer to her favorite book, linking her to the characters she wrote about and incorporating herself into their lives. She
hoped to be canonized by the Church for her devotion; by becoming a saint she would complete her own assimilation into the words
of the text she loved so much.

Kempe was not the first to explore this type of literary fiction—
Franciscan nuns had tried it two hundred years earlier, encouraged
by a popular religious text of the time, *Meditationes vitae Christi*. But
nuns were technically part of the official religious infrastructure.
Kempe was most decidedly not.

Even though the late medieval period in England was charac-
terized by a new emphasis on personal empowerment, like the
anti-musicomania of Victorian reformers five hundred years later,
with that new freedom came significant opposition from both the
church and the surrounding community. Not everyone was happy
with Kempe's explorations.

Kempe, at least by her own account, faced scorn and public hostility for her behavior. Writing of herself in the third person, she said
that at home in her village, "a reckless man . . . deliberately and on
purpose threw a bowlful of water on her head." At York, she claimed,
"she had many enemies who slandered her, scorned her, and despised
her." Several times she was placed under what scholar Gail McMurray Gibson calls "casual house arrest" while the authorities decided
what to do about her bizarre and disruptive emotional outbursts.
Kempe even alleged that her enemies in the community wanted her

burned at the stake, but that may have been hyperbole. It's difficult to tell if her contemporaries viewed her as a dangerous holy woman or just wildly eccentric, since she herself seems to have taken a fair measure of pride in her own oppression.

The Democratization of Fandom

The difference between Margery Kempe, Alice Drake, and a modern-day fan camped outside a bookstore for the midnight drop of the next J. K. Rowling book isn't a question of enthusiasm. It's one of access.

It's easy to attribute the modern explosion in fandom to the increased connectivity of a tech-savvy audience. In terms of scale, this is certainly true. But fandom is predigital. It's also prephonograph. It's even preliteracy. Margery Kempe, as a merchant-class woman in the fifteenth century, could neither read nor write. All of her stories were dictated to a scribe. By the 1800s, a fan like Alice Drake had significantly more opportunity to interact with the object of her affection—she could listen to music regularly as long as she had some spare change and a nearby orchestra. Each successive technological gain has made fandom both more accessible and more social, but it has been part of human cultural activity throughout recorded history.

Over the centuries, advances in transportation, personal wealth, leisure time, and autonomy have meant fans have gained incrementally easier and more frequent access to the things they love. The Internet removes the final barrier, reducing the effort required to almost to zero. For media lovers, most audio, video, or literary texts can be summoned with a finger tap. For fans of a brand, the Internet allows products to be discovered, compared, and ordered without a visit to the mall. For fans of an activity, finding instructions on how to do it (and others to do it with) is now trivial. For the celebrity-obsessed, the Internet provides a whole universe of access to the private lives of the famous—their creative process, daily routine, opinions, and the occasional naked picture.

Prior to the nineteenth century, there were a limited number of "texts," the official canon of work available to an audience, that encouraged this type of multichannel approach. Religion provides one of the few examples—Kempe couldn't read her Bible, but she could visit the locations mentioned in it, participate in rituals inspired by it, sing songs about it, and, of course, make up stories.

Broad cultural trends sometimes had the same effect. A fashionable French citizen who felt enamored of American culture in the late 1700s could travel to America and fight in the revolution against Great Britain, but many also wrote pamphlets supporting the cause; commissioned paintings about the glory of American principles; ate turkey, corn, and other New World foods; or wore tiny portraits of Benjamin Franklin in their hair. But these were exceptions in a world that placed little emphasis on such ancillary activities.

The modern term *fan object* is what we now call these centers of emotion and activity, pieces of culture that inspire both loyalty, and, more importantly, activity. When finding and being close to a fan object required so much energy, the result was a very limited range of audience engagement. Almost all of it relied on simple interactions: reading a book meant readers would travel to a bookstore or library, acquire it, bring it home, and then read it. Perhaps they talked to friends about it. They might read it again at some point. But unless they had access to their own printing press and a lot of spare time, few would try to add to it. The interaction was usually one-way. No matter how good the book might be, the barriers to joining in meant that it primarily inspired consumption, not participation.

Reading a book today can be as simple as clicking the Buy button in the Kindle app. As fans need less energy to acquire and experience fan objects, they have more energy to spend on finding new ways to express their love for them. They have responded to this extra time and energy by doubling down on supplemental activities. Any casual Red Bull fan can easily find and purchase the sugary caffeinated beverage they love, so very serious fans might display their ardor by attending an extreme sporting event sponsored by Red Bull while wearing a shirt with its logo. When fans of the Star Wars franchise have finished binge-watching, they have dozens of other points of access: books, toys, comics, fan conventions, drawings, amusement-park rides, video games, and costume contests. It's not just a set of movies, meant to be viewed and perhaps later viewed again. This is a world in which audience members can become fully immersed, one that they can make their own.

Modern marketing has stumbled upon the benefits of fandom, not for fans' ability to create worlds, but for their predictable buying habits. "Get the fans excited, and maybe they'll also give you money," so the wisdom goes. So much has been written about the need for audience engagement that it's rare for a large-scale media campaign to launch these days without the matching social-media outreach, a video contest, a crowdsourcing initiative, a downloadable mobile game, book tie-in, street-team postering, a booth at Comic-Con, an appearance in a popular video game, and a whole stable of paid bloggers, Instagrammers, and YouTube celebrities to name-drop the product. And if there's any budget left over, maybe there's a TV commercial or magazine advertisement. It's certainly a very literal interpretation of the idea of creating a "world" for fans to immerse themselves in.

It's true that fans—that is, empowered fans, fans with spare time and energy—do want to engage on more levels and platforms than ever before. But it's a mistake to take their enthusiasm as a license to push more product. Brands are used to thinking of their fan groups in terms of what's in it for their bottom line: the social buzz that will be generated and the locked-in purchases they can count on. Very rarely do they consider what's in it for the fan.

Fan enthusiasm is always predicated on the brand serving a very specific and very personal set of needs. Understanding these motivations and passions is the key to real and authentic fan interactions. These are the kind of interactions that lead to broader success for both the fan object *and* the participant. After all, both have significant investment in the fandom's advancement. As we'll see, the contributions of an active fan group, empowered by this newfound access, are worth far more than the number of their Instagram followers and the contents of their wallets.

Hatsune Miku: The Crowdsourced Superstar

Hatsune Miku is one of the most popular singers in Japan. She tops music charts and performs at venues around the country and internationally. She's opened for Lady Gaga. She's starred in commercials for Toyota, Domino's Pizza, and Google Chrome. A YouTube search for her name returns over a million and a half results (by comparison, "Janet Jackson" only returns just above half a million). Miku has long turquoise pigtails, stands 158 cm (or a bit over 5'2"), weighs 42 kg (about 93 pounds), and her birthday is August 31. She is a Virgo. She's sixteen years old. And she's been sixteen since her birth in 2007.

Miku is a computer program, the mascot for a vocal synthesizer that allows users to write songs and listen to them performed in the software's voice. An add-on piece of software creates music videos by animating a 3D form to go along with the songs.

The company that owns Miku, Japan's Crypton Future Media,

has been careful to provide almost no backstory for its mascot outside of matching her colors to the software interface that inspired her. Occasionally Crypton releases new clothing or a new vocal style (sweeter, perhaps, or more "vivid"), but her entire life has been created by fans.

Crypton has colonized a space that usually sits between the music industry and what's called character merchandising. Both industries are infamous for vigorously protecting their trademarks; control over access to their media and brand symbols such as logos and other imagery is their most valuable asset. Yet Crypton goes out of its way to encourage its customer base to spread Miku and her music as far and wide as possible.

The result is a fan object created almost entirely by its fan base. Miku's fans furnish her with stories, drawings, and, of course, songs, which number on Amazon and iTunes in the hundreds of thousands. Some of her fan-created repertoire is played during live concerts, where fans travel to watch her appear via preproduced video. Miku-licensed products, and appearances in video games and other media, allow for collections and engagement, and Miku websites allow fans to communicate among themselves.

When Crypton released the Miku synthesizer software, the company made a key decision. "[They said] you make the music; it's your music," explains Ian Condry, a cultural anthropologist who studies pop culture in Japan. "Theories are espoused within entertainment companies that you need a professional to create these characters, and Miku shows that's not true. People used to say that in order to have fans of movies, it was the story that was important. With comic books, they say you need great characters. With video games, you'd say you need a great world. What's interesting about Miku is that she has none of that."

Miku was originally a marketing ploy—a mascot on the cover of

Crypton's synthesizer software to help make it more approachable for a mainstream audience. "We were surprised by the speed and scale with which Hatsune Miku was adopted," explains Crypton's US/EU marketing manager Guillaume Devigne. "We had to decide quickly how to deal with a huge number of songs, drawings, and videos that were popping up all over the Internet."

Rather than risk the unpleasant prospect of fighting for legal control against a significant percentage of Japan's population, the company adopted an unexpected policy of "nonrestrictive use for noncommercial purposes," which allowed fans to create and distribute their creations for free. In American terms, it would be the equivalent of Disney saying to the world: go ahead and make Mickey Mouse do whatever you want him to do, as long as you don't charge for it. By coincidence, Crypton's decision coincided with a crackdown on copyrighted videos on the Japanese website Nico Nico Douga (now Niconico), a cross between YouTube and VH1's Pop Up Video. Record companies and production studios were demanding the removal of their copyrighted videos, and Niconico was desperate for material to fill the gap. Miku did the job nicely, first with songs fronted by fan illustrations and later with fully animated videos.

Niconico has since become the eleventh-most-visited website in Japan, and Miku videos dominate. Crypton Future Media has also opened its own sharing site, piapro.jp, and started a record label called KARENT to allow fans to distribute and sell their Miku-inspired work (while taking a cut, of course). Piapro.jp currently lists more than 5,000 songs.

Miku is a map for what interactions would look like if a celebrity had infinite time and reach, and her fans had infinite access: a fan object who is herself constantly re-created by fan tributes. That Miku is digital is almost incidental—if a popular singer such as

Taylor Swift had the ability to produce every single song written for her by her own teenaged fans and to make them instantly available to other fans, it's easy to imagine the craze that would follow. The activities of her fans have made Miku one of the most recognizable Japanese celebrities worldwide. And even though it was the original impetus behind her creation, sales of the Vocaloid software for which she was created are only one of Miku's many revenue streams.

At most Miku concerts, a large projection screen takes up much of the stage, and she is shown performing in 2D rather than as a full hologram. During her 2016 North American tour 36,000 of her most devoted fans crowded into arenas to wave green light sticks at the stage. At shows like this, there is no effort at realism. The dancing figure has a jerky, cartoony look, and she's twice as large as a real person. When Miku sings, there's no confusing her with a human singer; her vocal pitch is higher, and her pronunciation has an awkward, metallic edge. Still, all the trappings of a concert are observed: the live backing band, the Jumbotron close-ups, the antiauthoritarian feel. One of her most popular songs is "Secret Police," about a government agency that spies on its citizens; often the crowd is on its feet, shouting and cheering for the entire song.

At the end of the show, the audience's applause seems a bit like clapping at the end of a movie; it expresses a real appreciation, but the celebrity isn't on stage to appreciate it. It's just as much for the fans themselves, and for the creators who make the show possible. A journalist who attended a packed Miku performance at Hammerstein Ballroom in New York in late 2014 later wrote, "It wasn't Hatsune Miku that was impressive. It was the vibe, the environment—the fans."

"It just looks quaint and silly and ridiculous, but in fact, people are using it to explore very serious and deep issues," explains Condry. One of Miku's more famous songs involves a sixteen-year-old girl coming to terms with dying of cancer. Others deal with universal themes of loss, loneliness, self-esteem, and first love.

"She remains a close and familiar figure people can relate to, maybe more than the 'normal' human pop-stars. Since the fans create the content for Hatsune Miku, they live and express their imagination and feelings through her," says Devigne.

Fans seem to appreciate her unchangeable nature, the very inhumanity an outsider might find odd. Miku is a safe role model. Amy, a thirteen-year-old fan, put it well in a 2012 interview with *Wired*: "She's not going to die. She's not going to turn into Miley Cyrus, where she gets drunk or something."

In late 2014, Miku performed on *The Late Show with David Letterman*. A screen was set up in the area usually reserved for musical guests, and the lights dimmed to make the projected video clearer. She shimmied and kicked her way through "Sharing the World," a song that is technically in English although it takes some listening. At the end of the prerecorded performance, Letterman walked over to where she was taking her prerecorded bow. She waved and disappeared in a puff of digital smoke. Letterman took it all in stride. "Hatsune Miku, Ladies and Gentlemen. There she is. All right, that's fun. It's like being on Willie Nelson's bus."*

Having Fans Means Needing Fans

It's fashionable to tout the advantages of surrendering brand ownership to the audience. In theory it's a wonderful idea: give the most influence to those who are most likely to pay if they are satisfied.

---

* Disclosure: We were so intrigued by the Hatsune Miku phenomenon after researching it that our company, Squishable, is now a licensee of Crypton Future Media and makes a Squishable Hatsune Miku.

The greater their control over the object, the more it will resemble their wants and needs when it comes time for them to buy.

In reality, the interaction isn't so straightforward. The 2012 Creative Commons license for Miku's image includes the following caveat: "You must not distort, mutilate, modify or take other derogatory action in relation to the Work which would be prejudicial to the Original Author's honor or reputation." The company makes it much clearer on the website, directly prohibiting the use of Miku's image "in an overly violent context or in a sexual context."

Pornographic images and videos of Miku have flooded the Internet as her popularity has grown, ranging from the titillating to the downright dark. One fan-animated video of Miku's "World Is Mine" song features enough animated softcore to scandalize even the most open-minded of censors (it has more than a million YouTube views). Other works are significantly more brutal and bloody. Hentai sites, which specialize in manga-style porn, often have entire sections devoted to X-rated Vocaloid graphic novels. Both eBay and Amazon carry a number of unofficial body pillows showing the sixteen-year-old in various stages of undress and dishevelment. Crypton is not amused, but it's important to note that, as of yet, they haven't succeeded in forcing retailers to remove the listings.

As we will explore, relinquishing the reins of brand control comes with a nest of hidden issues. Fan expectations tend to skew one of two ways: either they are deeply conservative, making fans hostile to the changes required to keep a brand current, or they may demand the most extreme alterations to cater to their own, sometimes very particular, whims. The latter can mean trampling the qualities that made their fan object special in the first place. A media brand like Hatsune Miku can weather an unexpected porn storm or even thrive on it. An insurance company might not. A children's TV show could be ruined.

Nonetheless, fan objects and their fans can live happily in a state of friendly codependence if expectations are managed. Even with the risk of an occasional body pillow, today's audiences are encouraged to experience closer and closer levels of engagement with their fan object, on so many more levels than the basic, linear text. And this has caused an unexpected consequence. A fan object that *builds on* its audience *needs* its audience.

The Star Wars experience would be greatly diminished without the participation of the fans; few of us would go to an empty Star Wars convention. Monday Night Football is far more fun when the audience members use the official #MNF hashtag to discuss the game with each other. Miku does not exist at all without her fan group; she has no songs to sing, no music videos to show, no advertising clout with which to sell Toyotas, no backstory to help connect with potential customers. Her audience is creating *for* itself, and in doing so, they create the very materials that attract more *of* itself.

In a world-based story, the audience is as much a part of each other's experience as the fan text itself. Without the audience's participation in the story, there may *be* very little story.

As a culture, we're used to looking down on fandom. Our biggest critique, like that of the Victorian social reformers, is often a question of quantity. Fans love what they love too much. They watch too much TV. They play too many video games. There's a proper and improper way to enjoy a Coke: drinking a bottle of Coke is all right; collecting a million Coke bottle caps and using them for elaborate dioramas is not.

And yet, brand owners are increasingly reliant on these very people to support their businesses.

At the moment, fan objects and their fans still occupy two distinct roles within the world of consumption. There are makers, and there are buyers. The two rarely overlap. But as audience experience shifts away from mere consumption of a fan text and toward influencing, or even adding to it, the space between the audience and the fan object is narrowing.

What will happen as these two finally meet? When materials created by a fan group begin to smoothly feed back into the fan object, without the age-old barriers to entry and access?

We won't have to wait very long to find out. We are entering a period of convergence, of fandom singularity, where the distinction blurs between fans and fan object, between who is the creator and who is the consumer. This is a future in which the lines of communication between product and buyer go both ways.

This is a future in which everything is part of the canon.

CHAPTER 1

FANDOM IS A VERB

In the Presence of the Oracle

They come to Omaha. They travel by themselves, or with friends, or with family or coworkers. They come from New York, San Francisco, Capetown, Dakar, and Shanghai, their eyes red from long layovers in London and Atlanta. Private jets and large commercial flights, plane after plane sets off for the middle of America.

For some attendees this is event number twenty or more. Fellow travelers can be identified by their logos and their spontaneous conversation. "Are you going to the convention? Hey, me too!" They greet old acquaintances across the airplane aisle with a "Good to see you, you sonafabitch!" and wave to each other as they disembark. Most hotels in town booked out months earlier, and there's still enough reservation overflow to fill rooms half an hour away.

The next morning the line outside of the CenturyLink Center wraps around the corner. At least one couple has camped out overnight in a tent in front of the entrance. Excited first-timers begin arriving at four a.m. The doors open at 7:00 and the crowd flows through the metal detectors and into the main hall, a sea of blue plastic badges, pushing, laughing, and gabbling in anticipation. "This is my third year coming!" "I've been here fourteen times, what about you?" and above all, "Who do you work for?"

At 8:30, with all three tiers of the arena full and attendees still overflowing into a nearby ballroom, the giant screens show a celebrity-studded video. An altered version of the song "YMCA" blasts from the speakers, and the audience leaps into the aisles shouting the chorus: "We love the man-a-gers at B-R-K-A!" University of Nebraska cheerleaders run through the chairs, their thrashing pompoms held high. Waving and smiling under a multistory projection of himself, Warren Buffett takes the stage.

It's called the Woodstock of Capitalism. Every publicly traded company in the United States is required by law to hold a yearly shareholder meeting to vote on corporate policies, but few adopt the approach of Berkshire Hathaway: a three-day extravaganza that's part religious revival, part rock concert, and part business event. Each spring, tens of thousands of people travel to Omaha, Nebraska, to listen to "the Oracle."

Warren Buffett is a businessman, philanthropist, and poster child for slow-but-steady financial investing. Lore has it that he got his start selling chewing gum door-to-door as a kid. He's spent much of his life converting Berkshire Hathaway from a defunct Rhode Island textile manufacturer into the multinational holding conglomerate it is today. As of 2016 it owned, either wholly or partially, more than fifty subsidiaries, including GEICO, Dairy Queen, Fruit of the Loom, NetJets, the Kraft Heinz Company, Coca-Cola, Wells Fargo, American Express, and IBM. And Buffett—chairman, president, and CEO—is among the top five wealthiest humans on earth.

Unlike many corporations, such as the Walt Disney Company,

which moved its corporate shareholder meeting away from the Anaheim Disney park in 1998 after a particularly rowdy meeting, Buffett embraces the enthusiasm of his devotees. For some, this will be their biggest vacation of the year. The cost of entry to the annual shareholders meeting is a single Berkshire Hathaway stock certificate, but those without stock can easily buy a ticket, sold on Craigslist and eBay for $5 to prevent scalping.

"I've always known about it. There's this legend that's built up around it, but it never occurred to me I could actually go," says Christian Russo, a banker with a big-name financial company, who has traveled from New York City.*

His girlfriend, an executive at a major investment firm, was so excited at the idea that she bought BRKB stock so they could attend. "We could have just bought a ticket, but we wanted to do it right. It was like: I'm going to take my 401(k) and invest in Berkshire so I can see Warren Buffett. I know it sounds lame but it's actually really cool. You actually get to see Buffett. You're actually in the same room with him and 17,000 of your friends for nine hours."

The crowd in attendance this year is closer to 40,000—albeit not all present at the same time. It's a mixed group: some are middle-America moms and dads hoping Buffett will say something to make them rich. Some are Wall Street types, here for the networking. Some are here to publicize their own business ventures. A few may actually care about the official corporate business being conducted. Most of them will attend the hours-long Q&A session, where audience members can ask Buffett about everything from his stock picks to his political opinions.

"Imagine you could ask Spider-Man something," Russo

---

* Christian Russo is a pseudonym: his employer forbids him from being quoted on-the-record about these kinds of events.

explains. "Here you can actually do it! You just have to stand in line! But in this case it's not someone playing Warren Buffett, it *is* Warren Buffett, the actual guy!"

The morning kicks off in the arena with questions from a panel of journalists. They represent the usual financial news sources—*Fortune*, CNBC, the *New York Times*—as well as the shareholders themselves. One by one they step to microphones near the front of the room, where Buffett sits next to his partner Charlie Munger at a table laden with Coca-Cola and See's Candies, both Berkshire holdings. One shareholder asks Buffett to talk about natural gas and energy policy; another asks for Buffett's opinion on disclosing salaries for the presidents of Berkshire Hathaway's various subsidiaries. One daring shareholder says he feels like America is off course, and asks Buffett if he can push the president to change direction. Buffett says, "America is doing extraordinarily well," eliciting applause from the audience. Another question ends in a speech explaining why a college education isn't necessary for success. The arena explodes with cheers.

Buffett's answers are thoughtful and funny and can take up to half an hour each. Occasionally, he'll ask the opinion of Munger, who will usually reply some variation of "I think he handled it very well."

"You can tell he doesn't get paid by the word," quips Buffett, as laughter rolls through the crowd, echoing off the arena's ceiling.

Two seats away, a man in his early thirties is diligently tapping each question verbatim into an iPad. He's an investment advisory company employee based in Kansas. "I'm already part of the problem—I took, like, thirty pictures of him when he was in the hallway. Here, look," he says pulling out his phone and zooming in on the screen. "That's Warren, you see him?"

"I've been to the Grammys and to the Oscars. There's always a few empty seats. Here there are no empty seats," says another man nearby. "I feel wealthier already, just being here."

"Warren and Charlie we love you!" screams a middle-aged man from the upper stands.

In the convention hall next door, the other business of the Berkshire Hathaway shareholders meeting is well underway, in a commercial space the size of two football fields. Berkshire Hathaway boxers. Berkshire Hathaway cuff links. Berkshire Hathaway money clips, running shoes, bras, scarves, baseball gloves, cowboy boots, and aprons. A BRK-themed diamond pendant costs upwards of $500. There's a silver tray etched with Buffett's words, "It's not necessary to do extraordinary things to get extraordinary results." A Pandora bracelet, a silver circle with a custom-made Berkshire Hathaway bead, sold out yesterday. So did Berkshire Hathaway pajama bottoms printed with logos and dollar signs.

Each of the more recognizable Berkshire brand names has its own booth here, with its own version of Berkshire Hathaway paraphernalia for sale. Most have a line of shoppers down the corridor. At Heinz, devotees can buy Warren Buffett– or Charlie Munger–branded ketchup bottles and Buffett-themed boxes of macaroni and cheese. Oriental Trading is selling Warren and Charlie rubber duckies. At GEICO, shareholders can take a picture with a giant gecko mascot. Photos taken at Fruit of the Loom are overlaid so that they look like Warren Buffett is posing at the same table. The rolling ice cream carts of Dairy Queen are doing a brisk business.

The shelves at the 200-foot-long See's Candies booth are being stripped bare. Frantic stockers are shelving peanut brittle boxes as fast as they can. "It's always like this," says a blond, middle-aged stockperson as she rips open a new case. She throws the empty to the side and grabs another. By the time its contents are unloaded, the previous boxes are already gone. "People want it because it's Warren Buffett's favorite," she pants.

"This is what he eats? Are you sure?" asks a balding middle-aged man reaching for a box.

A tattooed twenty-something with multiple lip piercings mumbles his order to the cashier. A Buddhist monk in gold-colored robes wanders through the booth. A retiree in a wheelchair has so many purchases hanging from his push handles that it looks as though he might tip backwards.

Convention-goers are spread along the walls, sitting on the concrete floors in khaki trousers, power suits, yoga pants, and heels or flip flops as they chew through their rubbery sandwiches and pretzels, clogging the corridors and comparing loot. A shy teenager with a black T-shirt that reads "The Next Warren Buffett" blushes as she murmurs, "My dad bought it for me last year, so this time I *had* to come."

In his annual letter to shareholders in February, Warren Buffett congratulated attendees on their commercial zeal. "Last year, you did your part, and most locations racked up record sales." A blond woman stumbles by with two enormous cases of ketchup. An Asian businessman pulls down a whole shelf full of Berkshire Hathaway polo shirts. By late afternoon, the See's Candies booth is bare, almost completely sold out.

While events in the convention center wind down, some attendees crowd outside Buffett's modest house in the Dundee-Happy Hollow Historic District to take pictures. That night there's a barbecue at Berkshire Hathaway's Nebraska Furniture Mart, complete with dueling pianos and "Berkshire Weekend" discount prices. This is their biggest weekend of the year, to the tune of $40 million. Over a million dollars' worth of mattresses alone will walk out the door.

Meanwhile, competition is tight for Gorat's and Piccolo's, two of Buffett's favorite steakhouses. This weekend they're largely full of shareholders. In the weeks leading up to the event, the exact time he might be seen at each location is a carefully guarded secret. Rumor has it he's promised that he'll eat at both restaurants at some point and most diners are hoping to get lucky and overlap with his arrival. Reservations for Gorat's opened one month ago and within minutes callers could not get through. For the lucky few who did snag a table, many order Buffett's favorite: a T-bone, cooked rare, a double portion of hash browns, and a Cherry Coke, served on a Warren Buffett coaster. Some diners steal both the coaster and the menu when they're done.

"Only sissies get the small one," opines Buffett about Piccolo's root beer floats.

The next morning is the Berkshire 5K Fun Run, where participants are encouraged to show off their limited-edition Berkshire Hathaway PureCadence 2 commemorative running shoes. The starting gate is a giant cartoon of Warren Buffett in running sweats, topped with the words "Invest in Yourself." Warren Buffett himself fires the starting gun, and shareholders run alongside Berkshire Hathaway staff. All participants get a medal at the end before they leave.

At the Berkshire-owned Borsheim's Fine Jewelry and Gifts, a security phalanx watches the door. A shareholder's badge is the only entry ticket and the guards theatrically check each set of credentials before waving the lucky bearer through. The effect is one of exclusivity and privilege: this person is allowed in because she is special. At one point Buffett will take over as a clerk and shareholders can haggle with the guru himself. Twenty-six loose diamonds are for sale, each laser-etched with Warren Buffett's signature and priced anywhere from the equivalent of a used Toyota Corolla to a brand new Ferrari.

The adjacent mall has been largely shut down. There's a magician entertaining a small crowd, while over by the Pottery Barn, professional table-tennis players demonstrate their paddle prowess. Later on, Buffett will team up with Berkshire board member Bill Gates to play an exhibition match against US Olympic ping-pong player

Ariel Hsing. Sweat-pants-clad retirees and families with strollers mix with swarms of sorority girls from the nearby college.

"We've come every year for the last thirteen years. This is a family affair," says one gray-haired Chicago patriarch, gesturing to his wife and three kids. "It's like a rock concert. It's the rock concert of capitalism. It's like going on spring break, but when you went on spring break you didn't have money."

"Afterwards we're going to Pitch Pizza," says his wife. "[Buffett's daughter] Susie goes there. If there's a place the Buffetts go, it's gotta be good." She surveys the crowd, her lip curled in disdain. "A lot of people just bought one share of stock to come here. Look at these women, just here to pick up some high-finance dudes."

"Are you rich?" asks a man in his mid-forties. His name is Tommy, and he's making small talk while waiting to clear security. He's here with his small investment group. "We're similar to what Warren did, but I'm not as smart as him. I made my wife read a lot of his books. I told all of my friends, just follow this! There's no way you can't be rich if you just follow this! Everyone wanted to come, so we turned it into a big road trip. I was going to bring my copy of some of his books to get autographed, but I was too shy to get up in front of him.

"No hot tips that you can give us, eh?" he adds.[*]

Warren Buffett is eighty-three. "There's a certain, not desperation, but maybe urgency that's taking over the people who go. You're experiencing something that's not going to happen again. In a couple of years it will be over. This could be the last year," observes Christian Russo. On the way to the airport, Russo and his girlfriend will stop at a Dairy Queen.

---

[*]   All events occurred during the 2014 Berkshire Hathaway Shareholders meeting, but some quotations come from the 2016 Berkshire Hathaway Shareholders meeting.

Fans, Consumers, and Knowing the Difference

Technically, the Berkshire Hathaway Shareholder Meeting is a legally required corporate triviality. No shareholder is obligated to attend, with the possible exception of the few petitioners who file official resolutions to try to steer the company. And even they arrive knowing that their requests will almost certainly be denied. All the financial information relayed during these three days is included in the company's annual reports and financial briefings. Any pearls of wisdom Buffett drops are live-blogged by the *New York Times* and the *Wall Street Journal* or conveyed by the Fox News headquarters set up across the street. While ketchup might be slightly less expensive on the convention floor than at the local Kroger, the price is certainly offset by the cost of a plane ticket and lodging.

So these attendees aren't consumers. Or at least, they aren't only consumers.

A consumer of Tide Plus Bleach clothing detergent may love the brand. She may love the fresh sudsy smell and the whitening action's effect on their towels. And she may loyally buy Tide and only Tide for all her towel-cleaning needs. But if Tide changes its recipe to a smell the consumer doesn't like, that consumer will shrug and start looking for a new brand. Consumer interaction of this sort has a single outlet: if people like a product, they buy it. If they don't, they won't.

To bother branding a multinational corporate holding company at all is a little unusual. To brand it to this level is downright odd. Berkshire Hathaway attendees don't only appreciate the brand for what it does for them and their metaphorical towels; they've also reinterpreted what holding Berkshire stock means. It means financial freedom. Plucky American ingenuity. A chance to socialize with others like themselves. Vacation. Exclusivity. If the value of Berkshire stock decreases, they are unlikely to start shopping around for a better one. In fact, during the Great Recession in 2008, a common gripe among shareholders was that they didn't have enough resources to buy still more. The piece of paper that says "Berkshire Hathaway stock" is proof of an investment, but it also embodies a goal or even a mythos. It's something to believe in.

Consumers care about the product. Fans care about what that product stands for. These two groups of people have very different wants and needs. In 2010, a giant Dairy Queen spoon signed by Warren Buffett was auctioned to fans for $4,500. It's unlikely that the winner was planning to eat a giant sundae with it.

The Battle for Washington Square Park

Halfway across the country, the Sith are in deep trouble. They've gathered in Manhattan's Washington Square Park on a muggy August evening to challenge their eternal enemy, the Jedi. The odds don't look good.

The Facebook event page for "Lightsaber Battle NYC 2014" has almost 2,000 participants listed, and a sizable portion of those who RSVP'd have shown up. Hundreds of spectators stand on top of the cement benches that ring the park's main fountain, carefully out of range of the glowing plastic weapons flailed around by the crowd inside. Some of the swords are homemade, made of glow-sticks and tin foil, but most are a cheap telescoping plastic model dispensed from the back of a U-Haul truck on the north side of the park for $10 each. A number of participants have duct-taped two swords together to make a double-bladed saberstaff. They mill about under the light of the streetlamps. From the east side of the park there are chants of "Va-der! Va-der!" and from the west, "O-bi-wan!" as they await the signal to begin. The crowd is diverse—there are little girls dressed as Leia and tall men in kimonos and Darth Vader helmets. A number of fashionable women, stilettoes spread wide for balance, carry tiny dogs wearing Yoda sweatshirts.

At 9:20, a man dressed as Han Solo climbs onto a bench. As both sides shout their defiance, he nods at the Sith side and comments, "Wow, you guys are really outmatched!" Then, "3 . . . 2 . . . 1 . . . go!"

"Oh my god, people are really going to die," mutters a voice from the benches.

The two groups come together with the sound of a million bouncing plastic bottles, the front lines chopping at each other with a happy up-down motion. There's no room for finesse with bodies pressed so tightly together; most of the action happens in the air over their heads. The goal seems to be to come into contact with as many swords as possible. "Use the force!" shouts a woman. Off in the distance the crowd groans at a melodramatic death. A grinning elderly white man charges past in a wheelchair, sword aglow. "I think I'm dead maybe ten times!" Pieces of plastic fly through the air.

It's easy to pigeonhole fandom as the side effect of nostalgia. But even if this were true, the phenomenon's economic impact remains staggering. Almost all of the top ten movies of 2015, ranked by worldwide gross, were heavily fan-driven properties: *Star Wars: The Force Awakens, Jurassic World, Furious 7, Avengers: Age of Ultron, Minions, Spectre, Mission Impossible: Rogue Nation,* and *The Hunger Games: Mockingjay—Part 2.* Every single one was based on preexisting comics or sci-fi/fantasy books, or media franchises that already had huge fan bases before these movies ever launched.

Disney's $4 billion acquisition, and subsequent massive expansion, of the Star Wars franchise is a direct result of fan-supported activities. At the time of the sale in 2012 there were 17,000 characters listed in the *Holocron,* the Lucasfilm-maintained bible of all things Star Wars. The value of such a pantheon isn't in individual characters; it's in their huge variety. Robert Iger, CEO of Walt Disney, has focused on acquiring properties that have a wide-ranging mix of characters and backstories that can be used across all of the company's various channels. The TV shows and spin-off movies, the toys (both kids' dolls and adult action figures), the theme-park rides they can brand, the pins, the clothes. There's enough diversity of both character and recreation here to appeal to every member of an immense and engaged fan base.

Disney will not make a cent from the plastic fencers at tonight's event. Many of the "lightsabers" are unbranded and most of the outfits are homemade or bought for other occasions. None of the Star Wars movies are even shown. Like the attendees at the Berkshire Hathaway meeting, these Washington Square Park warriors aren't acting like consumers. Yet, on this hot summer night, their display is one of the most valuable brand-building activities possible, and Disney is getting it for free.

I Fan/You Fan/He, She, and It Fans

Fandom does not describe what someone is—it's something they do. It's a set of noncommercial undertakings in which enthusiasts participate. Fan-created performances such as the Lightsaber Battle make a product relevant and attractive to a broader audience. Their value is in the experience of participating. In fact, participation helps to differentiate between a fan and a consumer. Consumers give their money to a brand. Fans give their energy and time.

While there's often overlap between fans (who engage in activities) and consumers (who buy things), buying is not always a requirement. Active fans of the DeLorean automobile, made popu-

lar as the car-turned-time machine from the *Back to the Future* trilogy, are very unlikely to also be consumers: there are only around
6,500 DeLorean DMC-12s left in existence, and the company has
been bankrupt for several decades. But that doesn't stop thousands
of fans from flocking to DeLorean car shows, chatting on DeLorean
message boards, and putting up DeLorean-spotting websites. A significant number of the more than 1 million annual visitors to the
Guinness Storehouse in Dublin are young kids, an audience that (at
least theoretically) has never sampled the alcoholic products being
showcased.

There's a basic human instinct to form communities with other
individuals around the things they have in common such as geographic location, religion, gender, or class. Whether it's for the purpose of entrepreneurship, self-improvement, or to have a good time,
humans find excuses to come together. Today, their commonality is
just as likely to be a shared love of *The Empire Strikes Back,* a shared
enjoyment of kickball, or, for that matter, a shared fascination with
videos of cute cats doing quirky things.

Such common focal points are known as *fan objects*—a celebrity, brand, organization, pastime, or piece of media such as a
movie, book, or music that functions as a nexus of emotion and
activities. They are an important core, a center of gravity that both
pulls a group of people together and gives them something shared
to bond over.

Sometimes these fan objects bring with them a *fan text*—an official piece of media that allows fans to directly experience the fan
object. Sometimes the fan object *is* the fan text itself, such as in the
case of a beloved movie or book. Sometimes the relationship is less
direct; fans of a musician can listen to the fan text of their songs,
watch the fan text of their official music videos, or read the fan text
of their biography. Sometimes there's no fan text at all. Many activ-

ities, such as swimming, don't have much in the way of media available to help fans directly feel close to their fan object. It's difficult to be a hardcore swimmer without occasionally swimming.

A Sith arriving to a deserted Washington Square Park to challenge the Jedi would be a disappointed fan. She could wave a sword around by herself, but it wouldn't be the same. Our natural urges toward self-expression and interaction, for showing off who we are, are all predilections we can only fully explore in the company of others. As a result, fandom is inherently social: a performance needs an audience. Even though fandom often feels intensely personal, the activities that constitute it almost always exist as part of a shared experience. The image of a secret fan acting alone with no outside influence or interaction is largely a myth. Secret fans are more often still socializing and engaging with their fellow fans, but without involving their more mainstream social group. True solitary fandom rarely survives for long.

The most effective way to make fans out of mere consumers is by inspiring the audience to participate in activities, preferably ones that are separate from the mere consumption of a product, where they can identify as part of a larger group. These *fanlike activities* are the backbone of fandom.

Pilgrimages

Attendees of the Berkshire Hathaway Annual Shareholders Meeting in Omaha are participating in perhaps the oldest fanlike activity, older even than Chaucer's fourteenth-century travelers on their way to Canterbury. A pilgrimage describes a journey to a place, not because of its beauty or location or any other intrinsic value, but for what it represents. Its holiness. Warren Buffett's modest five-bedroom stucco house isn't particularly attractive despite belonging to a multibillionaire. There are a few security cameras and an unmarked security car parked outside, but those are the only signs of affluence. Yet even when he's away, fans can be found milling around on the sidewalk, seeking closeness to the guru by proxy. Gorat's Steak House has three stars on Yelp, and many of the reviews question Buffett's culinary judgment. It's very possible that without the Buffett connection the restaurant would not be selling out reservations weeks in advance. Many Lightsaber Battle participants traveled from New Jersey and Connecticut, a tedious feat on a late summer evening. The view of the World Cup through a high-def television is always going to be better than the view from the bleachers, but that doesn't stop the event from being one of the most sought-after sporting tickets in the world.

All fandom tends toward in-person interactions, whether it's attending the convention, standing in line for the book signing, seeing the singer in concert, finding the original brewery, or visiting the celebrity's childhood home. We want to prove to ourselves that this thing we care about is, at least in some sense, real.

Content Creation

During the winter holiday, some revelers decorate a tree. At Thanksgiving we roast turkeys, and on Valentine's Day we make cards. We bake a cake for birthdays and prepare our famous barbeque recipe on the Fourth of July. The making of personal works of creativity around patriotic and religious themes is such a natural activity that few of us really give it any thought.

As popular culture carves out a space among more traditional institutions, with it comes audience-made devotional objects. Fans can literally "pay tribute" to a fan object with their creative skills: the railway enthusiast who re-creates an entire train system in his backyard; the artist who draws a sketch of Taylor Swift as a Japanese anime character; the genius who takes a photo of a cat with both paws near its mouth and adds a caption that says "Invisible harmonica!"

Creative works by amateurs—a drawing, photo, piece of writing, or website—used to be easy to identify. The better the quality, the more likely it was to be officially sanctioned. But with increased access to professional-grade tools, that divide is shrinking. Fan-cut trailers for popular movies are often indistinguishable in quality from the original. The English band Radiohead actively encourages fan-made remixes of its music. The title sequence for Season 8 of the popular television show *Doctor Who* is based almost entirely on a fan-created video uploaded to YouTube.

Evangelization

"My club is awesome. You should totally join too." Almost every group, be it political, religious, or social, has some type of formal or informal recruitment system. Fan groups have the benefit of true believers, that core group of people with a deep emotional connection to the fan object. Fan evangelization follows many of the same impulses that drive religious recruitment. The fan who believes he has found the best ever Icelandic Death Metal rarely wants to keep that information to himself. For someone who's recently discovered the funniest TV show ever, convincing others to watch it too comes naturally. Many Berkshire Hathaway attendees have brought along spouses, friends, and coworkers in the hope of infecting them with Buffett fever. Part of the enjoyment of finding a new fan object is in the status it grants finders in the eyes of their peers. And of course, participating in a fan group is more fun with friends. For one thing it creates more fans to discuss it with.

Over the years a number of organizations have attempted to automate these evangelical urges. Early Facebook pages sometimes "like-gated" their content, so that potential fans couldn't gain access without first clicking the "Like" button. Facebook outlawed this sort of page design years ago, but we still contend with a legacy of "Like," "Tweet," "Pin," and "Email this" buttons today, scattered across the web like so many pieces of sticky digital candy. Games such as the infamous Candy Crush and FarmVille encourage evangelization as part of their game play by requiring a friend's input to unlock extra lives or abilities. And there are always websites and mobile apps that want to take the principle a step further, logging into our social networks either with or without our knowledge to evangelize our friends on our behalf. "Share your purchase," suggests the Amazon checkout confirmation page, along with a helpfully prewritten tweet and Facebook post.

Socialization

Interaction in a social group can feel like a challenge for some, and fan objects represent a powerful social lubricant and medium for self-expression.

A group of people with a passion for a specific fan object are likely to have other shared interests. Fans of a vegan lifestyle may also have a shared love of biking or yoga. Fans of English author Terry Pratchett's satirical fantasy novels are more likely to enjoy humorous Monty Python skits or movies directed by Mel Brooks. Commonalities like these offer jumping off points for discussions, friendships, and building a personal network. Using a fan object as a vehicle to discuss experiences and feelings can diffuse otherwise potentially awkward social situations. With a shared fan object, there is always a default topic of conversation. Interacting with strangers can be hard, but people wearing the same Star Wars outfits, holding the same lightsabers, and shouting mutually recognizable movie quotes aren't strangers in the traditional sense.

When a fan takes an online *Sex and the City* quiz and posts the result to her Facebook timeline, she's telling the world that she's a "Carrie," the driven-but-sensitive heroine of the series. In a regular conversation this person might have trouble announcing that she's looking for romance and excitement, but by publicly identifying with Carrie the fan's post subtly asks for commentary and approval from her fellow fans. It's probably just a matter of time before someone comments back, "Oh you so are, girl!"

Impersonation

Our bodies are a canvas we use to project signals about who we are and what we feel strongly about. Traditionally, flashing a group's "tribal colors" shows off our cultural affiliations. Face paint might provide clues about family origin and social status. The shape of a necklace pendant might signal others in the same religious community. In many cultures the color and cut of jewelry and clothing contains carefully coded information about the wearer's age, gender, profession, and relationship status. Few people would proposition a woman clad in a white wedding gown.

As our cultural affiliations have become broader, tribal colors have expanded to include new enthusiasms. Face paint can mean that the wearer is a Baltimore Ravens fan or obsessed with the band KISS. Wearing a replica of a "time turner," Hermione's golden necklace from the Harry Potter franchise, identifies the wearer as a devotee to other fans. And clothing, through screen and dye-sublimation printing, can identify the teams we want to win, the cars we wish to drive, the bands we've seen, our preferred beer, and our favorite BBQ joint. A truly subtle fan might even wear her fan object's signature perfume, sending out the signal that she admires Kim Kardashian odiferously.

Although some fans take their dress-up to the extreme by fully embodying the characters they love with *cosplay*, the art of constructing and wearing elaborate costumes based on favorite characters, it doesn't require going the full Elvis to tell the world about what we like. Sometimes it just takes a T-shirt with the right picture. Very few attendees at the Lightsaber Battle fail to wear at least some kind of Star Wars gear, even if it's just a colorful pin. A number of them even have Star Wars–themed tattoos.

Over the last decade, impersonation in the United States has taken over Halloween. There are still generic angels, policemen, and sexy kitties, but a large portion of the $2.5 billion spent on costumes in the US annually goes toward licensed properties. The Google Frightgeist costume search tracker reported that for 2016, three of the top five costumes were officially licensed: Harley Quinn, Wonder Woman, and the Joker. There are also costumes portraying corporate mascots like the Svedka vodka girls and Berkshire Hathaway's own GEICO Gecko, as well as products themselves, like a Crayola crayon or a Hostess Chocolate Cupcake. Progressive Insurance has a website devoted to dressing like its mascot, Flo the Progressive Girl, for Halloween, complete with links to download her signature buttons and nameplate.

Rituals and Traditions

Do something once and it's innovation; do it again and it's tradition. Fans excel at developing their own activities and practices to help them feel close to the object of their affection, often creating a customized vocabulary and rules for participation in the process.

Justin Bieber fans sometimes organize "buyouts" at the release of each new CD. Members of the million-strong Bieber Army rampage through Kmarts and Best Buys in a coordinated attempt to rocket the album to the top of the charts. And there's always the possibility that Bieber himself might notice and make an appearance. Very few of this thirteen- to eighteen-year-old age group have ever owned a CD player—they've come of age in an era where Pandora, iTunes, Spotify, and other digital services are the norm—so at the end of each shopping spree most of the CDs are collected and donated to charity.

But fan-made rituals and customs don't have to be so extreme. A book club that meets once a month; a tailgating party in the parking lot before each big game; dousing the coach of a winning team with Gatorade; the weekly screening of a specific cult classic movie—all serve the same purpose. They give members a sense of belonging and bind fans closer to a fan object by helping them incorporate it into the rhythm of their lives. Once something becomes habit, it is that much easier to maintain.

Creating Collections

When Bieber fans stage a buyout, or when Berkshire Hathaway shareholders buy bottles of ketchup with Warren Buffett's picture on them, they are engaged in ritual consumption. They are buying products for what they mean instead of what they do. For a consumer, the value of an object is in the purpose it serves. Tide Plus Bleach will make towels smell nice. But for a fan, the collection of objects such as toys, posters, ticket stubs, autographs, and other "proofs of participation" are valued for what they symbolize. A complete collection of rare Tide Plus Bleach bottles would probably be worth more if they were unopened. These are talismans of ownership. Fan collections are not unlike a voodoo doll: a product that's representative of a distant fan object can impart a feeling of ownership and closeness with the actual beloved celebrity, movie, book, or brand.

Fan collections can absorb vast amounts of time and money,

and often are prized for qualities like completeness, quirkiness, or the rarity of the objects. A collection of Star Wars–related products is great, but a collection of Star Wars–related PEZ dispensers is better. A complete collection of limited-edition Star Wars PEZ dispensers sold during the initial theatrical release of *Return of the Jedi* in 1983 might be the best, at least for someone who is looking to feel deeply engaged with her fan object. This is one of the few areas where social status in a fan group can be "bought." Fans feel even closer to their fan objects by engaging in *possession rituals*—organizing and maintaining the collection, positioning objects to best effect, documenting them, and creating display systems. Collections allow fans to relive high points in their own fan histories. A concert ticket stub is just a piece of paper, but seeing it carefully preserved in a scrapbook brings back memories of what it was like to be there long afterwards.

Why Do We Fan?

Rituals that directly involve spending money, such as the Bieber buyouts, are pretty rare. With the exception of licensed products such as costumes and toys, fanlike activities are technically valueless, at least when it comes to money. Very few fanlike activities are specifically intended to put cash into the fan object's pocket. The interplay between fanlike activities and monetization is much more complex than that found in a traditional buyer-seller relationship, but it's a strong one.

A 2013 study of Bud Light fans found that an increase in fan activity does lead to an uptick in sales, sometimes a larger one than would be expected from a standard advertising campaign. Over a one-month period, fans saw and were encouraged to share beer-related images on Bud Light's Facebook page, driving evangelization and socialization activities. The pictures were silly: one showed a hand picking beer bottles from a tree as though they were fruit, another showed beer pouring from a picture of a bottle on a smart phone. None had an overt marketing agenda in the old-fashioned sense of highlighting the product's advantages, price, or where to buy it. Nonetheless the four-week fandom-centric campaign led directly to a 3.3 percent increase in sales compared to a control group. It's a sizable figure for a brand whose parent company in 2013 spent $1.56 billion purely on advertising.

Turning Consumers into Fans

Sometimes the relationship between fanlike activities and fans' wallets is subtler still.

In theory, crowdfunding websites like Kickstarter, Indiegogo, and GoFundMe use the power of fan groups to raise funding for future projects. Each campaign allows users to pledge a certain amount of money and to receive tokens of appreciation in return. But in practice they often function like "preorder" systems: a Kickstarter to raise money for a book promises the fan a copy when it's completed. The fan has in essence bought the book, with the caveat that she likely won't receive it for months. Often as a thank-you fans will receive a bonus like free shipping.

From the point of view of a fan acting out of love, these kinds of discounts can be counterproductive. Sometimes they allow fans to feel like they are helping out a cause that they care about. But sometimes, instead of engaging with a fan's urge to participate in fanlike activities, they've only engaged with their old-fashioned consumer instinct.

Alternative and independent writers, musicians, and artists

comprise an industry that has seemingly tried every possible type of commercial relationship between creators and fans, with varying levels of success. Micropayments, charging pennies for each piece of content, are annoying. Paywalls, requiring a subscription to view content, prevent the curious from discovering material that could make them serious supporters. Advertising—selling banner ads and other sponsored space—has experienced a significant decline as ad spends are nudged away from hosting platforms and toward social media. Swag—selling branded shirts, mugs, stuffed animals, and tote bags—can help, but with less and less return as closets fill up. A person only needs so many tote bags.

Jack Conte, sometimes labeled in album reviews as the guy doing "all of those instruments," is a San Francisco–based musician and videographer. His personal style, both in his own work and as a member of his two-person band Pomplamoose, is aggressively indie. But despite a strong YouTube following, a weekly podcast, and a good tour schedule, by early 2013 he had yet to see the type of financial support he wanted. So he cofounded Patreon.

Instead of funding content creation through the sale of fan-text vehicles such as CDs, books, newspapers, swag, or ad space, Patreon adopts the patronage model: I admire what you do. Take this money and use it how you will. It's not exactly a donation, but it's certainly not a purchase.

"Art became fundamentally tied to commerce because art became tied to physical things that could be sold," observes Conte. It's a surreal marriage. A music fan who wants to show a band his appreciation and love might have only one option to support it: to click on the advertisement for American Apparel that appears on the band's website. The catchphrases "Shut up and take my money!" and "I'm throwing money at the screen but nothing is happening!" are often repeated in fan forums and on platforms like Facebook and Reddit. They represent real frustration: I want to help you, why won't you give me an outlet to do so?

"The desire to want to support an artist because their work speaks to you is an intrinsic emotional thing," says Conte. "I have over 120 subscriptions on YouTube, and occasionally, a video will pop up and I'll watch it and feel like it's a game changer in my life. If there were a button to give that person $1,000, I would press it."

Unlike Kickstarter and other crowdsourcing sites, Patreon primarily funds creators engaged in long-term, sometimes life-long, works rather than one-off projects. Fan texts, which are often released for free to the broader population, are funded as they are made. Only dedicated fans will opt to financially support something they otherwise can get for free—so the commercial relationship fans have with their fan object is, in some ways, the least important one. Yet, as of 2016, the Patreon website has over a million active pledges going to content creators, to the tune of over $6 million per month in support.

Patreon isn't the only organization to take advantage of the fan mentality for funding purposes. National Public Radio has been doing it for decades. A local NPR station is always free, but a portion of its revenue stream comes from "listeners like you." Historically, this works because its core audience is geographically centralized, which creates a group united around supporting the local station. Hometown pride is a strong motivator. But that's a fundamentally different audience from, say, a video creator with fans spread throughout the world. While there might be 100,000 people visiting the website daily, they're generally only engaged for as long as it takes to watch today's clip. Fans need to be encouraged to think of themselves as part of a group bigger than themselves, a group that's counting on each of them to do their part.

"People have been asking for something like this for years. [They say] I don't really wear T-shirts because I work in an office, and I don't really have room in my apartment for stuffed animals. I just want to support you." So says Jon Rosenberg, creator of the popular webcomics *Scenes from a Multiverse* and *Goats*, who has been using Patreon since late 2013.

Prior to the switchover Rosenberg sold advertising on his website, created toys and T-shirts to sell, printed compilations of his work, and appeared at comics conventions, all with diminishing returns. Selling to readers wasn't working, but appealing to their fanlike nature was intimidating. "I didn't want to use it as leverage against the audience, and I didn't want to guilt people—I didn't want to make it an unpleasant thing," he explains. "It's a delicate balance. You're asking people for their help but you're kind of demanding it too because you're saying: I'm not going to do this anymore if I can't get the support." He currently makes $3,094 a month through Patreon—enough, with the addition of his other revenue activities, to take care of his three kids, pay his mortgage, and draw full time.

"I would not be full-time employed by my comics if not for the generosity of my readers right now. It changes the comics from a loss leader into the product," he says.

Selling the Intangible

Convincing readers that their dollars are better spent as a pledge than a purchase is not a trivial task. More often than not, rewards are digital goods or exclusive access to the artist rather than paraphernalia. Products like the promise of extra videos, posts, or personalized haikus are popular. For $5 a month, fans get access to ongoing Google Hangouts with Rosenberg and to live streams of him drawing. For $100 a month, Rosenberg's fans get to have a beer with him at the Peculiar Pub on Bleecker Street in New York City. It's a level of access that's normally sacrosanct, but it's available as a Patreon perk to those who want it enough to pay. About one in ten of Rosenberg's 1000+ supporters support at this level or higher.

For the fans who aren't craving the opportunity for a traditional fanlike activity such as a pilgrimage or in-person meeting, the motivations are more varied. For example, some Patreon-style campaigns can offer opportunities for self-improvement. Corridor Digital, a team of YouTube video creators, offers supporters at the $20-per-video level "VFX school on a budget." They get a livestreamed tutorial about how to do video effects and a downloadable collection of related files.

Often, the interactions take on very personal meanings. Rosenberg's $2,000 milestone goal was entitled "Operation Kiddie Freedom." It was the threshold he needed to send his three kids to day care so that he would have more time to draw for fans. At the moment, Conte's personal Patreon page promises: "When I hit $7,000, I'll buy a new DSLR camera, and my videos will look awesomer." Patrons aren't just supporting art; they are sponsoring the creation of more of what they like.

"It's a self-identified crew of people who want to support and help us. Those people get a special place in my schedule and my mind as people who I really want to make sure are happy," says Conte. Fans buy the feeling of participation in an act of creation without having a direct role in what's being created. "In a sense, it's like walking into the San Francisco Opera and seeing a plate on the wall honoring someone who donated $4 million," he says.

Just as medieval patronage benefited the social standing of the patron, sponsoring creators on Patreon increases the social standing of the supporter, as public a badge as carrying a NPR umbrella. It's hard to overstate the importance of bragging rights among fellow fans. "Being a patron denotes some type of relationship, whereas a tip jar doesn't," says Conte. Most patrons have publicly viewable pages where they can show off which artists they support.

A lucky few Patreon artists are supported by superfans, those dedicated and serious members of a fandom who are willing to commit real time, energy, and attention to assisting and improving the fandom that they love. It is great to be supported by consumers, who want to buy the "extras" the artist is offering, and by fans, who want a feeling of closer engagement, self-improvement, or any one of a number of other personal motivations. But to have the support of superfans is valuable indeed.

Would Berkshire Hathaway superfans buy into a patronage model to support the multinational conglomerate corporation they adore? In a way they already do. Despite the vast amount of commerce that takes place on the convention floor, buying swag is not the prime motivation for most shareholders' attendance. Neither is ensuring that they remember their investment gains or losses; any financial app or budgeting website could accomplish that.

Like many Patreon patrons, a large number of Berkshire Hathaway attendees are looking for the chance to live vicariously through a person they support and admire. Some are there for personal growth. They use the experience as a learning opportunity to better themselves through a philosophy and a lifestyle they hope to attain someday. Others are looking for social status—bragging rights to hold over the friends and colleagues who stayed back home. The T-shirt they can wear to *next* year's event that will prove they're no longer newbies.

But everywhere in Omaha on this spring weekend, fans engage in a dozen different types of activities meant to strengthen an emotional connection with the fan object they love. And it's that active pursuit of closeness, not the number of times that they flash their credit card, that makes them truly valuable.

CHAPTER 2

THE RISE OF COMMERCIAL FANDOM

Click.

It was early in 2011 when Erik Karstan Smith decided to bring his two young children, Luke and Eden, to visit the San Jose Cemetery. Their great-great-grandparents were buried there, and it might be their last chance to visit their graves for a long time. Smith had recently lost his job as a project manager in an architecture office, and life as a stay-at-home dad, while rewarding, was not lucrative. In a few weeks the family would move out of their house. They were leaving San Jose, the city that five generations had called home for over a hundred years.

At two years old, Eden was deep into her princess phase. To celebrate the occasion, she chose a short-sleeved, gauzy dress, and butterfly wings that strapped to her back. Smith helped her paint two more large butterfly wings in purple and teal, drawn around her eyes like a mask. A headband added another two butterflies that rose, antennae-like, above her hair. The butterfly theme was by chance, but the symbolism seemed appropriate. "I wanted to kind of live that metaphor of a resurrection, because we were going to go through that process ourselves, of resurrecting our family in a new life," Smith remembers.

They arrived at the cemetery and headed for a large fountain with four statues representing Matthew, Mark, Luke, and John. "I'm not a religious guy necessarily, but I always love metaphor. I like symbology. [Eden] gravitated to that statue of John, and I thought that was pretty neat, because my great-grandfather's name is John. I really loved my great-grandparents; they were really special to me. I got chills. It was a really emotional moment for me, seeing her go up and hug the statue."

Without thinking, Smith grabbed his Polaroid SX-70, a folding single lens instant film camera. He raised it to his face, aimed it at the tableau, and pressed the button.

Click.

There she is, gazing off into the distance to the left of the viewer, wings extended as she grasps the marble folds of the statue's robes. The photo is yellowish and blurry, but it's still possible to make out the frozen droplets of water from the fountain and the stillness of the cemetery stretching off into the vast space behind her. She is centered within a familiar square frame of white, the bottom thicker than the other three sides. The top has a dark, drippy look, like the film is leaking out of the frame, distorting the sepia square, as though a second later the fragile moment will have melted away forever.

This is a photograph that should not exist. In February 2008, the Polaroid Corporation had made a grave announcement: it would be ceasing production of instant film for its cameras. The photography supplier, so iconic that its name was practically synonymous with the act of instant picture taking, had been all but destroyed by the rise of digital photography. Fewer buyers than ever wanted to work in a chemical-triggered medium that took ninety seconds to develop when digital technology offered so much more: cameras with built-in autofocus and white-balancing tools, instant previews, dozens of filters to process the image, and the ability to upload pictures to sharing sites. Nearly every laptop and phone had a camera, and none of them used film.

Polaroid's consumer camera production had already ended a year earlier, in 2007, so the remaining five factories that produced their instant film were fast becoming superfluous. The company was in serious financial difficulties; it saw no reason to keep production going for an unwanted product. Polaroid would fill its warehouses with enough cartridges to supply consumer cameras for one more year, but after that, there would be no more instant film. No longer would photographers be able to insert a pack of film into their camera, press a button, and seconds later be holding a colorful little square of paper and plastic immortalizing the moment. The film loved by Ansel Adams and Andy Warhol; the film sung about by Outkast, Blondie, Steely Dan, and the Dead Kennedys; the film that had provided a critical plot point in many a Hollywood movie; the film that had chronicled three generations of proposals, weddings, and births would be no more.

The earlier announcement about Polaroid cameras had caused concern, but the announcement about the film triggered a full fan-community panic. Within a month fans had organized numerous responses. Photography blogs encouraged fans to send Polaroid pictures to the company's headquarters in protest. Letters encouraged Polaroid rival Fuji Film to consider manufacturing an instant film that would work in Polaroid cameras. Polaroid fan Ali Kellogg started an online petition to save the film that ultimately collected 30,513 signatures.

Commentators in mainstream media lamented the loss. "There should always be a place for Polaroids because they create a feeling and emotion that's instantly appealing," implored photographer Karen Keats. "Digital cameras are boring," complained British journalist Tim Teeman.

The outpouring of emotion reflects the warm, almost childlike place instant photography occupies within the art landscape, at once kitschy yet intensely personal. "There are no negatives and no digital file, the photo you make on that spot is unique, and therefore feels precious. If you hold it in your hand and crush it, crumple it, it's gone. You can't get it back," says journalist Christopher Bonanos, who has spent years chronicling the history of Polaroid. "In some ways, it's closer to a painting than a photograph by our contemporary measure. There's a cost to each click."

Taking a photo with instant film is an intimate interaction. When a button is pressed, the shutter at the front of the camera opens for a moment, allowing light to strike a piece of film. It's absorbed by chemicals that are attuned to different colors of light. The iconic white borders on the film hold more chemicals that wash over the surface of the film, coloring each layer in the areas where it absorbed the light. A digital file is composed of ones and zeros, and even traditional analog photography involves transferring likenesses from camera to negative to paper. But the end product of instant film is a physical object that has absorbed the very light that bounced off the subject. It's a physical link back to the moment of inception: a made-to-order souvenir.

Instant photography offers a fundamentally social experience— not social in the modern sense of posting to a digital wall or texting a picture to a friend, but social in the sense of helping people to know each other better. Polaroids are for sharing in the moment. The rituals of development—waving the picture, handing it around, labeling it—are all small social interactions that create interpersonal bonds. It's likely that the subject may even have touched the picture, holding it, admiring the colors as they gradually turned from white to yellow to brown, and finally differentiating into full color. And of course, a risqué Polaroid picture is much more secure than a digital one.

As fans rushed to the stores to stock up on what might be the last film of its kind—in Australia, Polaroid film sold at 3.5 times the forecasted rate—the company braced itself for the barrage of disappointment. "We're trying to help what have been extremely loyal Polaroid customers to make our film categories last as long as we can," stated Tom Beaudoin, the president of the company at the time. Still, they held firm.

Florian Kaps was an instant-photography enthusiast and an online seller of Polaroid film who joined the save-instant-film campaign early on. If Polaroid film went extinct, not only would it render useless almost 200 million Polaroid cameras worldwide, it would also certainly impact his own business. Kaps was persistent enough to earn the attention of Polaroid management, who, perhaps in an attempt to temper the backlash, invited him to a party in June 2008 to mark the closing of the Polaroid factory in Enschede, Holland. It was one of the very last factories producing consumer-grade Polaroid film.

André Bosman was also there. It would fall to him, as a Polaroid production manager, to shutter the factory and make himself obsolete after twenty-eight years of service. At the party Kaps and Bosman lamented the coming loss of Polaroid film, a loss that represented a missed opportunity; at the time of the factory's closing, Polaroid was still selling 24 million film packs annually. The figure was well off the 100 million the factory had been designed to turn out in a year, but still a formidable number.

What about a much smaller operation? A gigantic organization needs a gigantic consumer base. But a small organization has a lot less bureaucracy to support. Bosman and Kaps, along with a few investors, returned to lease the now-defunct factory and set about trying to serve Polaroid's recently exited market. They called their acquisition the Impossible Project, with an equally impossible goal: to bring back instant film for Polaroid cameras and, in the process, create an entirely new generation of instant-photography fans.

At the beginning, the goal seemed as unlikely as their name. There were more than one hundred chemical components and several dozen physical ones in the film cartridges. "It was a very crazy supply chain that they had going," explains Oskar Smolokowski, now chief executive officer of the Impossible Project. "It wasn't just one factory; it was like twenty factories all feeding into this one factory."

Bonanos says, "There's a little pod of white chemistry at the bottom of the picture. And when the thing spits out of the camera, it goes between two rollers, which breaks the pod and smears the chemistry over the negative, and thus begins the processing. To get it to work the same way every time, the pod had to be manufactured so that [it] would burst exactly the same way every time, and it had to have just enough liquid in it that it wouldn't squirt out the top of the picture, but also enough that it covered the entire surface. Certainly, it doesn't sound so simple anymore if you're going to make a lot of them. If you're selling film where people are trying to record their kid's birthday party and they don't want to miss it, you've got to get it right."

By the time the Impossible team took over, nearly all the suppliers had long since moved on to other industries, and most of the factory machines were ready to be scrapped. It took two years for the Impossible Project to launch its first instant black-and-white film product.

The new film was not good. The prints were heavily sepia-toned and blurry. Chemicals often leaked out of the film, gumming up the camera innards in the process. It could take ten minutes to develop (color film, released later, could take significantly longer). Any exposure to sunlight could ruin the image. And, of course, there was no way to automatically share it to Facebook.

And yet the terrible film sold. Impossible called them "Pioneers," the instant-photography superfans who were willing to support Impossible through the labor pains of rebuilding their medium. These were the brave souls who bought the early versions of the film, a product that even Smolokowski admits was almost unusable. "The message was very much that we're working on preserving this beautiful medium. It's not there yet. There's no way for us to do this without you actually buying this film," he says. "We had tons of people buying the product, aware of the fact that it was sub-par, but knowing that they're supporting the cause of getting it back."

Releasing a product that barely functioned, especially when it was meant to replace a popular one that had been perfected over the course of half a century, was a risky move. No traditional organization could build a customer base this way. Established companies spend years, if not decades, on research and development before bringing a product to market; a small upstart like Impossible had no such luxury. Aside from the funding issues, their audience wouldn't wait forever. The longer it took, the fewer the number of Polaroid cameras that would remain to use the film.

Rather than hide the messy work of film development, Impossible embraced it. Every terrible, drippy, sepia-toned photo was a mark of progress. The fans rose to the challenge, and they snapped and snapped and snapped, and they sent their feedback back to headquarters. "The fact that it was actually a little bit harder to use almost became like a test of their skill," says Smolokowski.

The Impossible Project counts around 3,000 early Pioneers. As quality improved, the audience expanded to include younger fans in search of novelty and nostalgia; it turns out that hipsters love instant cameras. Within three years, Impossible's small team of chemists had used fan feedback to create an entirely new type of instant film while still getting as close to the original experience as possible. Photos were crisper and faster, with better color. "It was no longer a Polaroid photograph," says Smolokowski. "It was an Impossible photograph."

Dr. Frankenroid

On the day that Erik Smith visited the San Jose cemetery, he was shooting with very early Impossible film, a dicey move in light of the sunny weather and the humidity. But the resulting shot is a better picture because of it, the imperfections adding to the haunting stillness of the scene.

These days, Smith prefers to go by the name "Dr. Frankenroid" when online. The moniker was born in the late 2000s. During a trip to visit his grandparents, Smith's grandmother had pulled out her old Polaroid Impulse camera and took a few photos with her last remaining pack of Polaroid film.

"I had pretty much lost everything," he remembers. "We were just commenting on it, how it was terrible what happened with the economy. A handful of people were just ruining everything. People were running away with all the money; Polaroid was going under. It was just so sad because it was the camera that held all of my images. My childhood and my memories were there. How dare somebody not just ruin our lives but ruin an art form?"

With free time on his hands and a new sense of purpose, Smith tackled the challenge. "I was going to, like the great Dr. Frankenstein, stitch together my beast and combat this thing. Use it as a tool for informing people of the value of these cameras, the value of the history of Polaroid."

He began researching and collecting the old models. Soon he had enough to create an online Polaroid museum. Within two years he had become a self-described expert, a superfan to turn to when someone in the community needed information about an old Polaroid camera.

At the time, the Impossible Project was beginning to take its first steps, and as part of its Pioneer program, it created a contest. The first person to reach "Impossible Status" would be awarded free transportation to tour the Enschede factory. "This was my opportunity," Smith recalls. "I'd been cut down in my life. I'd lost my career. I'm going to show I'm a worthwhile person here. I'm going to win this contest."

The rules involved completing a number of fanlike activities, including uploading photos, recruiting fellow fans to buy film, and visiting some of the Impossible Project's brick-and-mortar stores. Smith was broke, so he set about selling his collection of cameras to finance his bid. By March 2011 he had completed all the tasks but one: he still needed to visit the Impossible store in Tokyo. With most of his remaining savings, he purchased his ticket.

A few days before he was scheduled to leave, the news was suddenly filled with images of huge waves and fleeing people, fires and crushed buildings in Japan. The 2011 Tōhoku earthquake and tsunami is today best known for causing the meltdown at the Fukushima Daiichi Nuclear Power Plant. The headlines were bleak: more than 15,000 dead, a quarter million displaced. Japan seemed like the last place in the world anyone would want to go.

Smith pressed on. His wife bought him potassium iodide pills to protect against radiation, and he boarded an almost empty plane to Japan. "Here I am," he remembers, "this Polaroid fool in the back of the plane doing sketches just trying to keep myself busy. I had two babies at home and my wife, and here I am throwing myself into this with no money."

Here's a snap of the airport upon his arrival in Japan, the room filled with Japanese people heading the other way. Here's a snap of his taxi driver as they headed toward the store. Here's a snap of the bemused concierge at the hotel he stopped at on his way back from the store, his task complete. The concierge is smiling and holding a brochure from the store that reads "Impossible."

Today Smith and his family live up in the Sierra Nevada Mountains in California, in an area with lots of local farms, trees, and fresh air. Smith is working on becoming a licensed architect.

"Photography is so much about capturing memory. It's personal, but then it becomes this objective thing that you can talk about or remember later. Memory is kind of like that, this kind of ghost that lives in our mind. It's not crystal clear like you get with digital photography. It's this fading thing that changes and is hard to grasp, and you have to look closer. There's something neat about that, I think."

Smith didn't win the Pioneer contest—he eventually lost on a technicality. But he believes that Impossible instant film brought him through a difficult period. "I needed something in my life," he says. "They did that."

The Future of Polaroid

Discontinuing instant film wasn't enough to save Polaroid. Following a series of ownership changes and mismanagement, the company went bankrupt in late 2008. When it finally emerged from the courts, it was not the same company as before. Gone was the cutting-edge technology and expertise that had made it a household name. With its namesake factories shuttered, its scientists had found new jobs and its distribution network had collapsed. All it had left was the name and residual goodwill on the part of fans.

The new Polaroid is largely a holding company for the intellectual property rights developed over an eighty-year run. The name, logo, and iconic white border are the company's greatest strengths. Sunglasses, T-shirts, cameras, and photo printing services all bear the Polaroid logo.

The Impossible Project is tied to the Polaroid organization in spirit and mimicry only; it's not a licensee of the organization, nor does it have an official contractual relationship with Polaroid. But Polaroid is lucky to have the Impossible Project around, because it allows the Polaroid brand to remain relevant to new consumers. Staying active within the public consciousness is its most valuable stratagem.

"The spectrum draws people in—the diamond, the Polaroid name, the iconic border. There's no question it resonates with people. I think people can't believe they recognize it. They go, 'Oh, that's Polaroid.' People know it and they're drawn to it," says Dov Quint, who has worked extensively with Polaroid-branded properties.

Modern Polaroid cameras are manufactured by a range of secondary factories that pay Polaroid to use its name for their products. Calling a camera a Polaroid gives it the veneer of history, an implication that this camera too is part of a classic photography timeline, even if the relationship is only a monetary one. The Polaroid Pic-300 Instant Printcamera has become a preteen darling. The Polaroid Socialmatic is a digital camera that prints pictures out on paper instead of using instant film, which means its relation to classic Polaroid cameras isn't even a technological one. In fact, few fans care about these cameras' purely contractual link with the Polaroid cameras of old. "You have younger people who have never had one of these, but have heard stories from their parents or grandparents, and they're like, 'Oh, my gosh, I need one of those. That's so retro and vintage,'" says Quint.

In 2011, three years after Polaroid declared bankruptcy for the second time, it ranked eighty-second on the CoreBrand Brand Power Rankings, higher on the list than Samsung, Verizon, Marriott, and eBay. The Polaroid of today has one of the more powerful brand names in the world, and its name is all it needs to stay there.

Fandom did not save Polaroid. Enthusiasm can't replace the fundamentals required to run a company—the expertise, the product knowledge, and a sound business model. If the core of a company has been disrupted, fan enthusiasm alone cannot keep it alive. But if there's the possibility of it surviving in a new form, fans can help discover what it will be. "This is no longer a mass-market product," explained Kaps shortly after he first started the Impossible Project. "It's something you're into and celebrate."

Fandom Is a Commercial Activity

At the core of almost every fandom sits a thing that can be exchanged for cash: a commercial product. It may be a movie, a book, an interaction, an experience, access to something special, or a pack of instant film, but at their most basic, fan objects are almost always designed to make money. Usually, the fan object's owners make a decision to hide or obscure the commercial implications of their own activities, the sordid monetary effects they hope to achieve from the goodwill they spend so much energy generating.

In March 2013, Coke deployed its "Small World Machines"— vending machines that allowed users to interact with a fellow soda-drinker hundreds of miles away—to shopping malls in India and Pakistan. The company claimed it would encourage communication between the two uneasy neighbors. Participants who "touched hands" through an interactive screen were rewarded with a free Coke. World peace and goodwill between nations aside, we all understand that the company's marketing department almost certainly measured the actual success of the campaign in terms of increased brand awareness, social recognition, and, eventually, units of Coke sold.

This is true even when (perhaps especially when) the fan object is an authentic, verifiable labor of love. The creators of the Impossible Project love—truly love—instant film. It's obvious in their attention to detail, their support for the community, and the financial risk they were willing to undertake. It in no way detracts from the earnestness of their mission to admit that if the Impossible Project is to succeed, they must also make money at it.

Fandom encompasses many definitions, and to pick only the ones that describe the soulless commercial aspects takes a lot of fun out of it. It definitely removes the personal passion, the very real benefits that exist for the fans themselves. But nevertheless, once all the goodwill and intrinsic rewards have been removed, we're left with a recipe for fandom that's purely scientific.

A SUCCESSFUL FANDOM =

CRITICAL MASS + EMOTIONAL RESPONSE + PLATFORM

A successful fandom involves a minimum required number of people who have enough of a positive emotional response to a fan object and access to a communications platform on which to express it. Or to put it another way: fandom is the natural output of enough people finding a place to express to each other how much they like a fan object.

Fans of instant film can easily partake in a basic commercial activity: buying film, taking photos, and then buying more. But when instant-film fans decide they want a more personal connection with the object they love, they have a wide variety of fanlike activities to choose from. They can talk about their photography in the forums on photo.net. They can do their own experiments with new films. They can get their friends to try them, too. They can show off their collections of vintage cameras to each other.

When enough of a population has decided that the original, intended interaction with a fan object isn't enough to fully explore the depths and variety of their affection, fandom is born.

What is the goal of all of these fanlike activities? It's tempting to call them ancillary to the primary commercial activity, fun but superfluous, a diversion for all those crazy folks who can get a little too wrapped up in things. But fanlike activities aren't busywork.

Creating Fan Context

Polaroid is a successful fan object: it has a large number of people who feel passionately about it, and they have found platforms on which to display that passion. The forums and critiques and experiments and museums and resale markets the fans created have given the brand a second chance. The fans didn't save it by walking into Polaroid HQ and offering their services as business managers. They did it by creating a new context in which the brand could continue to exist.

Context is all that extra "stuff" that surrounds a fan object and makes it more than a commercial entity. The rumors about it. The debates internal to it. The social media posts concerning it. The content created with and for it. The rituals and specialized vocabulary developed around it. The pilgrimages taken, and the conversations and documentation about each one afterward. Context is the glue that holds a fandom together. As humans we only have a single person's capacity to engage in commerce; we only need so many shirts, vacations, mp3s, or sodas. But context makes these commercial products relevant even when we're not actively engaged in the act of shopping. Even if every penny of a fan's income goes toward buying Polaroid products, there's only so much salary to go around, whereas the value of a successful fan context is immeasurable.

Snapping a picture of a cute puppy only takes a moment. It's enjoyable to feel the physical sensation of a "click" when a button is pressed, and it's satisfying to see the final print when it's done developing. But outside of the few people in your physical vicinity, no one else will ever share in that enjoyment (the puppy doesn't count). Posting that picture on a Polaroid forum vastly expands its reach, but more importantly, each post is a temptation for others to talk about it, offer suggestions, and share their own cute puppy pictures. For the picture taker, not only is that attention an enjoyable experience she'd like to repeat, but it also inspires others to do the same.

In certain cases, a context might be more powerful than the fan object it surrounds. For example, are celebrities people? Some are, but many celebrities are what historian Daniel J. Boorstin calls "human pseudo-events" who perform large parts of their lives with the aim of capturing media attention and reproduction. Their real power lies not in skills such as singing, athleticism, or modeling; given a large enough population, such abilities are relatively common even at the expert level. Their power lies in their context: their personal story, their flair, how they make people feel. Most celebrities are a complicated collection of rumors, fashion tips, social and political opinions, and licensing deals.

Is it even necessary to have a human being swimming around in all that context somewhere? Possibly not! The street artist Banksy has made a career out of anonymity. He may be a human, or he may be the product of an art collective, or a team, or a committee. More than a dozen writers created the works of Carolyn Keene, who is credited with the Nancy Drew mystery series. And creators of boy bands long ago learned to pick the context around their music group—the dance style, brand tie-ins, and the personalities their performers will portray—long before doing a casting call for the singers themselves.

The Marketing Arms Race

In the postmortem of Polaroid's downfall as a manufacturer (and resurrection as a licensing brand), one criticism is that the company never took the time to develop a robust context. "Polaroid's problem was that they kept thinking of themselves as a camera, but the '[brand] vision' process taught us something; Polaroid is not a camera, it's a social lubricant," notes Sir John Hegarty, a marketing executive with Bartle Bogle Hegarty, one of Polaroid's marketing agencies. And while Polaroid concentrated on the one product it was best known for, an increasingly sophisticated media audience moved on to new developments.

"Old Spice means quality!" says the narrator of a 1957 television advertisement for the long-standing men's grooming brand. A clean-cut Caucasian man stands at a bathroom sink, applying aftershave to his face and looking pretty happy about it. Next we see a picture of the aftershave bottle set against rolling ocean waves as the narrator assures us, "You'll really like that tangy Old Spice scent!" The waves fade to black as he asks, "What does all this luxury cost? Just one dollar! And never did a dollar bring you so much!" We zoom into a final view of the bottle's logo as our narrator brings it home. "Add spice to your life. Get Old Spice aftershave lotion."

The days of these straightforward advertisements, advertisements that say, "We have a good product and you should buy it," are past. The 2010 "Smell Like a Man, Man" Old Spice campaign kicked off with a TV ad, simultaneously released on the official Old Spice YouTube channel, featuring the shirtless former NFL practice squad wide receiver Isaiah Mustafa. The scene starts in a bathroom. "Hello, ladies, look at your man, now back to me, now back at your man, now back to me. Sadly, he isn't me." Mustafa is suddenly on a yacht. "You're on a boat with the man your man could smell like." He holds up his hand. There's an oyster in it. "It's an oyster with two tickets to that thing you love. Look again, the tickets are now diamonds." By the end of the scene he's on a beach, riding a white horse. He's holding a bottle of Old Spice body wash. "I'm on a horse," he points out. There's a logo.

As an ad campaign, "Smell Like a Man, Man" was wildly successful. The initial commercial won the Grand Prix for film award at the Cannes Lions International Advertising Festival and a Primetime Emmy Award for Outstanding Commercial, and received more than 50 million views on YouTube. And it did manage to modernize a brand that many associate with their grandfathers. But, as one critic put it, "What about *next* year?"

An increasingly connected and sophisticated consumer base demands advertising as engaging, entertaining, complex, and smart as they are. Without it, their attention wanes. Each time advertisers develop a new technique, platform, or tactic, consumers are quick to circumvent it. Less invasive methods like web banner advertising or a social media presence are often ignored. More invasive ones, such as video ads, can be skipped, and TV ads can be Tivo'd into oblivion. Only messages that truly delight and thrill have a chance of being heard above the noise, and, even then, the same strategy rarely works more than a few times.

The result is a kind of marketing arms race. Some commercial messages seem so post-ironic it can be difficult to tell what the advertisement is for and how we are supposed to feel about it. What does a video of Will Ferrell walking slowly through a field for thirty seconds want us to do? It's tough to tell (answer: it was an advertisement for beer). It's certainly far removed from "Old Spice smells good, and it's cheap, so you should get some." And even if the message is perfectly crafted to breach the audience's irony armor, it's difficult to identify the best delivery system. The readership for paper versions of newspapers and magazines continues to shrink, and the shift away from broadcast networks to on-demand services has drastically transformed the public's engagement patterns.

Of course, no one has stopped buying bath goods . . . or beer. But consumers have changed the way they decide. Millennials and other digital natives especially are more likely than past generations to look for information before making a purchase. That input usually arrives from review sites, social-media mentions, friends, news articles, rumors, and what that guy at that party said the other day. Thirty-four percent of millennials prefer brands that share information on social media, as opposed to just 16 percent of their older counterparts who do the same. In other words, as the effectiveness of traditional advertising wanes, consumers look to the brand's context to decide what product to apply to their armpits.

Traditional branding is a top-down effort that is generated, owned, and regulated by a brand's own marketing team. It can be carefully crafted to impart the exact nuance and timing required, and when an advertisement misjudges its audience, it can be withdrawn.

Context, by contrast, is generated by anyone with an opinion and can be much harder to control. Its reach is both broader and more robust, but, for the owner of a fan object, there's no way to steer context except in a very general sense of "Let's try this idea and pray that people run with it the way we want." Yet context does take a product and attach a narrative to it, and in doing so it often does the work of advertising more completely than any internally generated branding effort.

Fandom is *externally* generated branding. It allows fans to channel their natural urges toward self-expression and communication into the service of creating this all-important context. In a sense, the purpose of fandom is to project a personal meaning into what would otherwise be a soulless commercial commodity.

The Surge Movement

In 1996, Polaroid released its first digital camera, the PDC-2000. It was shaped like a military-spec airplane: rectangular and flattened, with futuristic bulges, and lenses sticking out of the front and back. At more than $2,000 each, its features weren't unique enough to reverse the corporation's flagging revenue, which had peaked five years earlier.

That same year the Coca-Cola Corporation released Surge brand soda. With its lime-green can covered with red explosions and a graffiti-style logo, Surge debuted as a direct competitor to PepsiCo's popular Mountain Dew. The liquid inside was grassy green in color, acidic and lemon-flavored. The unusually high sugar content led to the slogan "A fully-loaded citrus soda . . . with carbos! Feed the rush!"

In a pre–energy drink era, this was the perfect opportunity for an "extreme" style of marketing (in the mid-nineties, practically everything was *Extreme!*, from flavored corn chips to computer programming techniques). Advertisements for Surge portrayed race cars, skateboarding, military maneuvers, and other energy-consuming pursuits, activities that would find another home in marketing for caffeinated energy drinks a decade later.

For Sean Sheridan, Surge was the taste of high school. "My friends and I would always pile into two or three cars and caravan to wherever we were going. We'd go the same route, all the way around town just hanging out the window, yelling at each other. We would stop off at one of the nearby gas stations, fill up our tanks, and go and get a Surge."

Like many fan objects discovered during periods of personal growth, it is easy to associate beverages like coffee, alcohol, or soda with the coming-of-age stories and friendships of early adulthood. For Sheridan and many other teenagers at the time, Surge was part of new, intoxicating feelings of independence, freedom, and acceptance. "I see it as stretching your boundaries, an adventurous, close-knit-loyalty-to-friends kind of a culture. One of the things that you always had whenever you had a group of friends was a can or a bottle, or a two-liter or ten two-liters of Surge," says Sheridan.

Surge's own hardcore advertising had an unintended consequence: many teacher-and-parents' groups soon moved to ban it in schools and other kid-friendly locations. Reports of kids arriving to class hyperactive and wired were great for marketing, but terrible for public relations. "Geared towards thrill-seeking young people," warns a 1997 Associated Press article, "it causes students to talk more and misbehave." Coke protested that Surge actually had less caffeine in it than many other sodas on the market, and studies have since proven that sugar has no relation to hyperactivity. Still, the product's placebo effect was too powerful.

By 2002 Surge was on the decline. Although there was no official announcement, fans soon noticed stock disappearing from local shelves and drink coolers. Panic set in. "I put all my effort and weight into trying to keep it by making it as profitable as possible, basically buying it out everywhere I went, and making it known that that's why I was at that store," says Sheridan. He wasn't alone—as stock dwindled, hoarding became common. And then Surge was no more.

Coke launched other brands, and Sheridan turned to Dr Pepper and the new Vault soda, launched in 2005 with a similar taste, to fill the vacuum. But he didn't forget his first soda love, and a decade later he found himself searching online for others who felt the same.

The Surge Movement Facebook page was founded in 2011 by Evan Carr, a Californian in his early twenties. Vault soda had just been discontinued, and the time seemed ripe to revisit its predecessor. The goal was simple: get Coke to bring back Surge. By the time Sheridan discovered it, the page had already received significant attention from his fellow nineties-culture fans. Soon Sheridan, along with a third fan named Matt Winans, began serving as page administrators.

This Surge Movement community seemed different from the other Surge-themed pages and message boards that peppered the Internet. Remembers Sheridan, "A lot of the atmosphere coming from other pages wasn't really one of leadership. It was a 'Here's my page, check it out, I want Surge back' kind of thing. It wasn't a whole lot of back and forth engagement. One of our goals is to keep it personal. Make this not about 'Hey, we're these dudes who like Surge, lend us your power,' it's more about 'Hey, this is your fight. Let's all work together and collaborate.' We view all of the people who like our page, our base, as members, so their input is as important as ours. If you make it personal for people, they'll go above and beyond and do amazing things."

One of the first places their approach had a tangible effect was through what can only be labeled fan-generated customer service. When fans asked questions about how to become involved or expressed confusion about a policy, other fans would smooth ruffled feathers before the official admins even arrived on the scene. When an outsider would try to stir up trouble with a post telling the community members to get a life, it was these same fans who would warn each other not to be drawn in, with replies like "Stop being a negative nancy" and "Get off the page if it's a waste of time!" These superfans had spent enough time in the community to know the answers, and they also had internalized enough of the group ethos to represent it accurately. The result was that the message of Surge solidarity went out fast and thoroughly.

Those same regulars were instrumental in spreading the word to other Surge and nineties-related forums, convincing fans there to join the Surge Movement. Some created bodies of shareable content: photos of hands holding vintage Surge cans, drawings of the logo, Surge-themed Halloween costumes, food-pairing recommendations, and of course cat pictures. They also sent in suggestions. "One day there was somebody saying, "We should get a billboard and be like 'Hey Coke, bring back SURGE,' " remembers Sheridan. "And I was like 'That's kind of neat,' and then we moved on. Then somebody else, without any prior knowledge of the first comment was like 'Hey, we should get a billboard,' and after a few more of those we were like 'Maybe we should do that.' "

With only 13,000 community members at the time, the billboard idea was ambitious, but by early 2013 a community-created campaign on crowdfunding site Indiegogo was underway. Backers came from the community page. Fans told their friends. One backer donated $500. By January, the campaign had raised the required $3,745, and the next month a new billboard went up on the road outside of Coca-Cola headquarters in Atlanta, Georgia. It said, "Dear Coke, We couldn't buy Surge, so we bought this billboard instead."

Another fan suggestion culminated in "Surging days." Fans had always been encouraged to call Coke's customer service lines and request the return of Surge, but coordinated efforts meant that once a month, every month, a tsunami of requests would roll in. "After a while we started calling in, and I would get a couple of [Coca-Cola representatives] on the phone that would say 'Oh, is it the last Friday of the month already?'" Hundreds of personal hours were spent pleading, cajoling, and occasionally threatening, although the latter was usually discouraged.

"We got our occasional troll being like 'You're wasting your time on this. If you put all this effort into world peace everybody would be happy.' That really comes off to me as an excuse to never do anything. If you don't focus your energy on what speaks to you, then you're not going to focus your energy at all," says Sheridan.

In September 2014, Surge returned. Suddenly it was available on Amazon, the green shiny can, the vaguely citrus flavor, the bubbly grass-colored sweetness. The launch was subtle, relying purely on word of mouth, text, and private message, with none of the television ads and bravado that had attended its launch a decade and a half earlier. Thanks to a personal email from Coca-Cola North America president, Carr, as founder of the by-then 150,000-strong Surge Movement Facebook page, was the first to know. He and his two fellow community leaders were invited to attend the official relaunch at Coca-Cola headquarters.

The community went nuts. "We had a whole lot of people being like 'Don't tease me, this cannot be a joke. I'll come after you,'" remembers Sheridan. Screenshot after screenshot poured in showing Amazon checkout baskets full of Surge. The initial batch quickly sold out. And within days, there were photos of Surge fans across the world proudly displaying their purchase. Despite the soda's relative scarcity, many pictures showed fans popping open a Surge soda in the company of friends, spouses, kids, and pets. It was the kind of friendly, feel-good sharing that Sheridan remembered from his high-school days. One article crowed, "Those big on nostalgia can have themselves the biggest throwback Thursday (or any other day) of their lives."

Reliving the Past

Both Surge and Polaroid benefit from dreamy memories and strong lifecycle associations they impressed on their fans early in their lives. It's no secret why the eighties and nineties are such a rich source of nostalgia for today's adults. When the baby-boomer generation in the United States finally settled down to the business of reproducing in the early eighties, it caused an upswell in the youth population. This "echo boom" generation totals a whopping 27 percent of today's US population. Inquisitive, independent, riding the end of a wave of economic prosperity, it was a new type of demographic. For marketers, it was a gold mine with a number of interesting opportunities.

For example, Saturday-morning cartoons had existed since the 1960s as a way to consolidate children's viewing time for advertisers, but it took the arrival of this new generation for marketers to realize its full potential. The result was an unparalleled level of product exposure, broken down across different categories: sugary breakfast cereals and other snack foods, fast-food chains, and children's toys. Lots and lots and lots of toys.

In 1983, Ronald Reagan appointee Mark Fowler, an advocate of deregulation and a strong believer in the sanctity of market forces, was made chairman of the Federal Communications Commission. Fowler's time in office coincided with a rise in commercially driven TV for kids: *He-Man, My Little Pony, G. I. Joe, Transformers, Gummi Bears*. Suddenly, many children's shows had some type of commercial tie-in. In a recent documentary, creators of the comic-book-turned-phenomenon Teenage Mutant Ninja Turtles remember that they were encouraged to create the figurines concurrently with the TV show to give them maximum exposure. It wasn't exactly collusion—there was nothing illegal about such close collaboration between TV production companies and toy manufacturers, but it did create an extremely powerful psychological message. When children could watch the Ninja Turtle character Donatello save New York City in one episode, and then immediately find out that Donatello needed their help to do it again in the form of a plastic figurine, the line between TV show and advertisement had become blurry indeed.

Saturday-morning cartoons are no longer the cultural institution they once were. Increased regulation, the rise of on-demand media services, initiatives against childhood obesity, and a voluntary paring back by the children's marketing industry all heralded their demise. However, an entire generation—the Generation X and early millennial demographic—grew up in an intense environment of commercialized play. The childhood memories of many modern-day twenty- to forty-somethings are unusually saturated with Happy Meal toys, breakfast cereal and soda, and saving the universe with plastic action figures.

These memories are as legitimate as those of previous, less commercialized generations—the market-driven core at the heart of all fandoms does not invalidate the important cultural work they do. But it does create a thriving space for nostalgia and retro media that might not have existed otherwise. As the Saturday-morning cartoon generation matures into early middle age and begins to hit its peak spending ability, it's no wonder that mainstream culture has been saturated with echoes of what was once "kids' stuff." Any number of Saturday-morning staples have resurfaced in a live-action form aimed at nostalgic parents and their own new offspring: Scooby Doo, Alvin and the Chipmunks, the Smurfs, Speed Racer, Jem and the Holograms. Others are based directly on childhood toys: LEGO, Battleship, G. I. Joe. Transformers has had no less than four revivals. The TV show *My Little Pony* has relaunched in a blaze of glory and success; one of its most vocal fan bases is adult males (self-identified as "Bronies").

Of course, heavy commercialization isn't the only factor fueling nostalgia-based fandoms. Modern adolescence extends far beyond that of a century ago, when adulthood might begin as soon as the family needed money. The shift to compulsory education through age sixteen or even eighteen, designed to turn Americans into industrious and punctual workers, had the ancillary effect of encouraging a longer period of experimentation and self-discovery before the demands of the working world kicked in.

Today, the increase in college enrollment, followed by an increase in graduate school enrollment, temping, traveling, taking a gap year, and other pre-career activities, have enlarged the safety net. The result is a generation that's more playful, more social, more risk-taking, and arguably more creative than ever before. It's also a population whose delayed family responsibilities give them more money to spend on entertainment and nonessentials. Meanwhile, the recent cycle of economic recession and recovery keeps post-college grads at home longer than previous generations. Returning to childhood rooms and routines can't help but slide newly minted adults back into their childhood power relationships and habits.

The Internet Fixes Everything, Sort Of

In the rise of fan-led brand revivals, the Internet isn't a cause, it's a catalyst. Digital connectivity can't create enthusiasm out of nothing, but it can allow fans to act on their enthusiasm much more easily, just as it also gives those activities unexpected forms and consequences.

Surge is back because the Internet has shifted how groups converge and coordinate. Digital networks lower the discovery cost for fans looking to join a group: a few clicks of a mouse can inform anyone, anywhere, about membership opportunities at any time, instead of relying on word of mouth or traditional advertising campaigns. If humans have a natural urge to join others who have similar interests, the Internet decreases the energy needed to become a joiner.

But the Internet also allows for a broader definition of what joining might mean. A member of the Surge Movement can feel like part of the group by policing comments, traveling to take pictures of billboards, and submitting content. But members can also simply click the "Like" button on Facebook and feel good knowing that they've incremented the page's membership numbers by one, bringing it one point closer to a number that might convince Coke to resurrect the brand. These low-friction options for harnessing fan energy were hard to come by in the predigital world, especially when locating fellow enthusiasts was difficult enough to begin with.

Connectivity also removes the barrier of geography. Despite working together for years on a shared venture, the three admins of the Surge Movement community had never met in person before they shook hands at the relaunch event. Pre-Internet, communities often were forced to counteract geographic diffusion by coordinating large-scale conventions to bring fans together or by organizing local chapters that could support the enthusiasm in individual hometowns. Either way, such efforts required significant hierarchy and leadership to pull off, whereas a virtual gathering space requires very little of either.

Without the need for a strong, top-down governing body to

coordinate a geographically dispersed community, the Internet also reduces the minimum number of people needed to make a group viable and self-sustaining. That number might be as high as the hundreds or as low as two, but however many it is, it's less than it used to be. When less effort is required to hold a group together, fewer people are required to participate before the rewards grow great enough to keep fans coming back on their own.

Stigma and Nerdiness

Few soft drinks have a specific stigma attached to them. Neither do most forms of photography. But that's not the case for many fan groups—being labeled as a fan of romance novels, Death Metal music, or the TV show *My Little Pony: Friendship Is Magic* can have very specific connotations. Depending on their social group, a closet comics fan might prefer not to be seen going into the local comics store. It's certainly true of groups with a more risqué reputation, such as fans of nonmainstream sexual practices or fandoms that are considered unusual for a person's gender or age. While the fans themselves may feel no personal shame about their enthusiasm, they may still feel pressure to hide it from the world.

The anonymity of the Internet has gone a long way toward making those fandoms feel safe. It allows for less intersection between personal and professional lives, which means more freedom to explore and experiment. A work colleague might spot us going into a comic-book store, but it would take a lot more work to discover that we regularly visit comixology.com. Anonymity also helps to dismantle the easy categorizations that cause stigma in the first place; it allows a wider range of membership, and the more diverse that membership becomes, the harder it is to put labels on each member. But aside from providing a safe haven from stigma, the

Internet has had another, much further-reaching effect on the modern acceptance of traditional fandom.

The computer nerd of 1980s America was a stock character in pop culture. He—for it was almost always a young man—was an awkward figure with plaid pants pulled up to his chest, a white collared shirt, a bowtie, and a pocket protector to keep his many pens from leaking. Sometimes there were suspenders. His hair was greasy and parted in the center, his face pimply and fronted by thick black glasses, and his voice was high and stammering. Many a pre-Web sitcom had a token "nerd" figure, from *Saved by the Bell*'s Screech to *Family Matters'* Steve Urkel. They liked comics (ick!) and video games (ugh!). Entire movies were made from the premise— the 1984 comedy *Revenge of the Nerds* is the heartwarming tale of a hapless group of Poindexters as they attempt to understand college social life and have sex with some of it.

The nerd character was actually a twenty-year-old stereotype left over from an age when being a techie was often synonymous with being an academic or working for a government-funded science lab. By the early nineties many companies had sprouted a technical department to keep their new computers running, but their technicians' social status was often closer to glorified janitor: techies were support staff. Every company needed a few of them, but, outside a few specialized industries such as aerospace engineering, they certainly weren't central to a company's mission. The tech department was often in the basement, a closet, or an old, disused bomb shelter in the bowels of headquarters smelling of melted wires and stale potato chips. Very few elementary school kids spent their recess pretending to be programmers.

Then, with the mainstream adoption of the Internet in the late nineties, hundreds of thousands of exciting, high-paying technical jobs flooded the market. These were jobs central to the companies they represented, companies that were founded by programmers, whose first hires and most important positions were still more programmers and technical staff. These were, by and large, new companies whose jobs were relatively high risk. Entire websites such as Fuckedcompany.com tracked the failure rate as startup after startup came and went.

High-risk jobs are perfect for younger workers who aren't afraid to take a position that may be gone tomorrow. The average age of the stereotypical computer nerd plummeted faster than his rising stock options, and it also mutated. He—it was still usually thought of as a he—certainly wasn't an academic. If anything, he probably dropped out of college to make his first million. But he was cultured, well dressed, and had an edgy haircut. An early association with tech centers in San Francisco and Seattle meant he was also probably politically liberal and urban, with the healthy dose of self-esteem that comes from early success. He probably went rock-climbing or skateboarding in his spare time.

With the rise of the Internet and related technology booms, being a tech nerd was suddenly a comfortably upper-middle-class position, synonymous with high-paying and decidedly white-collar jobs. Working with technology had become a highly desirable career for oneself or a potential mate.

It's not surprising that many of the pastimes traditionally associated with being a nerd experienced a sudden rise in respectability at the same time. Partially this was a result of this particular population's newly won financial success and their ability to spend it on their hobbies, but mostly it reflects a new normalization of the nerd's social status. Nerds had gone from janitors to rock stars; being a tech nerd was now socially acceptable, and so too were their traditional fandoms such as video games, comics, and science fiction.

It's interesting to note that traditionally "nerdy" fandoms that were *not* generally associated with this particular demographic experienced little upgrade in status. Fandoms like Japanese anime, which tends to have a younger audience, and the creation of fan fiction, which primarily attracts female writers, benefited from the lower barrier to entry created by the Internet, and they did see an increase in membership during this same time period, but neither experienced much of a change in their social acceptability. To admit to writing a fan fiction story based on the shows *Supernatural* or *Doctor Who* can still cause giggles in much of mainstream society. It's a reaction that's become much harder to trigger by admitting you spent last evening watching the latest Avengers movie.

Fan enthusiasm made Polaroid a household name, but now that Polaroid is no longer relevant as a manufacturer, the company has been given a new lease on life thanks to the nostalgia of a wealthy, playful, and socially connected generation. Surge benefited from all of these phenomena as well. It received the impact of childhood nostalgia, an increase in economic agency, improved connectivity and anonymity, and the rise of nerd culture—the group with whom ultrasugary "energy" sodas have historically been most closely associated.

In September 2015, Coca-Cola announced that Surge was once again back in brick-and-mortar stores. Shelves across the country would be filled with lime-green cans. A bottler in St. Cloud, Minnesota, reported it had run through its entire year's supply in two weeks. Its director of sales apologized. "I'm the guy to blame for running out," he said in an interview. "I put together the forecast. I figured 4,000 cases would get us through the rest of the year. I didn't realize the size or scope of the Surge fan base."

CHAPTER 3

FROM CONVENTION TO CONVENTIONAL

"We Have a Place for You Here"

On that first day I was very shy. I had a coin purse in my bodice and I sang my song. "Apples, fresh apples, come buy one from me! Try my cold juicy fruit picked off me own tree! Apples!" And a man came up to me but I wouldn't look at him. Remember I was shy. And he handed me a quarter. I saw the quarter. I took the quarter, put the quarter in the little coin purse, put the coin purse back in my bosom, reached to get an apple, handed him an apple without looking at him, and I heard him say, "I don't want an apple." And then I looked at him. "What?" He said "No, I just wanted to see you make change." I put the apple back, and after that I've looked everyone in the eye. It just kind of like woke me up to have a good time.

Judy Kory, on playing the Lord Mayor's wife
in Faire, An American Renaissance

I n the summer of 1963, the residents of the Hollywood Hills neighborhood of Los Angeles could often be seen outside in the surrounding hills, hammering together planks of wood and sewing colorful pieces of fabric. Hippie-style camper vans dotted the landscape. A vast construction site was emerging at Oliver Haskell's Ranch a few miles north of the town, seemingly staffed entirely by colorful bohemians.

These talented young people normally would have been hard at work in the nearby movie industry, but the country was still reeling from the Red Scare of the 1950s. Conservative politicians had taken full advantage of Cold War–era hysteria about communism, and the resulting blacklist of suspected sympathizers had abruptly ended or paused the careers of a considerable portion of the movie industry. Suddenly, it was the early sixties and a huge group of actors, set makers, costumers, and other creatives had found themselves unemployable in Los Angeles.

Many of them saw no reason not to lend their talents to a groovy new project run by local children's-theater teacher Phyllis Patterson. Patterson was known for an unusual curriculum based around group improvisation, slapstick comedy, and mobile set pieces. Her Laurel Canyon neighborhood, a West Hollywood bedroom community, had been hit by the latest round of anti-Communist layoffs, and as her children's workshops became more popular, the idea of using her class to make a political statement began to take shape.

By spring, Patterson had developed the concept of a "Medieval Faire" using the props and skills her students had developed in class. She and her husband pitched it to the local radical radio station, KPFK, as a fundraiser. The station's lawyers offered a critique: the medieval period was not known for its human rights successes. The concept was immediately changed to a Renaissance festival to reflect a "rebirth" of liberal values.

A call went out over the KPFK airwaves. Five hundred volunteers were recruited from neighbors, the parents of Patterson's students, and their out-of-work colleagues to create sixty booths and hundreds of costumes. Craftspeople from the local artists' commune were enlisted to sell their pottery and hand-loomed blankets. Hundreds of psychedelic-style posters were printed up. "Jog Your Deep and Mery Way to the Renaissance Pleasure Faire and May Market!"

Jugglers! Belly dancers! Wenches! Knights! Fools! Queen Elizabeth! In its first weekend, 3,000 people visited the faire. By year two, the size of the faire had doubled. A larger site was found. KPFK changed its unofficial slogan to "A Renaissance in Radio," and soon other towns across the country were creating their own events.

The Renaissance faire is a uniquely American phenomenon, one that has little in common with its fifteenth-century European inspiration. The jousting tournaments, craft vendors, harp and lute music, and woodsy location might evoke a village feast day in Merry England, but there the similarities end. The language is 100 percent American, albeit sometimes with a Beatles accent. The wording is a sort of faux King James English filled with *thou*s and *prithee*s. Entertainers and wandering improvisers don "garb" rather than historic clothing—costumes that have more to do with sensual or symbolic characteristics of the part they portray than with anything their Renaissance counterparts might have worn in public. The smoked turkey legs that have become synonymous with half a century of Renaissance faires are, not to put too fine a point on it, from a particularly New World bird.

The purpose of the early Renaissance faires wasn't historical re-creation exactly, certainly not once the Pattersons began to expand the concept beyond its politically inspired roots. The population to whom the early festivals most appealed was not academics. It was rebels.

It may be going too far to say that the Renaissance faire invented the sixties, but it certainly gave a huge boost to what the sixties meant. For the local alternative communities, the faire was a chance to retreat from a world that made them feel unwelcome. Inside those gates, they could mix with others like themselves, don liberating, playful costumes, and try out new forms of sexual experimentation, professional fulfillment, and drugs. The bright colors and loud music, sexy dancers, and infamous after-hours parties were a refuge of counterculture. On the outside, long hair and a beard might mean distrust, or possibly even arrest. Inside, they could make someone Robin Hood.

It was at the faire that hippie men first tried on tight velvet leggings and flowing shirts with brightly colored patches. Soon performers like Jimi Hendrix were dressing up in gold brocade jackets and red silk, sashes and bows. For ladies, faire versions of Renaissance clothing often allowed women to go braless, to express their sexuality, and to experience an unprecedented level of physical freedom. The corsetry and flowing fabric of Renaissance garb also accommodated a much larger range of body types than was found in the pages of 1960s *Vogue* magazines. As Jenna Dawn put it in an interview with Faire chronicler Rachel Lee Rubin, "It was a heady experience—the first time I got any attention from men! . . . It was quite an awakening. It helped to save me." A 1996 article in *Spin* magazine (by popular author Elizabeth Gilbert) puts it even more succinctly. One patron explains: "I'm fat. I have a lot of problems with self-esteem in life. But when I put on this costume I'm gorgeous." In the early years, nudity wasn't uncommon.

Early faire sexuality in general seemed far more free and easy. Costumes and other trappings of innocent play allowed forms of otherwise taboo experimentation. In a decade when homosexuality was still a jailable offense, many first homosexual experiences occurred at the Faire under the safe guise of portraying a character. A strong BDSM community sprung up, making use of the faire's playful take on corporal punishment and its many leather vendors.

Professionally, the faire supported careers. Roles for out-of-work actors were just a beginning. Magicians Penn and Teller performed their first gig together at the Minnesota Renaissance Festival. The Flying Karamazov Brothers got their start at the Northern California Renaissance Pleasure Faire, eventually going on to Broadway. Many present-day alumni of the Big Apple circus, Cirque du Soleil, and other members of modern vaudeville have their roots at a Renaissance faire.

As the faire grew it expanded to new locations and evolved, fostering a community of like-minded artists. Whether they were selling ceramics or sandals or wooden trinkets, these craftsmen revived a waning American crafts movement. The classic counterculture publication the *Los Angeles Free Press* got its start as the *Faire Free Press*, when founder Art Kunkin dressed up his two young daughters in garb and entered the fairgrounds armed with his first printing. Faire news on the outside ("Shakespeare arrested for obscenity") yielded to real-world news in the form of articles about alternative filmmakers and radicalistic groups on the inside.

As fans recall those early days, they echo themes of self-discovery and relief—and of belonging, sometimes for the first time ever. "To us, come Sunday night, you realize that wow, I've left my village again and now I have to go make it in this outside world so that I can make the money to go back to my village," remembers faire alum Sean Laughlin in a recent documentary about early faire life.

For many, the faire offered a family of a sort, bound together by a rejection of the world outside the gates. Members of the faire quit their jobs and began new lives on the inside, married fellow faire workers, and had faire babies who themselves became faire workers.

William Barrett of performance troupe Cock and Feathers recalls, "You could be something that you couldn't, that you were afraid to be, out there."

Filmmaker Doug Jacobson, who has been documenting the faire for years, observes, "The Renaissance Faire motto was, you are a misfit; you're an outcast; you're awkward. You're discarded by society. We accept you. We have a place for you here."

Fandom as Utopia

Academics are known for reevaluating their interpretations of social phenomena. It's what keeps them employed. Since the 1950s, new interpretations of what the phenomenon of fandom means show up every few decades, igniting new waves of interest in fan studies, and how fans should be treated and supported as a result.

Since their beginning, fandom academics have separated the study of fan cultures into roughly three historical phases based on the thinking of the period and the observed behaviors of fandoms at the time. Call them first-wave, second-wave, and third-wave interpretations. Or to give them our own names, let's dub them "fandom as utopia," "fandom as societal re-creation," and "fandom as identity."

"Fandom as utopia," one of the earliest attempts at understanding fan behaviors, is the tendency to ascribe idealistic motivations to a fan group and its members, to portray fandom as a place where marginalized members of society can experience love and friendship far away from those who would judge them. It's a common mantra: This fan group is different from other fan groups. This fan group is a safe space, where we treat each other better. The members of this group are kinder, nicer, more tolerant, more interesting, more intelligent, more creative than outsiders. The members of this fan group may have been misunderstood by mainstream society, but here we have built an even better one.

In 1973, more than 6,000 people assembled at the Commodore Hotel in New York for Star Trek Lives!, one of the earliest fan conventions for the TV show. During an interview, one woman explained her group's philosophy: "We try to measure our behavior according to the Vulcan ideals of tolerance. The idea that we can coexist with each other, not just passively, but that the interactions of people who live differently can produce something greater than the two could have produced by themselves."

Fans of broader science fiction often point to the genre's optimism and hopefulness about what the future could be . . . if only the rest of the world would listen to them. It's a concept applicable to any range of subcultures. Fans of pop singer Lady Gaga are encouraged to see themselves as advocates for civil rights, just as fans of the yoga apparel brand Lululemon have a wide range of health-minded beliefs that include positivity, work-life balance, friendship, simplicity, children, and also yoga.

Thinking Different

When Apple, the multinational technology company, launched the iPod portable media player in 2001, its white earbuds quickly became a token of membership. As one blogger at the time put it, "Once you start to notice them, you realise that they are everywhere, worn like badges of pride. iPod owners give each other knowing glances on the bus or in the Post Office queue—'Ah, another believer.'" The signature white Apple earbuds acted like a secret handshake, a visual marker that said: "We are alike. The outside world may not understand us, but we are both special and different."

"Think" had been an official motto of IBM for almost a century when, in 1997, Apple tasked its new CEO, Steve Jobs, with turning the failing company around. The resulting, now-legendary marketing campaign was called "Think Different." It was a way to place Apple in direct opposition to more mainstream computer companies.

Rather than highlight the brand's technological superiority, "Think Different" highlighted its idealistic superiority. In print advertisements, on billboards, and in TV spots, the centerpiece was a set of simple black-and-white photographs of progressive heroes such as Albert Einstein, Jim Henson, Mahatma Gandhi, Martin Luther King Jr., and Jackie Robinson. To keep from appearing as though they were exploiting the people featured, donations of equipment and cash were given to each participant's charity of choice. In one advertisement, the pictures show while a voiceover narrator says: "The misfits. The rebels. The troublemakers." These are the people who "see things differently," the ad continues. The ones who cannot be ignored "[b]ecause they change things. They push the human race forward."

The "Think Different" campaign is credited with giving Apple new momentum, just as many core users were contemplating a shift to Windows or Linux-based systems. But the campaign did more than that—it established the concept that Apple users were better that other computer users. More creative. More intelligent. A misunderstood minority whose amazing genius would soon be appreciated by the world. And, more importantly, it was possible to self-select into this brilliant aristocracy with a purchase.

Long after the end of the campaign, *our users are special* has remained an important theme for Apple.

The utopian theorists have a point. A feeling of refuge from the outside world is integral to many fandoms. The more alternative the fan object, the harder it can be to feel accepted away from fellow fans, and the more necessary the safety of a like-minded group.

Rennies (as faire fans often call themselves) have certainly felt their share of stigma and backlash from mainstream culture. As early as 1967, Phyllis Patterson faced major political challenges. Her mainstream neighbors had begun to protest the faire as a cesspool of drug use and promiscuity. Local authorities announced mandatory fingerprinting for all faire artisans. A newly created "special use permit" for the faire space was blocked by a group of local fundamentalist ministers. Impassioned speeches begged the local chamber of commerce to protect law-abiding citizens from the "weirdies" and "undesirables" who would surely threaten homes and property. Arrest rates of attendees were so high that even local judges expressed concern. Police helicopters flying over the faire became so commonplace that actors learned to improv them into their scripts by pointing and shouting, "Dragon!"

While Rennies might allege that the scorn and condemnation was a judgment against their idealism and countercultural tendencies, it likely came down to something much simpler: their social class.

Classy Fandoms for Classy Fans

High-class taste is frequently a euphemism for tastes that broadcast access to money or social capital. Avant-garde French films are classier than stoner comedies because they require an expensive education, or at least the leisure time to become self-taught, to appreciate what's going on. The subtle reference to a month spent in a Tuscan village is classier than a mention of a weekend at Disney World. Cantonese food at that one hidden little gem in Hong Kong where you have to wear a tux to be seated, they don't really take outsiders but my assistant can get you on the list ... is more classy than a takeaway of Chinese noodles from the local mall's food court, even if—and this is important—the mall version actually tastes better.

Stigma against a fan object often has less to do with the value of the object itself, and everything to do with the perceived social status of its fans. The more blue-collar the fans, the less the worth outside society attributes to the fan object.

From a strictly commercial point of view, the horrorcore music duo Insane Clown Posse may bring in more revenue than the famous Takács Quartet string ensemble, but the former is given significantly less cultural credibility. Succeeding as a pro wrestler with the WWE requires skill and training, as does becoming a Shakespearean actor, but only one of them would probably be welcome at a high-society cocktail party except, perhaps, as a novelty.

In a fandom-as-utopia worldview, embracing cheap popular culture is scandalous but empowering. Having been excluded from formal culture through a lack of social, cultural, or financial capital, these oppressed outsiders scratch value out of the only outlet remaining to them. This is fandom as a form of rebellion, fans who say, "Society says I'm not worthy of attending their snazzy opera, but I can have just as much fun with a midnight showing of the gender-bending sci-fi classic *Rocky Horror Picture Show* at the local cinema. I can make my own utopia over here, using the tools you don't care about."

How accurate is this worldview? It's difficult to say. Certainly class issues of this sort are well in evidence at Renaissance faires. To this day faires are still often staffed by itinerant workers and artists who follow the seasonal cycle from north to south and back again. As modern-day carnival employees, they often have few financial resources; some even lack a permanent residence for the off-season. Many are unsalaried workers without an economic safety net, which means that the tribal colors of the upper class—a sophisticated education, physical status symbols, and long-term health and aesthetic maintenance—may be out of reach.

In one telling example, at the New York Renaissance Faire overweight female fans are sometimes referred to as "Sloats." It's not just a pun ridiculing their scanty outfits and overflowing corsets; it's also a sly poke at the local village of Sloatsburg. As a tiny middle-class settlement, built in the shadow of the affluent gated community of Tuxedo Park, Sloatsburg is a prime target for class-based uneasiness.

Dropping out of mainstream society has a price. As Steven Gillian puts it in the documentary *Faire: An American Renaissance*: "[You] quit college, cut the soles off your shoes and join the circus. And you were only going to do that for six months, and lo and behold, now you find yourself [working] the beverage crew. You're delivering ice. You're sixty-seven years old. You don't have health insurance. But, then, maybe it's also a case of what the fuck, I'm having a good time and I don't care." Of course, "what the fuck" may be a reasonable philosophy when the rest of the world has already labeled your subculture, as one critic puts it, "fat middle-aged people in odd outfits acting weird."

Fandom as Societal Re-creation

In the late seventies and eighties, Renaissance faires began contemplating ways to broaden their appeal. By then, hundreds of festivals had sprouted up around the country, from single-weekend shows at local fairgrounds to multimonth behemoths with designated land and permanent structures. But despite their ubiquity, many privately owned faires were struggling with financial difficulties. More and more began consolidating under corporate ownership, and holding companies soon operated multiple faires all over the country. Add to the mix an aging festival population and an influx of harder drugs, and the time seemed right for standardization and commercialization.

Regimented, structured, insured, and profitable, the newly reworked faires quickly expanded to a wider audience. While many still used local craftspeople, some operations opened to a flood of cheap Chinese imports. Some long-time vendors were pushed out, replaced by stalls hawking Vegas-style plastic drinking tubes and T-shirts screen-printed with medieval-themed vodka ads. Corporate sponsorships from companies like PepsiCo and Delta Airlines became commonplace. Family-spirited discounts and theme weekends attracted a more mainstream, budget-conscious clientele that had no interest in paying premium prices for one-of-a-kind crafts. As actor Billy Scudder put it, "The faire scene was a love-in; now, it's a business."

The free-spirited volunteer network that had made earlier faires so successful dwindled, as did the open-door policy allowing actors, musicians, and artists free access as long as they were willing to contribute their time. Says Jacobson, "Those people started going, 'Well, hey, you know, I would do this shit for little or no money just to be part of this, and now you are telling me I'm not valuable anymore.' If you create something that is part of somebody's identity, then when it becomes more popular and other people start showing up who aren't authentic and don't care about all the past indoctrination, those people will start to rebel and get really upset."

Utopian-style fandoms often take antiauthoritarianism as a given. In 2004, the Renaissance Entertainment Corporation, then owner of the Northern California Renaissance Faire, announced it was closing because of profitability concerns. Seeing an opportunity to put power back in the hands of crafters and staff, community member Lisa Stehl managed to save the faire by turning it into a participant-owned event. Yet she soon found herself fighting the same anger that had been directed at the previous owners. "These people want to kill their savior," says Jacobson. "They are very opinionated people, and they are very dramatic, and they will get upset, and they'll try to just take shots at the person in charge." It mattered not that they were now themselves the authority figures; resentment had become a cultural norm. No matter how noncommercial their origins, many fandoms follow a similar trajectory.

The Desert Ain't What It Used to Be

Burning Man, the infamous creative camping event held each year in the Black Rock Desert, is part art show, part wilderness survival retreat. Each year, nearly 70,000 attendees flock to this dusty patch of sand in northern Nevada for a week of socializing and partying with their fellow "Burners" and to show off monumental art projects that are often the culmination of a year's worth of work.

The origins of the event are humble—a solstice bonfire among friends, which slowly grew into a temporary city of freethinkers. Aside from an admonition against guns in camp, the only official rule early on was, "Don't interfere with anyone else's immediate experience." Kindness, openness, sharing, these were the attitudes to aspire to. In fact, all the hallmarks of the early Renaissance faire period can be found in abundance: relaxed sexual attitudes, nudity, drug use, personal creativity, and people having a great time, freed from the standard mores of society.

To keep from going the way of similar-sized festivals, such as Comic-Con, which many have accused of devolving into a pop-culture wasteland, the camping ground of Black Rock City is ostensibly a commerce-free space, where only coffee and water—

indispensable after a night of partying—are sold. Many attendees bring food and crafts to give away or barter, but no money can
change hands. Those found selling goods are evicted from the
event. Participants tape over even the smallest logos on equipment,
and, despite the heavy involvement of Silicon Valley, very little
overt patronage is in evidence outside of a little networking and
recruitment. Yet, even here, where anticommercialization is the one
unbreakable rule, things are changing.

"At Burning Man, the Tech Elite One-Up One Another" shouts
the subheadline of a *New York Times* article from the summer of
2014. Recent years have seen the rise of turnkey camps, luxury
encampments set up by paid staff before the arrival of their wealthy
owners. These private oases of comfort often include private air conditioning, private showers and toilets, and entertainment centers.
The inhabitants can arrive by private jet, sometimes accompanied
by their own personal butlers, chefs, masseuses, and paid entertainment. Some deals even include premade art pieces for them to show
off. The cost for a truly luxurious, custom-made Burning Man experience: $25,000 per person, or more.

Such camps have been accused of violating the spirit of Burning
Man, claiming all the fun of a camping trip with no dedication to
the event's underlying principles of self-reliance, ecological commitment, and sharing. Sometimes RVs will be circled up to exclude
passersby from a camp. Some attendees retain bouncers to deal with
anyone who looks like he doesn't belong. A number of camps have
even been accused of draconian work conditions, although it's difficult to know if the workers are honestly facing exploitation or if they
feel exploited in relation to the original spirit of the event.

Burning Man takes place in a desert. A wind-scoured, unfor-
giving desert where temperatures routinely reach a hundred
degrees and dangerous dust storms are common. Getting there

is not cheap, and survival for a week requires planning, endurance, and a decent amount of cash. Nice RV rentals from nearby Reno soar up to $8,000 during the festival. Even in the simplest of camps, this is a truly expensive slumming of the type that normally requires careful preparation, spare time, and access to the specialized equipment and supplies needed to survive in a remote and unforgiving environment. Standard tickets cost $390 each.

The financial ability to drop or outsource family and social responsibility for a prolonged period of time narrows the eligible population even more. A full week of vacation (plus travel time) is a luxury generally only available to employees with paid leave, or those skilled enough that they can afford to quit their jobs once a year. Few single mothers of three working night shifts as a waitress to make ends meet will ever see the tents of Burning Man. It's an experience that's largely open only to the financially stable, or those with access to a financially well-off social group that can subsidize their stay.

The 2014 Burning Man census found that more than 35 percent of Burners made more than $100,000 a year; by comparison, only 8.5 percent of Americans did the same. A disproportionately high number of attendees were millionaires.

"The tech start-ups now go to Burning Man and eat drugs in search of the next greatest app," said Tyler Hanson, a paid "Sherpa" at a turnkey camp. "Burning Man is no longer a counterculture revolution. It's now become a mirror of society." In the summer of 2016, one turnkey camp was even vandalized by disgruntled Burners who cut electricity wires, dumped potable water, and sealed camper doors shut while the well-heeled owners attended a dance party.

That's because fandom isn't utopia. Or, perhaps, it isn't only utopia, certainly not for everyone, and even when it is, it's never one for very long. Every ideal world is subject to the dangers of its own success. There is always an inevitable gentrification that comes with successfully colonizing a previously borderline cultural space.

As academic thinking on the fan phenomenon shifted in the eighties and nineties, "second wave" fan studies emerged to rethink fan-group creation. It had become clear that fan motivations were more varied and complicated than a selfless devotion to utopian ideals. A more Machiavellian explanation was needed.

This is "fandom as societal re-creation." In the new interpretation, fan groups were no longer a shelter for people rejected by an uncaring mainstream. Instead, fan groups were a chance to re-create the mainstream system around different criteria: a new hierarchy where the creators might this time get a chance to be on top. A high-schooler who felt picked on and rejected, socially or romantically, for valuing brains over brawn might join the chess club. "In chess club," our stereotypical nerd might think, "*I* get to be the one who picks on the newcomers who are still learning the game. And maybe in *this* setting, someone will decide I'm impressive enough to date."

Few subcultures of any type pass up the opportunity to divide themselves into a hierarchy based on perceived status and clout. Even at Burning Man, that bastion of social egalitarianism, newcomers unprepared for the harsh environment are sometimes labeled "Sparkle Ponies." It's not a compliment. In gaming and technology, fresh faces are "Newbies." At the Renaissance faire, woe to attendees who try to buy their way into the hierarchy by purchasing an entire set of garb without first doing the background research.

It's difficult not to detect elitism in the tendency to label which fans are more experienced, more real, more authentic, or "better" fans than others. For every fan who joins a movement for utopist reasons, there are others with baser motivation. And sometimes the reasons for becoming a fan straddle a little of both worlds. While Apple computer users may or may not be part of a new creative aristocracy, the social benefits of displaying one of the most recogniz-able, most expensive technology brands cannot be ignored. Apple computers often cost hundreds of dollars more than their closest competitors' models with similar specifications. Dell, HP, Lenovo, and Asus all offer less expensive laptops with faster processors. Apple software interfaces have a reputation for being easier to use, but the fanaticism they inspire can seem out of proportion to their technological properties. However, unlike Dell's or Lenovo's, the exteriors of Apple products are immediately identifiable in a way that shouts its high-priced identity to the world. Those white ear-buds, that glowing case, the iconic colors and logos of an Apple phone or laptop make it more than a piece of equipment; it's also a status symbol. Few other technology brands embrace this level of visual branding, but it's a core component of Apple product design. It's difficult to entirely discount the economic prestige signaled by an Apple purchase.

In the case of the early Renaissance faire, the motivations for some fans may have been even simpler. Outside the festival gates, attracting a social standing, and with it a member of their preferred gender, might be difficult. Inside, there was significantly less com-petition. As Jess Winfield of the Reduced Shakespeare Company put it, "It was a place where geeks and misfits and people who didn't fit in their everyday life could go and get laid."

It's certainly a different interpretation of the "renaissance" of idealism that made such a difference to American culture in the six-ties and seventies.

The Revolution Comes with Purple Hair

"At one point, if you wore a miniskirt, you were assumed to be a hooker. You couldn't find stiletto-heeled shoes or spike-heeled shoes. You'd have to go to a thrift shop. Or, do what we did, and dig in basements of old shoe stores that had stuff they forgot to throw out from the sixties." Tish Bellomo looks to be in her fifties, but it's difficult to tell. There are few pictures from the past forty years of her or of her sister Eileen, who goes by "Snooky," without both of them sporting wild, fluorescent-colored hair. Snaps from the eighties show it layered, feathered, and back-combed into a fiery mane. At the moment, it's bright pink with a green streak at the front.

"We used to go to stripper stores," says Snooky. "We found these great stashes of all these pointy-toed Beatle boots that no one else had. We found a big stash of black jeans. Everybody would hear about it and come for them. Then we found a big stash of stiletto shoes."

"And a basement full of go-go boots. We essentially hit the mother lode there," remembers Tish.

In the mid-seventies, just as the Renaissance faire was edging into the mainstream, Tish and Snooky were living in New York City's East Village. The American punk scene was in full swing thanks to performers like The Ramones and Patti Smith, and the music club CBGB had become the (arguable) epicenter of the movement. Located at the corner of Bowery and Bleecker streets, it hosted everyone from The Talking Heads to The Misfits to The Police. And starting in 1974, Tish and Snooky spent their evenings there as backup singers for the band Blondie.

The punk movement had a lot in common with the hippies of a decade earlier—the same youthful rebellion, the provocative clothing and ostentatious hairstyles, a do-it-yourself approach to music creation, a relaxed attitude toward drug culture, and an affection for BDSM-style paraphernalia.

With bands forming faster than they could be named, supplying the music was not a problem. But supplying the gritty, urban trappings of a punk lifestyle was a little more difficult. Leather, spikes, stilettos—all had few mass manufacturers in America at the time. When fellow scenesters started asking the sisters where to buy their signature style, Tish and Snooky decided to supply it. They borrowed $250 from a family member, raided the same amount from Snooky's savings, and—with friend Gina Franklyn—rented a small storefront on St. Marks Place, and opened a punk-clothing boutique, likely the first in America. At their mom's suggestion, they named it Manic Panic.

Having no business experience forced them to rely on their own taste. "People would try to sell us stuff that they told us would really sell well. Maybe it would have, but if we didn't like it, we wouldn't sell it. We only sell stuff that we would wear," Snooky remembers. "Johnny Thunders [came in], trying to sell us a saddle because he wanted money. We wouldn't take it, because we didn't want to sell a saddle. I wish I had that saddle now."

One of the first items they chose to carry was a line of bright, semipermanent hair dye from England. The East Village took notice. Then the press took notice. In little time, shoppers were making pilgrimages there from uptown, then from New Jersey, and then from Japan and the Netherlands. "All these people started coming in, and at that time, we had hardly anything to sell because we had hardly any money," says Snooky. "I was like, oh, my God. What's going on? Why are all these people coming?"

By the early eighties, Manic Panic was synonymous with crazy hair color. It was a verb: to Manic Panic someone's hair was to turn it Wildfire Red or Atomic Turquoise in the same way that "to Google" has come to mean searching online. The Manic Panic storefront became so iconic it was used in the opening credits for the 1980–81 season of *Saturday Night Live*. When MTV showed up a few years later, there was only one place to visit for those who wanted to look like they'd stepped out of a music video.

In the meantime, the St. Marks store itself was becoming a center for punk culture. Members of the B-52s remember making regular pilgrimages. So did Cyndi Lauper and The Ramones. It had a family feel. Says Tish, "Our store wasn't just a store. It was like a clubhouse, a hangout for people, like a social scene where people would come because it was cool. It was this gathering place for bands and fans." On Christmas Eve they would stay open late, and friends and musicians would pour in with wassail and cupcakes. "Everybody would get all emotional and teary," remembers her sister.

As a concept, it certainly evokes what their hippie counterparts would have called a good vibe, or as Tish puts it, "This is the feel-good hair dye." Through the years, both sisters have continued to perform with their band the Sic Fucks, and the brand remains heavily involved in charity work.

Today, Tish & Snooky's N.Y.C. Inc., the sister-owned corporation behind Manic Panic, concentrates primarily on hair dye, and operates out of an office in Long Island City. The New York City clothing store is long gone, a victim of Manhattan's rising rents and the brand's need for warehouse space, but there's still a small retail area near the front for those pilgrims willing to make the trip to Queens. Inside, one wall is covered with tributes and gifts from grateful fans. One customer has sculpted them a giant tub of Manic Panic. Some fans make them handmade jewelry, others make paintings, many of them portraits. "They're a little scary," admits Tish, but she and her sister hang them up anyway.

There are also plenty of notes about personal experiences. "There was one girl who wrote to us and said she was suicidal. She dyed her hair, and it made her so happy, and took her mind off of her problems. It just made her feel good," says Tish. She recalls one elderly Canadian woman who reported that she had felt invisible and lonely before she dyed her hair purple: "She said it changed her life. All of a sudden, people talked to her and wanted to take a picture with her. Everybody was friendly to her. She just had so much fun. It was just the sweetest thing."

"It really does change the way you feel when you change your hair color. I love my hair pink. I just love it. When I come into work here, I look around. At least 50 percent of the people working here have beautifully colored hair. It just makes me feel so good every morning. It just puts a smile on my face. When I see all the pretty colors, it just makes me kvell," says Snooky.

Fandom as Personal Expression

The story of Manic Panic certainly sounds like a utopian fandom, but it's not. Not exactly. Despite the early ideology of the movement, the personal stories of belonging and refuge, by the late eighties drugs, the AIDS epidemic, and mental-health issues had taken a heavy toll on the first-generation punk population. It was not a scene of idealism.

Possibly as a result, the significance of Manic Panic products began to change dramatically in the nineties as models and sports figures made brightly colored hair safe for the general population. The memories of punk's early days may remain, but there's a key difference in how contemporary Manic Panic fans interpret the hair-dyeing experience. For one thing, the meaning of crazy-colored tresses has become much more diverse. Today, it would be impossible to pigeonhole someone with a bright green dye job. He might be showing solidarity with urban youth, or it might be St. Patrick's Day. A band member might dye her hair orange and blue to show her allegiance to alternative social norms, but she just as easily might be a fan of the University of Florida's football team.

And yet, this isn't exactly re-creating society. There are certainly elements of it—punk popularized the term "poser" in the English language (from the French *poseur*, pretending to be something you're not). To accuse someone of posing is a challenge to his fan bona fides; to accuse him of going through the motions, of not being as true a fan. It's a classic method of pulling rank over those "beneath," especially those of the wrong gender, race, or class. Yet, when it comes to hairstyle, the mainstreaming of unusual dye jobs has been largely embraced, even by many who were part of its original punk genesis.

Today Manic Panic seems free of much of the usual baggage that accompanies a multidecade phenomenon. It even successfully survived losing its physical claim to authenticity—the lease on its original store—with very little fan backlash against its products.

It's also survived extensive commercialization. Manhattan has almost no traditional shopping malls, so when mass stores such as novelty chain Spencer's Gifts and teen clothing store Hot Topic started ordering Manic Panic, at first there was no hint that the brand had broken into the mainstream. Manic Panic was suddenly available in almost every suburban mall in America. There have even been occasional licensing deals—a line of hair salons in Japan, a few cosmetics, a brand of wine, an occasional T-shirt. Yet, in general, the name Manic Panic is still synonymous with the dye that Tish and Snooky made famous.

Manic Panic is less a story of mass co-option and more a history of intense personalization. Modern fans use the product for the same purpose as their punk predecessors—to show off their unique sense of style. But the definition of who's allowed to be unique and what that means has expanded.

This is third-wave fandom, fandom as self-expression. This most modern theory of fandom rejects the definitions of earlier decades—the rosy vision of a perfect utopia, an oasis for the lower classes, or the self-promoting, hierarchy-obsessed world of re-creation. In fact, many modern fans would be surprised to hear their hobbies and enthusiasms described as class- or status-inspired at all. That's not to say that some modern fans don't feel like outcasts, or that they don't gain confidence by victimizing others. But current definitions of fandom—what academics call "third wave"—rely more heavily on the purpose that fandom fulfills for each partic-ipant. The longing for a safe space away from the world has ceded ground to one concerned much more with personal expression than how that expression appears to others.

Pigeonholing fans into any particular lifestyle, class, or set of motivations is not as simple as once believed. We now understand that *everyone* participates in one or more subcultures, often many at the same time. A specific set of tribal colors can no longer be assigned to a single group membership. Or, to put it another way, class remains a strong societal force, but dividing out *which* sym-bols represent *which* class is harder. A pair of ripped jeans might be a pointed critique against modern trends toward disposable goods, or it might be a pair of predistressed Gucci Genius jeans (retail price at one time was $3,134) signaling an attraction to luxury items.

A recent study, amusingly titled "Negative frequency-dependent preferences and variation in male facial hair," points to a great exam-ple of this: the fewer the members of society with beards, the more attractive beard-wearers appear to potential mates. The beard indi-cates that the wearer is outside of the norm. Being in opposition to the majority style makes it a wearable symbol of alternative philo-sophy and lifestyle. When too many people have a beard, the reverse becomes true, and clean-shaven chins become a symbol of rebellion instead. There may even be a point over which society rocks back and forth—so-called "peak beard"—when wearing a beard shifts from rebellion to conformity and back again. It certainly muddies the water for anyone using facial hair as a clue to decide if a guy is appropriately alternative or not.

To make the situation more complicated, in a society where everyone chooses to rebel in some ways and conform in some ways, it can be difficult to know who counts as mainstream and who doesn't. Few fandoms fit into a strict "us versus them" philosophy because, while the Internet has made it so much easier to define "us," it has become increasingly hard to determine who is part of "them." In 1960s language, the fight against The Man has become more complicated than it was when lines could be drawn around groups of "hippies" and "squares." It's a rare modern individual indeed who can fit everyone's definition of mainstream.

Everybody vs. The Man

J. K. Rowling's Harry Potter books tell the story of a young, unloved orphan who suddenly discovers he's a popular and powerful wizard destined to save the world. Suzanne Collins's Hunger Games trilogy tells the story of an impoverished teenager who suddenly discovers that her natural abilities make her the perfect figure to lead a rebellion and save the world, or at least, her nation. In Stephenie Meyer's Twilight book series, a shy wallflower suddenly discovers that her amazing smell allows her to befriend and influence a powerful array of vampires and werewolves, and save (at least her part of) the world. The TV series *Hannah Montana* tells the story of an awkward young high-schooler who is secretly an ultra-mega-pop star, beloved by millions. She does not save the world, but she probably could.

Exceptionalism describes the rise of storylines that portray early teen wish-fulfillment fantasies. The plotline usually goes like this: a young, unloved, or bullied outsider discovers that he or she is actually a secret princess, wizard, celebrity, savior, witch, god, super-hero, or alien, or has some other unexpected ability that makes him or her very special. These characters are thrown into a new, exciting world in which they are beloved and admired. There is often a romantic love triangle. In the end, they save the universe and find acceptance on their own terms, with a new group of friends that truly understands them.

Exceptionalism carries a valuable message of control, acceptance, and power during a period of development when we all feel powerless: about our social life, our future, even our own body. Most exceptionalist plots also contain a revenge fantasy against those who dared to underestimate us. Such plots have been a staple of science fiction and fantasy writing as far back as Susan Cooper's *The Dark Is Rising* and Orson Scott Card's *Ender's Game*, but their sudden, overwhelming popularity in young-adult fiction has taken many observers by surprise. The phenomenon has been variously attributed to a new cultural fascination with celebrity, the rise of reality television, the navel-gazing effects of social media, or some combination thereof.

No matter the cause, rebellion—here, stories about people who succeed by being countercultural—is now big business. Take, for example, the evolution of Disney films: early Disney animated films such as *Cinderella*, *Snow White*, and *Pinocchio* all stressed the benefits of kindness, patience, bravery, and loyalty. But by the Disney Renaissance period in the late eighties and nineties, movies like *The Little Mermaid*, *Aladdin*, *Beauty and the Beast*, and *Mulan* offered heroes with a different set of values: independence, self-reliance, and embracing dreams even when it meant disregarding authority figures. The centerpiece of the Disney smash hit *Frozen* is the now-infamous anthem "Let It Go," an ecstatic tribute to the benefits of telling the world to go to heck (this is still Disney, after all). It's an empowering message, and it's a lucrative one. As of 2016, *Frozen* was the highest-grossing animated film of all time. Few parents of anyone ages two to twelve have not been subject to at least one viewing.

When citizens of Hollywood Hills petitioned their chamber of commerce to save them from the hippies in 1967, it's unlikely that they could have imagined a future in which rebellion itself had become safely middle class. Perhaps more than safe—healthy even. Experimenting with the bounds of authority is an important part of modern coming-of-age narratives. The very word "alternative" no longer means "dangerous and subversive." More often than not, it's a term that stands for "strong and independent."

And in the meantime, selling the trappings of that rebellion has become a huge business. Renaissance-style bodices can be bought in any Victoria's Secret lingerie store. Stiletto shoes and studded black leather regularly tour the catwalk in Milan. Blue, purple, and pink hair dye shares the shelf with platinum blond and medium brown at local pharmacies.

We stigmatize fandoms at our own peril. Who knows what currently downtrodden movement will be considered an important sector of the economy next?

In her fight to preserve her creation, Phyllis Patterson eventually broke through the political roadblocks. The Renaissance faire thrived, but it took far longer for local residents to admit that the impact on the tourism industry, land values, theatrical performance, the crafting movement, and modern culture in general made it a worthwhile commercial effort.

Within only a handful of decades, the economic landscape had shifted. In 2007, on the other side of the country, the following letter arrived at Manic Panic headquarters:

Dear Friends:

Congratulations on Manic Panic's 30th Anniversary! New York is the world's most exciting city. We are the American cradle of punk rock, home to a very colorful cast of characters, and (as anyone who's seen our busy streets at rush hour knows) a place where life is sometimes manic and panicked. Therefore it's no surprise that our residents have become so fond of your hair dyes, clothing and cosmetics, not to mention the huge boost you've provided to our local economy! . . . I know you'll make our great city even prouder in years to come. On behalf of the city of New York, please accept my best wishes for continued success.

Sincerely,

Michael R. Bloomberg, Mayor

CHAPTER 4

WEARING OUR FANDOMS ON OUR SLEEVES

Frida's Margaritas

Frida Kahlo is giving away margaritas. They're churning out of a slushy machine, a lime-green frozen mixture sloshing against the plastic sides of the container. They taste . . . very nice, actually. They would be at home in a nicer college bar on Cinco de Mayo: clean and citrusy. Frida Kahlo Tequila: "100% Blue Agave. Ultra premium tequila in Blanco, Reposado and Añejo captures Frida's Passion for Life and satisfies your taste buds with the essence of Mexican culture." The matching website concurs. "You already enjoyed Frida's iconic paintings. Now enjoy her passion for life. Tequila!"

The artist, iconic and iconoclastic, glares from a poster in her colorful dress and unmistakable black unibrow. Industrial-strength spotlights burn up above. On one pedestal, there's a plastic Frida Kahlo doll. There's her signature, printed onto a pair of Converse sneakers. There it is again on a pair of cowboy boots. Glossy brochures show Frida Kahlo–branded beer, Frida Kahlo magnets, Frida Kahlo mouse pads and calendars. A Frida Kahlo corset from

La Perla. A Frida Kahlo Mastercard design. Her face on a blouse from the popular clothier Zara. The official slogan, plastered everywhere, reads, "Frida Kahlo: Pasión por la vida!"

The actual Frida Kahlo was a complicated figure: feminist, political activist, Mexican patriot, and, of course, brilliant and tortured artist. Polio, followed by a body-shattering traffic accident, left her in pain for much of her life. A tumultuous marriage to fellow superartist Diego Rivera was rife with intrigue on both sides—she had affairs with numerous men and women; he had affairs with, among others, her sister. She was a devoted Communist and an active supporter of Joseph Stalin, yet she was also the lover of rival Marxist revolutionary Leon Trotsky. Through it all, she painted, mainly self-portraits of the tragedies and loneliness of her life: Frida Kahlo as a young girl with a grinning skull instead of a head; Frida Kahlo bleeding from open wounds in her leg and foot; Frida Kahlo wearing a necklace of thorns; Frida Kahlo covered in blood on a hospital bed after a miscarriage. By the time she died at the age of forty-seven—whether from a pulmonary embolism, the official finding, or an overdose is still debated—she had created dozens of these portraits of pain.

"She was very much into aromatherapy," states the official press release for Frida Kahlo 100% Natural Skin Care. Products such as the company's signature Omega-3 antiaging and antiwrinkle face creams contain ingredients like rosemary oil and Japanese green tea. In 2007, Naturals Skin Care, Inc. licensed the use of Kahlo's name from her official brand-name owners, the Frida Kahlo Corporation, along with the company's "Pasión por la vida" tagline.

It's the second day of the Licensing Expo[*] here at the Manda-

---

[*] The majority of Licensing Expo events described are from the 2014 conference, but some quotations and specific events occurred during the 2013 Expo.

lay Bay Convention Center in Las Vegas, Nevada, and today the Frida Kahlo Corporation is hoping to entice other manufacturers to follow in the steps of Natural Skin Care. Tucked into the side of the "Characters and Entertainment" area, the Frida Kahlo booth is bright with colors and imagery direct from Kahlo's Mexican context. Sales representatives pass out pamphlets and slushies to the crowd as they wander by on their way from the Power Rangers booth to the elevated Sea World platform. "Have you heard of Frida Kahlo? She's gotten really big with a new generation. She's actually trending right now on Twitter. We're having a lot of luck with the eighteen-to-twenty-five age range," says one of the reps.

Fandoms for Sale

The Las Vegas Licensing Expo fills the entire convention center, positioned next to the Shark Reef, the casino's showcase 1.6-million-gallon aquarium. Out on the Strip, the heat makes the air shimmer and the entryway is filled with kids pushing their way into the air conditioning and up the escalator to ooh and aah at the fish. Walking in the other direction, thousands of manufacturers, brand owners, and media analysts will head down, past the posters and statues of Thomas & Friends and Bon Jovi, and into the cavernous space that is the south convention hall. Inside it looks like an extremely tasteful flea market, but the commerce here doesn't require inventory. Despite the visual similarity to pop culture–themed conventions such as the San Diego Comic-Con, the merchandise on sale here is very different.

This is where fandoms are bought and sold.

Licensing is the commercialization of a fandom. For many brands, celebrities, and media properties, their most valuable asset is often not their product; it's their audience. When an audience grows large enough, it becomes worth quite a lot of money to manu-facturers and other brand owners. Licensing offers other businesses the rights to purchase and use a property for a new purpose.

Licensing has become so commonplace that we often don't even notice it. Placing a Chicago Bears logo or a Mickey Mouse face on a shirt or baseball cap is a win-win for everyone involved. The prop-erty licensor gets cash, at rates that are generally anywhere between 3 percent and 22 percent of the product's wholesale price, with almost no additional work on its behalf. In return, the manufacturer gets an in-demand article of clothing to sell and a built-in fan base to sell it to. Consumers get a trendy tee.

For a movie, a large, enthusiastic fan group with money to spend may be worth much more than ticket sales. The animated feature film *Despicable Me* was a success at the box office, bringing in $543 million gross worldwide. But at the Licensing Expo, it begins a sec-ond incarnation as a licensing property. Two standout items within the movie were runaway hits with consumers: a fluffy unicorn doll (that inspires the young character Agnes to exclaim, "It's so fluffy I'm gonna die!") and a group of yellow Minion henchmen who speak gibberish-sounding Minionese. Both have seen new incarna-tions in a wide variety of merchandise, including Halloween cos-tumes, duct tape, folding chairs, backpacks, Tic-Tac mints, and of course, T-shirts.

"It feels like everybody has a Spider-Man T-shirt. In middle school you wouldn't be caught dead wearing a [comics or cartoon-themed] T-shirt, that was like the kiss of death. But there's not that level of shame in anybody born 1990 and on. It's not an embarrass-ment to them. They embrace this. I think you would almost be ostracized for *not* having a Captain America T-shirt. It's become so universally loved and accepted that you're almost the odd man out for wearing a polo with nothing on it. Or a blazer—God forbid you put on a blazer." So says Jesse DeStasio of Striker Entertainment. As Vice President of Business Development it's his job to connect licensees, that is to say, fan object owners, with potential licensors looking for properties with which to brand their products.

"Early on in my career, one of the biggest brands I worked on was the Twilight film saga. Nobody saw it coming. The conventional wisdom said, 'Girls don't buy products; girls are going to the mall to meet boys. They're not going to buy a T-shirt.' Then it became a huge global phenomenon, and it ended up being highly merchandisable. What [Twilight writer] Stephenie Meyer did is she captured something universal: Twilight is really about the first time you have a crush on someone. That all-encompassing feeling of newness and desire—usually when you're heading into puberty. And it's confusing and depressing and obsessive. The way Bella longs after Edward and feels confused about Jacob, we've all had that, male or female," he says.

"Ultimately, girls identified with Bella. I think that they wanted to have a little piece of how they felt when they read the book or saw the movie in their day-to-day life. If you think of the idea of a 'totem,' that's what a consumer product is. It's a little totem for the brands or the characters that you love, that you need to be reminded of."

In licensing terms, a movie like *The Twilight Saga: New Moon* (or *Despicable Me*) is an advertisement, the bait that draws consumers toward a huge moneymaker: related consumer goods. What may have started with T-shirts and posters now covers nearly every type of product. There are Twilight key chains, rings, necklaces, lunch boxes, jewelry boxes, puzzles, water bottles, purses, wallets, action figures, candles, belts, trading cards, throw pillows, umbrellas, watches, tote bags, duvets, hairdryers, makeup, and an official Twilight wedding dress.

By the time that *Minions*, the third Despicable Me movie,

launched in July 2015, Universal had already seen $2.5 billion in retail sales of products related to the movie franchise. Universal itself sees only a portion of those sales as royalties, but it's still a formidable number.

Of course, the Holy Grail for both licensors and licensees is the evergreen property—a brand that requires no introduction. "When I think of evergreen stuff, obviously Star Wars comes to mind. Hello Kitty, LEGO I think is pretty much golden, anything they touch is great. It's always beloved, it will always be on store shelves. It is not dependent upon trends. It will always survive. The brand may ebb and flow but ultimately you're always going to have the interest of the buyers," explains DeStasio.

Four hundred and seventy licensors are in attendance, representing the rights to more than 5,000 brand names, celebrities, media properties, art pieces, and anything else a manufacturer might want to turn into a lunch box. Each booth, some of which cost tens of thousands of dollars to construct, shows off the advantages of licensing a particular property. Walls display artwork, statistics about the size and enthusiasm of its fan group, and plans for future expansion and advertising. The Kahlo booth is more approachable than most; many display only a tasteful logo, white walls, and a security guard. Admission into the booth of a sought-after property such as Cartoon Network, BBC Worldwide, Grumpy Cat, or Pokémon usually requires an appointment.

The Characters and Entertainment zone has any number of other celebrities, media properties, and personalities. The Endemol Licensing booth represents the TV shows *Big Brother*, *Deal or No Deal*, *Fear Factor*, and television host and personality Steve Harvey. Core Media Group is trying to license Elvis and Graceland, *So You Think You Can Dance*, and boxing legend Muhammad Ali. Around the corner, Live Nation Merchandise offers up the rights to Nirvana, Coldplay, Lynyrd Skynyrd, and the Wu-Tang Clan.

A huge two-story booth by toy manufacturer Hasbro comes complete with crystal chandeliers and custom wood floors. Giant pictures from the *My Little Pony* animated show dot the walls. In front, two ladies in pastel dresses demonstrate *My Little Pony*–themed makeovers. A half dozen middle-aged women in corporate suits have lined up to get a pink-and-purple hair extension clipped into their somber curls and pageboy cuts.

Stonyfield Organic is offering to license its name to other food products that need an in with the coveted "mom" demographic. Their licensing agent, Brandgenuity ("Where can we take your brand today?"), is also offering the rights to Playtex feminine products, the History Channel, and the Juilliard School. Coca-Cola, with $1.3 billion in licensed product sales annually, has procured an entire island to itself. Convention-goers crowd around it, holding up cell phones to snap pictures of an a cappella group singing corporate jingles. The video game Tetris shows off its successful licenses for underwear, mugs, stress balls, and scratch-off lottery tickets. The Boy Scouts organization wants new clients to join its 150 existing licensees, who already produce products like granola, cookware, and walking sticks. The very rugged-looking Trademarking Resources booth (Jeep, HillBilly Beverages, and the National Rifle Association) currently hosts two midriff-flaunting booth girls. They pose for pictures in front of a display of gun-themed pet products, sunglasses, lighters, and a gun safe called the NRA Fatboy Junior.

Walking the padded carpets between the aisles from one end of the Expo to the other can take thirty minutes. As an industry show, the crowd is quiet, businesslike, and middle-aged. The average attendee has a comfortable waistline and fashionable glasses, staring down at padfolios or catalogs as they power-walk from meeting to meeting. Others crouch on the carpets around the power outlets, rumpling their suits in an effort to charge tablets and cell phones. Snatches of conversation float up from the murmuring groups: "Try saying something that isn't a threat but sounds like a threat, like 'We will consider avenues outside of the US' or something" and "Let's go after Urban Outfitters again."

To find out what is actually going on inside the private meeting rooms nearby, it's necessary to read the daily convention newsletter. Peanuts and sports brand Umbro will be making Snoopy-themed soccer wear. Sega Europe has high hopes for the retro appeal of Sonic the Hedgehog. 1928 Jewelry has just signed on to create a line of necklaces and earrings based on *Downton Abbey*. The animal-welfare activists at the ASPCA are hoping to put their logo on a wide variety of toys, housewares, and jewelry. Actress Gwyneth Paltrow has made a speech about the importance of taking brands global. "My hope is that we'll continue to reach more people in more places with things we love and want to share," says the pull quote.

"A licensed product is likely a guarantee that you're going to sell ten times the amount, just by virtue of recognition, just by virtue of being able to get in front of the buyers of retail stores," observes DeStasio. "Every single product and every single package and every item that's put on a shelf is a little tiny billboard for your brand. Just having somebody walk past the shelf at a Hot Topic and seeing your logo, that face-to-face interaction, that's extremely valuable. Especially in an increasingly digital world."

The winners here are rarely unexpected. In 2015 the top-grossing licensor was Disney, with $45 billion in sales, and the top-ten list is peppered with the likes of Mattel, Sanrio, Warner Brothers, and Major League Baseball. Car manufacturers like General Motors and Ferrari do well, as does health guru Dr. Andrew Weil's Weil Lifestyle, to the tune of hundreds of millions each.

For licensors, the Expo is their best chance to buy a new personality for themselves. They must choose with care the products to associate with; these are the coattails on which their brand will ride for the next year. While each contract is an attempt to borrow the fans of the licensor brand, it also changes what the brand means. Nerds candy is a box of sugar crystals covered with acidic candy coating, but with one signed clothing contract, Nerds is also a fashion statement.

Rounding a corner on the north side of the Convention Center is a spacious white booth. It sports a wall-sized photo of Pope Francis and the tagline "End of the World Pope." A number of attractive Italian ladies in matching skirts and pumps are eager to be helpful. "This is our big reveal. I think it's bringing people together who wouldn't be into it," says one. The pope is listed in the directory under "Characters and Entertainment." He is licensing his name, signature, picture, and official slogan ("Pray for me") as it pertains to—and as a benefit for—his favorite football team, San Lorenzo. His likeness graces backpacks, shirts, sweatshirts, notebooks, and rubber bracelets.

It might feel a little disquieting to see a dollar value placed on our enthusiasms, memories, loyalties, and even spirituality. These properties, and what they stand for, are deeply personal to many people. It's our first time watching *Star Wars* or taking that spring-break trip to Disney World. It's a memory of baking Toll House cookies with a grandmother. It's our community or spirituality. It can feel dystopian to think of all of these personal associations in terms of their commercial value, as something that can be sold to the highest bidder. It's easy to imagine shadowy figures conspiring in a boardroom to decide what we will love and cherish next year. But that's not exactly the case.

"I just bought a pair of slippers off of Instagram. They're the best shoes I've ever owned. Would I have been more inclined to buy them if they were Metal Gear Solid branded slippers? 100 percent. I couldn't have clicked that button quicker," says DeStasio.

"We live in a chaotic world where we are at the mercy of any number of variables. We are not in control of whether we live or die. This collective compulsion, the idea of displaying and curating things, is a way of having order in a universe where there is no order," he muses. "It's a reminder of what that brand evokes in you."

In one sense, it's true that one of the main purposes of our beloved fandoms is to provide positive emotional associations for other products that we otherwise wouldn't look at twice. And yet, fan experiences and feelings of identity and membership are very real. The fact that those same experiences are sometimes the result of a handshake between businesspeople rarely has any impact on the way they make fans feel. Fans are experts in taking what they want from a property and interpreting it for their own purposes. What a fandom means to people, and the important role it plays in helping them express themselves, is deeply personal and authentic even if the origin may be more contrived.

Saving Great Britain

Populations pass in and out of fandoms depending on what they need at various points in their own personal development. Scholar Matt Hills even postulates a fandom autobiography—a chart showing how someone's deepest fandoms line up with periods of personal change, strife, and growth. We might become fans of heavy metal in a reaction to the first wave of hormones in our early teen years, fans of baby-toy brand Skip Hop when looking for guidance as a first-time parent, and fans of Harison's Yellow, an early American breed of rose, as a way to spend our time in retirement.

Fandoms can be temporary or permanent, but they are always

timely. In this context, fandoms become almost a form of self-help, a way to work through or experience new periods in life. A way to "become a better you."

Great Britain's relationship with the memory of World War II is complicated. While the fighting didn't finish Great Britain off, it did add a touch of humiliation to an already tragic situation. A country with a strong ethos of cultural superiority had barely survived annihilation by an enemy that was inarguably better equipped, trained, and organized. And their rescue came thanks to an uncultured upstart of a former colony, at that. Great Britain was a traumatized nation, its people shorn of their sunny supporting lands, sifting through the rubble of their homes, reliant on foreign aid for the very food they ate.

And then, then something wonderful happened: onto the gray bitterness of 1950s British literature arrived James Bond. Bond, the archetypal superspy. Bond, the international traveler. Bond, the master of lethal, ultra-advanced weaponry. Bond, the well dressed, the epicure of fine food and wine, the seducer of women, the powerful and well-trained strategist, the winner against all odds. Most of *Casino Royale*, the first book in the Bond series, takes place in France—a trip that would have been financially out of reach for most Britons. Bond enters a poker tournament, and an American gladly hands over a bulging envelope of cash in deference to his superior skill. In one scene of lavish extravagance, he even *eats an avocado.*

"*Casino Royale* was to the beleaguered nation a salve," argues author and historian Simon Winder, in his book *The Man Who Saved Britain*. It wasn't just escapism; James Bond introduced an alternative narrative of British power. Espionage—fast, exciting, honorable—is the opposite of the grinding war of attrition that eventually won World War II. In this new version of British supremacy, the United Kingdom might be little, but unbeknownst to everyone it was still doing amazing things. Not for Bond the parades and public accolades of heroes like Superman or John Wayne's cowboy characters. He worked in secret, behind the scenes. "Bond may have been a one-man band, but as he toured the colonies that Britain had ceded to America, readers at home were reassured that at least we'd retained our sense of style. He epitomized the cozy fiction of the lopsided Anglo-American alliance. The Yanks might have become the masters, but only the Brits really knew how to behave," wrote William Cook in the *New Statesman*.

It's hard to overestimate the reviving effect Ian Fleming's creation had on British culture. He was the right man, at the right time, and certainly in the right place. He offered a reason to go on.

Humanity has always asked questions about the way the world works, and how we should act to survive and succeed there. How should we behave? Where do we belong? What's happening to us? These questions have traditionally been answered with mythology, the stories and warnings supplied by religion, local community, and family. Myths are an easy shorthand for teaching cultural norms. Knocking on wood to warn off the jealous fairy folk reminds us, "Don't take your good luck for granted!"

Modernity isn't satisfied with these answers. In a time when transportation is ubiquitous and changing location is common, sources like extended family groups, traditional geographic community relationships, and religion have become a weaker influence than in past generations. We understand now that no single information source is infallible. For many, rebelling against their family, hometown, or childhood spirituality is an important part of their "becoming an adult" process. As traditional mythologies give way, it makes sense that we should look to other sources for answers to these very human questions.

The 1986 fantasy movie *Labyrinth* is a cult favorite among many a Generation Xer. The story of a young woman's fight to free her brother from the clutches of the evil Goblin King is simple and charming, and its heroine Sarah was a first crush for many. The online repository fanfiction.net has almost ten thousand *Labyrinth* and *Labyrinth* crossover pieces of fan fiction—derivative stories detailing the further adventures of Sarah and her brave band of misfit friends.

It doesn't take long to notice a trend. For every fan-made story about the characters fighting a new villain, there are five that detail Sarah's struggles with everyday problems. Moving to a new goblin town. Dealing with elf bullies. Sexuality. Depression. Anxiety. Abuse. By the time we get to stories describing Sarah's nervousness about complications in her first elf-pregnancy, and how she feels about the goblin doctor's insistence on bed rest, it's obvious that whatever is going on here is a lot more personal than a mere adventure story.

It is no secret why Ian Fleming created James Bond when he did; he himself was active in the war, and the bleak new world that emerged from it was hardly a victor's prize. "If Fleming was born when the British Empire was at its apex," wrote Cook, "Bond was born just as its power began to wane." James Bond hit the English national psyche at a time when it needed a realistic hero for its new reality.

Bond's popularity turned him into a major national export—Bond movies, along with the international success of the Beatles, quickly rewrote what being British meant to the outside world. And Bond helped rewrite what being British meant to the British as well. Winder notes, "Nobody else—writer or writer's creation—has more powerfully engaged in managing that vast shift from Imperial state to European state. Fleming somehow, through some kind of heroic version of his wartime work, moved everyone on."

Something becomes a fan object by filling a deep-seated need in a fan's life. Maybe the fan is looking for a new philosophy or perspective, or a new friend group, or just a new way to spend time. In this sense, fandom is very much tied to fans' current situations and feelings about their lives. It will ebb and flow as a fan's life changes and evolves. Fan objects offer modern mythologies, the stories that tell us how we should approach the world right now, at this point in our personal history.

Fandom Is Healthy

How much agency do we have in choosing our fan groups? How much conscious control do we have when it comes to the things we like? Most of us likely don't care about the underlying nature of our affiliations, just as we may never consciously consider the physical, psychological, or social benefits we receive from them. It's easy to read purposefulness into the choosing of new fandoms during times of uncertainty, but in reality the process is often subconscious. Our own brains know what we need, and our brains find it for us.

In the mid-2000s, researcher Daniel L. Wann and his collaborators conducted a number of studies into the advantages of sports fandom membership. In one, Wann surveyed 155 university students in Kentucky (59 male, 96 female) about their level of involvement and identification with the fan group for a local sports team. Then he asked them questions about their social self-esteem and general satisfaction with their lives, rating their feelings on a scale of low to high. As a control, the students were also asked about their feelings for a distant sports team, one they cared about but, for geographic reasons, could not engage with its fan groups as fully.

The results were clear. High team identification, that is, "the extent to which the fan views the team as an extension of his or herself," leads to higher levels of social and personal self-esteem and well being, and higher levels of positive emotions. Fans are less likely to feel alienated or angry overall, and less likely to report emotions of loneliness, depression, or fatigue. These results aren't just a side effect of a general interest in sports. Fans who care about a team, and are able to access a group of fellow fans such as themselves, are truly happier, more well-balanced people. And that's even more true when the team is on a winning streak.

Daniel Wann posits a complex feedback interaction, which he calls the "Team Identification–Social Psychological Health Model," that allows sports fans to use their affiliation to live happier, fuller lives without ever consciously choosing to do so. These are the feelings of belongingness and camaraderie triggered by following a local team. It's easy to locate fellow fans of the Ravens in the team's hometown of Baltimore. Many people on the street wear jerseys and hats with the logo on it, and the team's activities often come up in conversation. Many local habits are formed around rituals involving the Ravens, such as going to games, tailgating, or hosting viewing events. "In environments such as this, fans of a local team can feel part of something grander than the self. They gain vital connections to others in their community and a feeling of camaraderie," explains Wann.

Teams lose, coaches leave, scandals occur. In a group setting, fans learn valuable psychological compensation techniques. These are practices such as how to distance themselves from stressors. How to engage in "retroactive pessimism" (revising their memory of how hopeful they were after a disappointment), and outgroup derogation (taking out frustrations on a ritual enemy instead of on themselves or each other). In a group setting, they can feel good about themselves when their team is successful and learn how to control their feelings when it isn't.

We are descendants of apelike creatures who survived because they were willing to identify as part of a larger group with a shared purpose. As we have become more sophisticated, those urges haven't gone away. Identifying with a social organization helps individuals form the connections that lead to better mental health. While few people today feel the need to invoke religion to summon the tribes for mating or mammoth-hunting purposes, tight communities of friends based around shared commonalities—what sociologists call "families of choice"—still have huge tactical advantages.

As described in chapter 1, socialization is one of the most basic of fanlike activities. Using the existing framework of a subculture is a fast way to quickly build trust, gain acceptance, pass on important information, and learn new skills in a safe environment. And as anyone who has ever been to a fan convention can attest, it can certainly provide valuable mating opportunities.

Marketing professors Bernard Cova, Robert Kozinets, and Avi Shankar call this a transcendence in conformity, the romance of feeling like part of something bigger than ourselves. It's an exhilarating yet comforting feeling. And it's one that can be triggered by becoming a member of a new religion or a new political movement, becoming more involved with a local sports team, or by joining the Corgi Nation (fans of the little stubby-legged herding dog from Wales). All these groups exploit this feedback loop from our ape-ancestor brains. It's no wonder that they bestow similar positive psychological benefits.

We're All Individuals Together

In an episode of the animated TV series *South Park*, the elementary-school character Stan asks a group of Goth kids how he can defy mainstream society and become a nonconformist like them.

Between flips of dyed black hair they tell him, "If you want to be one of the nonconformists, all you have to do is dress just like us and listen to the same music we do." While it's written for laughs, there is truth here. There are few actions more fiercely individualistic than choosing an unexpected group with whom to conform. It's a whole lot easier to express our unique individuality if there's a larger community backing us up, reassuring us we're still socially acceptable.

Fandom emerges from two very different motivations—the need to identify with a fan object on an individual, personal level, and the urge to feel like part of a larger group where members share similar traits and goals. We want a sense that we are unique and special, but we also want a sense of belonging. Fandom spans this paradox nicely. It allows us to show off our unique individuality while at the same time feeling protected by a larger, supportive group.

Identity leisure describes the process of trying on different personalities to find the best fit. It's not uncommon to pass through dozens of different subcultural identities during our lives: a Goth phase, a hippie phase, an indie music phase, and probably a dozen others, before our personalities settle down (at least until the next period of upheaval).

Fandom involves identifying with different fan objects, each of which comes with a new social group, new activities, and new ethics, social norms, and values. Experimenting with various fandoms is a way to answer the question "Where do I fit in?" It lets us move quickly from one concept of self to another and allows us to experiment with new philosophies, politics, love, friendship, and rebellion, in a series of supportive environments.

Showing fellow community members that we too belong to the same group as they do is an important part of identity building. As we choose fandoms with which to link our sense of self, even temporarily, we look for ways to express our affiliations to the outside world. While die-hard fans may go out of their way to create home-made fan tributes—clothing, accessories, artwork—most tradi-tional consumers prefer to purchase their tribal colors.

The Licensing Expo provides them. Those purveyors of fandom are counting on the group loyalties of fans to sell their T-shirts, posters, earrings, wallets, belts, toys, and frozen food. The fans are counting on the purveyors to give them thoughtful products they can use to show off those same affiliations.

Harry Potter and the Fair Trade Chocolate

As fandom becomes a central part of identity, it's natural for fans to begin experimenting with the meaning and purpose of their groups. What that identity, in fact, means. A shared identity is a very power-ful, empowering thing.

Call it a side effect of fandom as utopia—so many fan groups have internal mythologies that revolve around idealism that they become a natural jumping-off point for Good Works. Just as com-munity groups like the Shriners, Kiwanis, and even the Freema-sons often find social causes to rally around and support that are largely unrelated to their core activities, fan groups have become unexpected rallying places for seemingly completely unrelated social causes.

When the social-justice issue benefits the fan object this is no bad thing. Pop singer Lady Gaga has doubtless gained at least some audience share through her status as an icon of the LGBTQ civil rights movement, as did the performer Madonna before her. In these cases, the fact that their fan groups grew beyond their original brand identity has positive potential benefits.

Chocolate slavery—the use of forced child labor in the produc-tion and harvesting of cocoa beans—is awful stuff. Kids as young as five are abducted or sold as a workforce on the West African cacao plantations that feed the rest of the world's candy bar cravings. Chocolate is a $100 billion industry, and activists and journalists who attempt to report on the practice are sometimes targets for intimidation or violence. Yet, in late 2014, one organization, the Harry Potter Alliance, did manage to make some headway. Their campaign was called "Not in Harry's Name."

At first glance, the connection between cocoa farms and the Harry Potter media empire seems tenuous. Warner Brothers, which owns the licensing rights for the Harry Potter movie franchise, sells Harry Potter–themed "chocolate frogs" in some of its stores and theme parks. Harry Potter fans go to theme parks, and they also sometimes eat chocolate. It's not the most obvious correlation. Nevertheless, for almost half a decade the Harry Potter Alliance had been engaged in a vigorous crusade to persuade Warner Brothers to make chocolate frogs—and other Harry Potter–themed chocolate merchandise—fair trade.

Reading Harry Potter for the first time was a defining moment for many millennials. It's a true world-based fandom; its context is fantastically broad. Almost anyone can relate to it in almost any way they want. There's something in it for underdogs, overdogs, costumers, cooks, craftspeople, thespians, academics, athletes, rebels, romantics, and shy wallflowers alike. This is a fandom that, for a couple of years in the mid-2000s, inspired an honest-to-goodness religion based around the character Severus Snape, complete with visions, divinations, sexual rituals, and an order of completely earnest nunlike disciples. The rest of the fandom nicknamed them the Snapewives.

The HPA was founded in 2005 by a group of Harry Potter superfans, including comedian Andrew Slack and members of the tribute band Harry and the Potters (known for such songs as "Voldemort can't stop the rock" and "The economics of the wizarding world don't make sense"). Their stated intention is to help spread the high morals and ideals as found in the Harry Potter books. They run a conference called the Granger Leadership Academy, named after in-canon do-gooder Hermione Granger. "Your entire life you've been told stories about great heroes—now it's time to become one" promises their website.

Paul DeGeorge is one of the cofounders. "We're not specific to one issue. The Harry Potter Alliance is not an organization that just works strictly on LGBTQ rights or something. We're a multi-issue org, and we look for that connection to the work, and our reason why the fandom should be invested in it."

The relationship between the HPA and the Harry Potter franchise is a complicated one. Fans want to have an impact, but they don't necessarily want to oppose the brand on a consumer level, say through a boycott. To outsiders it might seem like a situation of wanting to have your cake and eat it too, but that's not quite the case. For consumers, making themselves heard is just a matter of choosing the next best product until demands are met. Fans don't always have that option.

The HPA encouraged Warner Brothers to look into the labor practices. Warner Brothers replied that they had a report saying the practices were fine. The HPA demanded to see the report. Warner Brothers, possibly sensing a slippery slope, refused. There was a widespread petition and video campaign. "Albus Dumbledore asked us to choose between what is right and what is easy. We ask you to do the same. Show us the report," the petition demanded. Lawyers were contacted. Even J. K. Rowling was pulled into the fray.

On December 22, Warner Brothers wrote a letter to the HPA acquiescing. The letter was short and terse. "Thank you for your partnership throughout our discussions on this important issue. We value and appreciate the collective voice of the Harry Potter Alliance members, and Harry Potter fans all over the world, and their enthusiasm and love for the world of Harry Potter." All future chocolate would be UTZ or Fair Trade certified.

"WE WON!" crowed HPA's blog post announcing the victory.

Warner Brothers is a huge, multibillion-dollar behemoth of a company, and Harry Potter–themed chocolate barely even rates a mention on their lengthy list of monetization activities. They can afford to be responsive to fans seeking to change a small portion of their business model. It's a small price to pay for keeping millions of engaged and loyal Harry Potter fanatics flocking to their theme parks, using their key chains, wearing their necklaces, bracelets, and T-shirts, waving their replica wands, watching their movies, and, of course, eating their chocolate.

You Like The Smiths? I Like The Smiths!

"Do you like the Smiths, Morrissey, and/or making out and stuff? If you answered yes to just one of these questions, then you should totally come to 'Heaven Knows I'm Miserable,' a magical night combining Smiths and Morrissey music with speed dating...."

Thus begins the pitch for what may be a uniquely Brooklyn phenomenon (the pitch ends, "come or I will stab you"). Speed dating, the act of spending a few minutes with each of a large number of potential mates, round-robin style, is a staple of romantic comedies and sitcoms. There's Jewish speed dating, speed dating for athletes, speed dating for ballroom dancers, speed dating for chefs, and at least one theme park that has speed dating on a roller coaster. Dates there last as long as the coaster ride: forty-nine seconds.

A speed-dating event aimed at fans of melancholy rocker Steven Morrissey is hardly the most unusual of the bunch, but it may be one of the few that that makes serious romantic sense. While it's not impossible to imagine roller-coaster riders falling in love based on a shared appreciation for an increased level of G-force, Smiths fans are, at least potentially, self-selected to share a reasonable number of traits.

The crowd at this particular event was tattooed, awkward, and unapologetically hipster. In other words, a demographic potentially too shy to congregate without an excuse. Some potential daters had crossed two rivers to travel there from distant New Jersey. The participants traded quips, trivia, and quotes. At least one couple bonded over stories about crying.

Music-based dating is an extremely niche field, but the concept of using our fandoms to prescreen a population for kindred spirits is not.

Christian Rudder is a co-founder of OkCupid, one of the largest and most active dating websites in the world. When creating the tools that eventually became OkCupid, he and his co-founders particularly wanted to match people based on subtle but important personality traits that might not be apparent from a standard profile. The result was a series of personality quizzes and questions to help coax out what makes each user tick.

In the profile area, daters are encouraged to fill out responses under "Favorite books, movies, shows, music, and food," "I'm really good at," and "The six things I could never do without" to showcase their personality. This leads to a dating profile that's lighter on self-description ("I'm nice, I'm funny, I like to travel") and heavier on proving it ("I volunteer in soup kitchens, I do amateur standup comedy, I just got back from trekking Mongolia"). It's what an elementary-school writing teacher might call "show, don't tell."

Engine42 is a male looking for females.* He wants the world to

---

* Names and logins here are modified to protect the users' privacy.

know how much he loves Clint Eastwood movies. Lately he's been reading books about Chinese medicine, and dabbling in Thoreau, Kerouac, and Hunter S. Thompson. Circuiter says he spends a lot of time thinking about the politics of Batman. Unicornlvr hosts gaming conventions and owns a Google Glass, but he's quick to clarify he's also profeminist. THEDOCTORW sports a Doctor Who–themed T-shirt in his profile picture. Watcher75 is at a Yankees game. IDeeJay is DJing. Says Hightek34, "If you still watch the Matrix like it was the first time and wonder if you will ever meet anyone who understands the philosophy behind the Matrix I am your woman :)."

This is not an accident, says Rudder: "Pictures at Machu Picchu or in front of the Egyptian pyramids is a shorthand to announce to potential dates that 'I love to travel' or 'I'm willing to go on an adventure.' When people are sharing their passions, there is a lot of potential for connection."

A casual study in 2012 found that men spend just under a minute reviewing a dating profile, while women spend a bit under a minute and a half. It's barely longer than roller-coaster speed dating.

The rise of the social web has exponentially increased the number of new people we encounter every day. A century ago, outside of urban centers, the arrival of a stranger in town might be rare enough to merit discussion for weeks afterward. On OkCupid, with fast enough fingers, it's possible to "meet" hundreds of strangers in an hour. But at the same time that the number of new meetings is skyrocketing, the amount of exposure we have to each new person has significantly decreased.

In Jane Austen's *Pride and Prejudice*, the main character, Elizabeth Bennet, spends months trying to discern the true natures of the young gentlemen newly arrived in the neighborhood. The result is a series of gossips, letters, whispers, quips, proposals, and long, elegant conversations. Eventually, with the help of an aunt and uncle, four sisters, a few close friends, some helpful servants, and her parents, she figures it out. The modern romantic has a couple of pictures, a few lines of text, and, if the 2012 study is correct, about sixty seconds. Communicating enough detail to attract someone in such a short amount of time requires a bit of help.

Fandom as Identity Shorthand

During hunting season, orange jackets help separate a hiker from a deer. In many parts of the world, some type of leg covering is necessary for heat-retention or antichafing purposes. Baseball caps protect the wearer from the sun; even the fanciest watch also helps the wearer keep track of time. Parabolic skis are better at carving snow than straight skis, which are better than planks of wood strapped to someone's feet (which in turn are better than just falling down a mountain).

But aside from the pure utilitarian purpose of a product's colors and design, the main objective of most individual taste is to declare and maintain position within a group. We pick the products with which we surround ourselves based on the story they tell the world. *Any* shirt can help us avoid hypothermia. A NASA logo shirt identifies us as the type of person who supports science, exploration, or possibly, ironic retro hipsterdom. The value isn't in the thing itself; it's in the story it tells the world. A headscarf, bindi, or six-sided star pendant announces a very specific type of affiliation. So does black lipstick, a Green Bay Packers jersey, or a Hermès Birkin bag.

Aside from any utilitarian issues (a T-shirt would need to become pretty extreme before it stopped doing the basic job of covering the wearer's chest), purchasing decisions are a highly personal form of self-expression. Knowing which brands, logos, and styles to associate with acts as an important form of currency, but it's also a chance to flaunt those all-important badges of membership that tell the world, and ourselves, who we are.

Brand paraphernalia, the products that make up the commercial base of many a fandom, act as tokens of identity and membership. They are tickets of entry, proof that the owner understands enough about a subculture to bear its mark. These "functional artifacts" are the tribal colors by which a group can identify fellow members. And, unlike traditional tattoos and other markings of tribal membership that must be earned through rites of passage, these are tribal colors that can literally be bought.

Identity shorthand is a term that refers to a quick, efficient way to communicate who we are to the outside world at large. It's not a new concept, but the Internet has universalized it. Online, the more traditional markers of age, class, wealth, education, politics, and geographic location disappear. Our likes have become stand-ins for the self we wish to present to others. A curated list of favorite media is more than a conversation starter; it's a bite-sized encapsulation of how we picture ourselves, or at least who we want to be.

Jane Austen herself spent many a paragraph capturing her plucky heroine Elizabeth Bennet's personality: "She had a lively, playful disposition, which delighted in anything ridiculous," she is "considered a local beauty" with "fine eyes" and a "light and pleasing" figure. Faced with a modern reduced word count, we might instead encapsulate this as, "She was into *Archer*, beauty blogging, and yoga." When it comes to naming our favorite book, a choice like *Pride and Prejudice* is meant to send a very different message about the profile holder than, say, *Atlas Shrugged* or the Bible.

One of social media's great successes has been what scholar Clay Shirky calls the "obsessive dollhouse pleasure" of getting our profiles to look just right. We curate the digital version of ourselves, picking and choosing the items it displays with as much care and concentration as Miss Bennet ever gave her exciting young gentlemen. This is particularly true on sites like Facebook, which literally asks us to tell the world who we are based on our "likes."

With so much emphasis placed on seeking to break down stereotypes, it's ironic that one of the main purposes of many subcultures is to provide access to a potential group of friends about whom certain assumptions might be made. To put it another way, fans use their hobbies as a way to prescreen for the type of people they'd like to meet. After all, if we already have this in common, what other opinions and lifestyle choices might we also share?

Of course, identity shorthand also weeds out people who might be a waste of time. As Christian Rudder puts it, "If *World of Warcraft* is really important to you, you shouldn't hide that fact. It's counterproductive. There are plenty of people that don't like *World of Warcraft*, [and] those people aren't going to like you when push comes to shove. The dating pool is big, so the more specific you are, the better off you'll be, whether it's weightlifting or traveling a lot, or *World of Warcraft* or BDSM or whatever."

As with all fandom displays, it's a balancing game between extremes. A profile can try to catch as many potential matches as possible by leaving out potentially stigmatizing obsessions (such as a deep and abiding passion for Jane Austen), or it can let the freak flag fly. A fandom that is too generic tells prospective partners almost nothing. Too specific, and the fan risks being pigeonholed. The latter approach might mean a lower number of potential dates, but the ones it does attract are more likely to be compatible. It's a trade-off. "I think you should put your best foot forward on online dating profiles. You should make sure that it's your foot though, that it's not some made-up fictitious version of yourself," says Rudder.

In one well-documented anecdote, a World Champion player of

the fantasy card game *Magic: The Gathering* made the grave blunder of daring to leave his pastime out of his OkCupid profile. Even though he was personally attractive, professionally successful, and socially active, one of his dates was so mortified that she wrote an indignant tell-all about her ordeal for the tech blog *Gizmodo*. It's almost too easy to imagine a similar story set in the early civil rights era when a date suddenly learns she has been "tricked" into dinner with someone of an unacceptable race, religion, or class. Whatever the reason, the lesson is clear: it's often better to weed out the judgmental majority long before things progress to the level of an in-person experience.

Fans often pick branded goods that represent stereotypes they want to associate with. A profile picture of a woman wearing a Han Solo tank top might come with a set of assumptions. She's a sci-fi fan, but a bit edgy. There's a chance that she's tech savvy. She values independence. A woman wearing a Captain Picard shirt, from Star Trek, may be trying to give off a slightly different set of signals. Her fandom is a less mainstream option, so, even though she's still a sci-fi fan, there's a chance she's a bit more geeky. Less trendy. She also may be more idealistic. Perhaps she's into science. Or, as licensing agent Jesse DeStasio puts it, "You'll probably have a different assumption if you see a girl wearing a Dallas Mavericks T-shirt versus a girl wearing a Batman T-shirt."

"There's a code that you're relaying in your dating profile," says Virginia Roberts, a.k.a. The Heartographer. She almost always prefers letting the dirty laundry, whatever it may be, all hang out. Roberts has made a career out of helping the romantically awkward bait their online dating profiles to catch just the kind of people they're fishing for.

One trick is the Easter egg method—to pepper a profile with fandom references that an insider would immediately understand but an outsider wouldn't necessarily notice. A hardcore vegan might mention how much she likes seitan. A rabid Apple fan might slyly reference receiving blue iPhone messages. Such a note establishes the person as Team Apple without sounding like a boring tech blogger about it. Fans of the cult TV show *Arrested Development* might drop a quote like "There's always money in the banana stand." Calling out fan elements is a signal that says, "We probably have something in common."

As long as there are new studies about what exactly causes the sparks *d'amour*, daters will continue to tweak the faces they choose to show the world. OkTrends, the data blog that analyzes the statistical dating behavior of OkCupid's user base, recently announced that profile pictures contributed to a much larger percentage of reader opinion than previously thought. Or, as they put it, "So, your picture *is* worth that fabled thousand words, but your actual words are worth . . . almost nothing." It's no wonder that so many users have felt inspired to embed their all-important fandoms directly into their primary profile image, the first photo a prospective mate might see.

In his profile picture, Cosmic-space sports a NASA T-shirt. He's looking for a liberal left-wing lady who's searching for knowledge.

Making Fandoms Worthy

Dating—and socialization in general—takes fandom-as-identity to its furthest extremes. It's the difference between buying something that the wearer finds funny, and buying something that the wearer hopes will tell other people that they know it's funny.

Not all fandoms, even the very popular ones, have enough *je ne sais quoi* in them to serve as an identity for their followers. The ones that work have been carefully curated to do so, with just enough insider context to communicate through the limited medium of a T-shirt, quotation, or logo. For fan-object owners, getting to this stage is the final goal. It requires a fan group dedicated enough to bring their own context along with them. After all, without a bruised and yearning British population to inspire, James Bond is just a rather mean bureaucrat.

Media properties, imbued with detailed characters and vibrant stories, are relatively easy identity fits. Their stories of rebellion and exceptionalism offer a way to align ourselves against our own perceived challenges. Character assortments let us pick whose traits we find most appealing: the rebellious pilot or the dutiful captain. But all fan objects have the potential to be identity-building. Sports-team fandom often merges a storied history with characteristics of the local community. Each celebrity has a personal narrative with which we might feel an affinity. Every choice comes with its own built-in set of characteristics for us to broadcast to the world.

Building fandoms that can be worn like a badge of membership requires a detailed context. Just like the best dating profiles, they find that sweet spot between being so generic that a brand means nothing and being so hyperspecific that no one other than the wearer can interpret the qualities represented. And they embrace the context the fans have bestowed upon them. It's that fan meaning that sells the T-shirt.

Back at the Licensing Expo in Las Vegas, men and women in business suits are haggling over what logos will grace T-shirts, hats, necklaces, watches, and lunch boxes over the next year. Little House on the Prairie has agreed to put its name on a line of quilting fabric. Pokémon's Pikachu will be offered in Build-a-Bear workshops. Skater legend Tony Hawk's name will appear on boys' clothing, shoes, and accessories at Walmart. Everywhere there's the quiet bustle of contracts being signed and money changing hands, the logos practically arcing through the air as they jump from buyer to buyer. Three and a half million OkCupid users are counting on them to pick the right ones.

CHAPTER 5

MEMBERSHIP AND STATUS IN THE HAPPIEST PLACE ON EARTH

Down the Rabbit-Hole

The White Rabbits are on the move, a horde of motorcycle vests and black T-shirts spilling out of the party and onto Buena Vista Street, joking and jostling each other. The majority are tattooed. Beards abound, piercings are serious, hair is shaved or wild or bleached. There must be two dozen of them surging down the middle of the road. A couple of late-night tourists press against the closed storefronts to give the group room.

"Apparently people are afraid of us," jokes a man somewhere in the middle of the pack.

"Afraid of us, as a club? I'm friendly as fuck!" announces a muscular blond woman with a giant tattoo of a Kodiak bear head across her neck.

They squeeze through the gates, keeping each other within shouting distance as they reach the exit turnstiles. Hands grope for cigarettes and lighters as they wait for the rest of the human comet tail to catch up. One member stoops to pick up a forgotten candy wrapper and drops it respectfully into the trash.

"Everyone here? All right, heading out!" comes the call from the front. Cigarettes are stubbed out. Then, as a group, they turn toward Disneyland, where twenty-three FastPasses will grant them wait-free access to the Space Mountain roller coaster.

The White Rabbits are one of hundreds of Disney-themed social clubs that operate out of the Disneyland Resort in Anaheim, California. They can be seen clustering at the bars and smoking sections of Disney's California Adventure. They take over rows at shows like Disney's *Aladdin—A Musical Spectacular*. They fill entire trains at the Haunted Mansion. They know about the special Lilly Belle car on the Disneyland Railroad, the fabled basketball court at the top of Matterhorn Mountain, and the tough-to-find air-conditioned room in Cinderella's castle. They know the cleanest and emptiest bathrooms at any time of day. They travel in packs, threading through Disney's sweating weekend crowds like dolphins through shrimp, weaving in and out of store and restaurant shortcuts with a confidence born of long experience.

Appearances aside, they aren't biker gangs. In fact, members are quick to correct any use of the "G" word at all. Nevertheless, they have adopted traditional biker-gang lingo, using terms like "prospecting," "patched-in," and "sergeant-at-arms." And of course, the matching vests: denim jackets with the arms cut off, embellished with biker-style patches declaring to all the world that these are the official members of the White Rabbits, Sons of Anakin, Mickey's Little Monsters, The Hitchhikers, The Mousefits, Robin Hoods of Disney, or Triton's Mermaids.

Disney is watching. "If you're a new club coming into the park, you're going to get this plainclothes undercover Disney FBI/CIA dude. He's going to act all casual and he's going to say, 'Hey, I see you're part of a social club. That's really cool. My brother's part of a social club. Do you mind if you turn around so I can take a picture of your patch?' And they'll take pictures of your patch and they'll keep you on file."

So says Jake Fite, age forty, give or take a decade. Fite is a mountain of a guy with a giant smile and a full blond beard. The effect is of a big friendly porcupine. He's been coming here since childhood, a story he seems to share in common with much of Southern California, although most people's stories don't culminate in ruling over a horde of 150 group members. As leader of the White Rabbits, one of the largest Disney social clubs, he spends his weekends here at the parks presiding over his tattooed tribe: planning the club's activities, keeping order, and dispensing justice as needed. "Everything is managed," he says. "There's some people in the club that think this just magically happens. That's my role in the club, just to make stuff happen. All they have to do is show up and have a good time."

As they plow through the drifts of families waiting for the Paint the Night parade en route, Fite points out areas of interest: here's a historic spot, there's an image of Mickey hidden in the sidewalk. This ride always breaks down. That one never has a line. He knows his Disney. "Jake! Hold up!" someone yells from behind.

"This is my life," says Fite. "Walking ten steps and then someone yells, 'Hey Jake!'"

In Tomorrowland, the Space Mountain ride attendant is overwhelmed at the size of the arriving mob. He resorts to schoolyard etiquette, asking everyone to raise an arm, counting them through the gate by hand one by one. "Can I be in your group too?" he jokes as they file past.

They gossip about their collections of Disney paraphernalia. They gossip about rides. "My nail is going to fall off." "I can't drink vodka." "I was like, come back when you have some facial hair." "She's such a lightweight." Then they're at the front of the line, filling the loading area with denim vests and good-natured trash talk. It takes three separate trains to whisk the entire group away, down the roller coaster track and off into the dark.

The Gangs of Disneyland

Disneyland is an urban theme park, an easy half hour's drive (without traffic) from downtown Los Angeles—in southern California driving terms, practically next door. The millions of people located nearby make Disneyland's attendance demographic very different from that of its sister resorts in Orlando and Paris, and Disney social clubs are a phenomenon almost entirely exclusive to the resort in Anaheim. An unusually large portion of park-goers are locals with season passes rather than tourists who might visit only once in a lifetime. It's not unusual for a guest to drop in just for a specific show, or to eat lunch.

The Anaheim park is also tiny relative to Orlando's Disney World. Prior to the creation of the new Disney California Adventure it was estimated that the entire Disneyland park could fit inside one of the Orlando resort's parking lots with room left over. Disneyland's centerpiece, Sleeping Beauty's Castle, is smaller than many of the hotels nearby. It's a bite-sized attraction, friendly rather than majestic. The park has aged well, but nothing can change the compact, cozy, retro feel of Walt's very first attempt.

The result is an unusually loyal fan base, even within the intense world of Disney fandom. This is the park that originated "Dapper Day"—a biannual fan-created tradition when park-goers dress up in vintage formal wear. And Galliday, an unofficial Doctor Who–themed dress-up day, as well as Tiki Day, Harry Potter Day, and Raver Day. Dressing up is built into park culture—for every little girl in a Cinderella dress there's a teenaged couple wearing matching T-shirts that say "He's my Anakin" and "She's my Padme," or a whole family decked out as the Incredibles.

It's a good environment in which to don an item of apparel, such as a motorcycle gang vest, that might be rather risky to wear outside of the park walls. But which vest? At last count there were more than three hundred social clubs to choose from, although some are defunct, and others have only a handful of members. Disney's context is so huge that it practically forces specialization. The Hitchhikers Social Club began as a club for Northern Californians. Pix Pak Social Club is for members who are especially into Pixar. The Darkside Social Club and Sons of Anakin are both for Star Wars lovers. The Mickey's Empire Social Club is pirate-themed. VooDoo Crew claims to be more family oriented. The membership of the White Rabbits draws heavily from those employed in the service industries.

Patches go on the back of the vest, leaving the front free for other badges showing rank, position, nicknames, and, of course, collectible Disney pins. Lots and lots of pins. Many members' vests are so tightly packed with metal they're practically bulletproof. Almost every store in the resort carries some, and limited-edition pins are released on a regular schedule throughout the park. eBay does a brisk secondary trade. Aside from the monetary outlay they represent, pins give off a complicated set of signals about the member's self-image, level of commitment, and history. A pin tied to an event, such as Disneyland's Diamond Celebration, its sixtieth anniversary, announces: That's right, I was there when it happened.

Then there are the less expensive buttons—simple, round, hand-pressed on little personal machines—that the social clubs themselves use to trade with each other and to hand out to curious tourists. Some of the buttons are almost as collectible as official Disney pins. In a sly stroke of gamesmanship, one large group happily trades out Darth Vader buttons with the phrase "IDRYBSSC" on them. It stands for "I don't recognize your bullshit social club."

The entire vest is steeped in enough symbolism to rival the most medal-heavy military uniform, combining the romance of group membership with the thrill of self-expression. It's the physical embodiment of fandom as identity. And, hey, it also looks cool. As one Sons of Anakin member puts it, "People come up to me and say, 'We love your gear, where can we get one?' The attention is flattering. Do you think I'm wearing this vest in 102 degree weather for fun?"

The Rules of the Road

The tall young man was patched into Mickey's Empire just eight months earlier. He has a large tattoo of Ariel, from *The Little Mermaid*, on his bicep. It's actually a tattoo of a pin: his ultimate pin, one that is especially rare and expensive. Someday it will be his. In the meantime, his vest is covered with other *Little Mermaid* tributes. "I like the whole rebellion thing with *The Little Mermaid*," he says. "She really spoke to me."

His club is mingling with the Sons of Anakin in the shade, across from a statue of Walt Disney. There are fewer tattoos and piercings here, but more exciting hair—blue, purple, and fluorescent red. Some members have removed their vests in deference to the incredible heat. A plastic lightsaber is part of the Sons of Anakin outfit—their website says officers are required to sport a standard-issue red Darth Vader one—and every once in a while someone will telescope theirs out to gesture at something. "I want some orange iced tea!" says a member. Whoosh, out comes the lightsaber, pointing toward his intended destination.

"I was taking a picture in front of the pumpkin and this guy was like, 'Oh these gangs!'" complains a Son, "And I was like, 'It's social clubs!'" Out in front of the castle, sunscreen is melting down the cheeks of tourists as they pose for red-faced selfies.

"Everyone here? All right, let's go meet some princesses!" Lightsabers waving high in the air, the groups set off toward the Royal Theater.

In the past there have been rumors of interclub violence and turf wars within the park, something group members vehemently deny. There's plenty of fraternization, but almost no crossover. At least one group, the Main Street Elite, is rumored to have discouraged its members from mingling with other social clubs, so says gossip. Then again, no one seems to have seen that group around for a while.

Elena Salcedo is a member of Mickey's Empire. She's petite, with purple hair, and looks more like someone's sweet younger sister than a potential gang member. She's making her way through Fantasyland to join the rest of her group over at the live show "Mickey and the Magical Map."

"I have family who've been an annual pass holder for many years. They would always talk about Disney. Disney, Disney, Disney," she recalls. "Once I got older and I started making my own money I was able to purchase a pass. That's when I started getting into the movies, the music, the shows. Any kind of merchandise out there: hats, clothing, just anything. It started with my family being so into it, and then I kind of just grew into it myself. All of a sudden, I started noticing a lot of groups wearing vests with little designs on their backs. I started wondering, what is that?"

Instagram is the platform of choice for most social club members and it's where Mickey's Empire originally caught Salcedo's attention. After two months of lurking, she finally made her move: "I went up to the members and I asked them, 'I've been following you guys for a while. I'm very interested in seeing if I could hang out with you guys. I want to be part of this. I want to belong to a group that believes in and loves Disney as much as I do.'" A little girl in a tutu drops her water bottle, chasing it across the Main Street sidewalk. Not missing a beat, Salcedo scoops it up and returns it to her. "Nobody is going to judge you. You have great company. It just makes you happy you know?"

Mickey's Empire membership comes with obligations. Members must wear the vest at all times within the park boundaries. They must meet every Sunday at five p.m. to go over club business. They must allow tourist families to go before them on the rides. And of course, they hold all things pirate near and dear. "One of the things that we try to do a lot is ride the Pirates of the Caribbean ride," she says. "That's one of our rituals." Their organizational structure is nautical—they have three captains and a first mate—and their emblazoned logo is an image of Mickey himself with a pirate hat, eye patch, and sword.

The club fills up an entire bench in the third row of the amphitheater. A boy one row in front is turned around in his seat, wide-eyed. His mother keeps glancing back at the imposing row of vests and trying to distract her spellbound progeny, but he's having none of it. Mickey bounces on stage to introduce the loose plot that will allow a half-dozen Disney movie characters to make brief musical appearances. The target age seems to be about five, but it's clear that this is not an ironic event for Mickey's Empire. One of the club's captains is nodding along to "Under the Sea." A huge man with a buzz cut sitting further down the bench greets the appearance of Pocahontas with a murmur of "Best princess ever...."

Mickey learns an important lesson about being yourself, or possibly tolerance. Paper streamers explode from above onto the crowd. The captain gathers the streamers landing on him and gives them to the ecstatic little boy, helping him loop them around his neck into a giant lei. This is definitely the best day of the boy's entire life.

Mickey's Own Private Club

Club 33 is the only place on the inside of the original Anaheim Disneyland park where it is possible to procure alcohol. It is private, both literally (it inhabits a hidden nook high above New Orleans Square) and metaphorically (basic memberships are rumored to cost upwards of $12,000 a year, with a waiting list more than a decade long if it even exists at all). Allegedly, the membership includes A-listers like Tom Hanks and Elton John. An eighty-four-year-old life-timer was recently banned for allowing a set of passes for dinner there to be auctioned for charity.

Access is granted through a little brass intercom at the side of the door. Inside, visitors who didn't take the dress code seriously may be given a "shawl of shame," to cover their bare shoulders, like a big scarlet letter branding them as ignorant outsiders. As exclusive hideaways go, it isn't exactly the library at the Vatican, but not for lack of mystique.

The main bar certainly is lovely, all stained glass and crystal and gold and swooping lines of dark wood, filled with the type of oversized antiques that seem like stage props. Dark little nooks are accented with paintings that move if you wait long enough. Everything is just a little bit larger than life, like a cozy sound stage or a theater set. It's beautiful. But there are plenty of other classy bars that are just as beautiful, none of which require the equivalent of in-state college tuition for access. The allure here is not predicated on the gorgeous chandeliers.

The clientele this afternoon is middle-aged and affluent, wearing quiet hairstyles and twinsets. There is a scattering of modest pearls, tasteful watches, and absolutely enormous diamond rings. Every now and then a gust of air circulates the rich, sweet aroma that can only come from fantastically expensive whiskey served neat. Some of the members do sport an occasional mark of affiliation, such as a subtle Disney gold bracelet or Club 33 baseball hat, but it's hard to imagine any of them with pierced eyebrows.

This afternoon we are here by invitation. With so many White Rabbits, it seems almost inevitable that some are friendly with acquaintances who have Club 33 access. "Initially, when we first started coming, we did wear the vest and we didn't think much of it," says Fite. "But, word on the street was that some of the members were feeling a little uncomfortable, so I just made a blanket statement to everybody in the club, 'Hey, any guys who happen to go up there, just don't wear your vest. Either drop it off at a locker, or just fold it up and put it over your arm. Just try to blend in a little more.' I thought it was in our club's best interest to be a little bit more incognito."

Missie L. Fite, Jake Fite's other half and a fellow Rabbit, agrees: "I think there are misconceptions at first. Maybe people are a little intimidated by us in the beginning. Then when they finally get to know us, they're like, 'Oh, these people are pretty rad!' "

Outside we pass two college girls in sequined mouse ears taking pictures next to the large white-and-gold plaque with the number 33 in it. They're in the wrong spot; the plaque is a decoy. The real entrance is a nondescript door underneath the overpass a few doors down. It's more subtle, but there's still an obvious "33" worked into the stained glass above it. Club 33 may be a private location safe from the curious, but to keep its allure it must also *keep* the masses curious. Walt Disney, the man, understood like few others how to invoke the mythic. "With 33, it's a different perspective than what another visitor would see because not every guest can get in. It's very special. You feel special to be there. And you're thankful for it," says Missie.

Trent Vanegas, sergeant-at-arms for Sons of Anakin, has friends who have been asked on dates to Club 33. Occasionally he's been invited to tag along. So far, he's declined. "That feels kind of smarmy," he says. "Club 33 is like the Holy Grail for me, but I want to do it the right way. I want it to feel right." When questioned later, a number of attractive Disney fans do show signs of swooning when Club 33 is mentioned. Others mention attempting to bribe their way in with money or cigars.

Trent's group is sitting on the floor of "The Disneyland Story presenting Great Moments with Mr. Lincoln," one of the few large air-conditioned spaces in the park besides rides. Vanegas is hanging out over by the early concept sketches of Disney attractions. He's in his forties, with a fashionable haircut and a large tattoo of a star on his neck. By day, he's a celebrity-gossip blogger.

He and his fellow officers are nervous. They're about to talk to their president about an "internal issue" they've been having. The vice president was home yesterday in bed with a fever, but he'll be dragging himself in for the confrontation despite the broiling heat. Trent declines to share what the president has done, but whatever it is, it's not good.

Discipline and enforcement vary from group to group, as do the rules that trigger them. Some groups mandate specific codes of conduct; some disallow drinking. Almost all require a strict adherence to park rules.

Consequences for breaking the rules vary. "Overwhelmingly, punishment consists of probation, which means the member cannot wear their vest in the parks at all," explains Vanegas. For really bad infractions, there's always expulsion; upon being patched in, all Sons of Anakin members sign a contract acknowledging that they don't actually own their patches. If the club ever kicks them out, they have to turn the patches over for a 50 percent refund. Group members are conscious that the park could easily reconsider its laissez-faire attitude on social clubs, and no one wants to be the troublemaker who ended the fun. "There's never been instances where there's been a fight or there's been an arrest or anything like that," Vanegas says. "It's Disneyland. If you're at the point where you want to fight with someone at Disneyland, you're doing it completely wrong."

"Everyone's Friends with Everyone"

This afternoon the Rabbits have taken over Sonoma Terrace, a bar across from Pacific Wharf, in Disney California Adventure. Five tables have been pushed together, and from all directions come the vested masses greeting each other with "Hey, brother" and "Good to see you, man!" They're a diverse group, although most do share a general rockabilly aesthetic. There's a Rabbit behind the bar too, albeit without a vest—a number of members work here.

The social strata here are thin and unsubtle. An Ace patch identifies the bearer as one of the original twelve founding members. Many old-timers have their nicknames on the vest, with patches that say things like "Tramp" and "Grizzly." After that, picking out who has the clout can get harder. Fite is technically the Ace of Hearts, but he has four vice presidents who represent the King of Clubs, Spades, Hearts, and Diamonds. There are Queens and Jacks for members who contribute their time for charity and group events.

The titles help maintain decorum. "If it's just one guy telling another guy, 'Hey don't do that,' they can blow them off and say, 'Who are you to tell me what to do?' If we have a hierarchy, they are above you. They can step in if someone's going out of line and say, 'Hey listen, you can't do that' or 'You drank too much. You're being a fool. Take off your patches because you're reflecting badly on the whole club.'"

Three new recruits huddle at the end of the table, carefully sipping beer from their plastic cups. They're here to see about joining. The well-groomed young couple seems a little overwhelmed, but the smiling black-haired man is shaking hands and introducing himself to everyone who comes near.

"It's hard to find friends when you're brand new out of the military," says Aaron W., a Rabbit for less than a year. He had moved from Georgia to San Diego, but soon found himself unemployed and in a dark space. Then, around last Halloween, a couple of acquaintances invited him to the park. "I was in shock. It's November, they just put their Christmas decorations up," he remembers. "It felt like I was finally home where I belonged. It got me out of my funk just seeing how kids were happy there." That same day, he upgraded his ticket to a season pass, putting down $130 despite his lack of a job.

"I wanted a group that could be a family, but also be willing to help out other people in need. That's how I met Jake, and I was like, this is a good group. That's why I chose the Rabbits, because one of the values I wanted was to help people and have a family. Without a family, you can't really feel good," he says.

The language of family is heavy in many joining-up stories. "You get to hang out with a big group of friends, and everyone's friends with everyone," explains another Rabbit. "I didn't have any brothers and sisters growing up. The bond, the connection we have, it pulls you in." They go to ball games or camping together. They come to each other's rescue when there's a bad cold or blown-out tire. They take turns live-streaming rides for members who can't make it as often.

As for the three new recruits? "Well, they seem cool so far," says one long-standing member, nodding at them in encouragement. "We'll accept whoever as long as they're not a dick."

In comparison, some groups have joining-up rituals that border on the Masonic. They can take months to go through the full process. One member of Mickey's Raiders, an Indiana Jones–themed social club, later described his initiation: "To become official I had to find three hidden Mickeys. I found one in the fireworks, and one hidden on a building. Then they'll give you little tasks, like riding your least favorite park ride. Mine was the Tower of Terror." Like the movies the club is named for, there is a scavenger-hunt mentality to it all. "The treasure is us. We are the family they missed. If they accept the treasure, they will become worthy," he explains.

In the background, the Pixar Play Parade goes by, with swimming fish and ants and caterpillars and furry monsters. Inside the bar, evening plans are made. Dinner over at Cocina Cucamonga Mexican Grill, then maybe a trip on Ariel's Undersea Adventure, before heading to the Mad T party.

"Why did I pick the White Rabbits? All the other ones were prudes and jerks," explains a Rabbit, sipping his beer. "It's all about collecting buttons with them."

It Hit Me Like a Bolt of Lightning

Becoming a fan can be a transformative experience, deeply personal and potentially life changing. The stories of how we discover the objects that furnish our fan identities are as much a part of our personal mythology as the story of how we met our significant other or chose our career.

Fan origin stories generally fall into two categories. Most common is the sequence of events experienced by many Disney social club members: the "social-first method." Someone hangs out with a group of people—family, an extended friend group, or colleagues from work—and as they grow closer they find themselves drawn to the things the group likes. Eventually they find themselves enjoying them too. Socialization is a basic fanlike activity, and the more we have in common with fellow fans, the better friends we can be. We take on the tribal colors and symbols of the group to show other members that we belong.

When Elena Salcedo of Mickey's Empire was first exposed to her family's love of Disney, she knew little about it. It took years of exposure to their enthusiasm before Disney turned into the passion for her it is today. A new student at the University of Kansas might find herself becoming a fan of the Jayhawks. Someone whose friends play Pokémon Go may feel inspired to learn the game. A newcomer in a group of opera lovers may grow to appreciate Pavarotti. While their deep feelings about these fan objects are very real, the most important thing about the fandom is that it gives the fans a connection to their group.

Then there's the other type of fan story. An individual, perhaps by chance, experiences the fan object for the first time. Aaron W., alone and "in a dark space," happens to visit Disneyland during the holiday season. Pow! Suddenly, like a bolt of lightning, the feelings are there, an instant connection, an immediate emotional outpouring. The teenager who reads his first Batman comic and falls hard for its gritty themes of rebellion and justice. The American serviceman in France during World War II who wrote home to describe his culinary epiphany upon eating gourmet cuisine for the first time. When a fan object strikes a chord in us, it creates a feeling of rightness, of deep connection. Not only does the unexpectedness pack a punch, it also goes right to our core sense of self.

Because "bolt-of-lightning" fandom stories often occur outside a built-in community, there can be a period of lonely isolation before the newly minted fan is able to connect with other like-minded souls. When the connection does come, the discovery that she isn't the only person in the world who values her new obsession is often a relief. This incubation period has shortened since the advent of the Internet, where finding fellow fans is just a matter of choosing the right search terms, but it's still there.

Why Do We Fan?

Creating a strong fan group requires understanding what brings potential group members to their fandom. How did they get here?

What are they looking for from those feelings of intimacy with a fan object, feelings that are no less real for being one-sided? Fan-group members must profit from their membership, but, more than that, the nature of the profit must match each member's motivation to join. No one participates in fanlike activities just for the heck of it.

Any number of Disney social club members tell stories of how club membership helped them come out of their shell, or beat the blues, or how it improved their self-esteem. For a lot of fans, finding their fandom is a life-altering event. It helped them find themselves. It helped them feel like a better person. This is especially true of "good for you" fandoms that encourage self-improvement, such as listening to New Age or religious music, participating in activities that encourage the intellect, or fandoms like running or dance that help participants get in shape.

It's not uncommon to hear what some academics label "tales of the miraculous"—fans who attribute pseudomagical powers of positivity to their fan object: Listening to that band got me through a bad breakup. Seeing that athlete work so hard helped me through a difficult medical issue. That comic book saved me when I felt hopeless about life.

For some, fandom acts as a way to develop a skill set. Content creation, leadership, and evangelization—all of these are an important part of fandom, and many professional resumes are augmented with skills that were originally developed in service of a fan object. Not to mention that fan knowledge and socialization can act as an important way to build self-confidence and networking. With so many White Rabbits in the service industry, it's easy to imagine a member who is looking for a new job reaching out to fellow Rabbits for their advice.

For some, the lure is the playfulness. Fandom can be a place where the grownup rules are suspended, where we can stop pretending to be adults, and revel in the delightfulness of enchantment and mystery and fantasy. Finding a space away from the mundane lets us access those childlike, playful emotions we might not otherwise be able to reach.

And then there's the search for family. It's almost impossible to find a close-knit fan group that *doesn't* use the language of family and take a familial role in each other's lives. Of course, since fan groups are such fertile ground for romance, sometimes the "family" can become literal. There were five separate weddings planned within the White Rabbits in 2016 alone, all to fellow club members.

Love-Bombing the Firestarters

For Jake Fite, building the White Rabbits up to the level where their activity could become self-sustaining was a matter of constant content creation and interaction. "We started a Facebook group for club members, and we hit Instagram hard. I knew that in order to make this work, it had to be interesting for people. I would be in there every day. If you go into a group, and you see what's going on, and then you come back the next day and there's nothing new, you're going to stop coming back to that group page. It took a long time to finally grow it to the point where now I could probably step away from it, and there's enough stuff going on in there that it would just sustain itself."

Fan-group development is an "emergent behavior," a phrase borrowed from science to explain why there is no single recipe. Only once a group has formed is it possible to look back and understand the many conditions that made it possible. Providing the basic elements—such as platforms for personal display and fan socialization—may allow the formation of a cohesive unit, but not always. But no matter its path, the first challenge to any new fan group is reaching the minimum viable number of members to become self-sustaining.

Fandom is social; a fan who has no other fans with whom to fan doesn't stay a fan for long. A good fan community recognizes that reaching self-sufficiency will take a while, and finds a way to benefit members without requiring critical mass. Early activities should have a low barrier to entry, and they should be enjoyable even without the input of other group members.

Encouraging early group members, the all-important firestarters, is the most important tactic in the group-creation arsenal. Many group owners resort to "love-bombing," a term borrowed from the language of cults to describe how they bombard early members with displays of approval and attention to keep them engaged.

Giving fans diverse ways to participate, at varying levels of involvement, helps a fan group become self-sustaining faster, and provides for a more robust fandom overall, one that requires less love-bombing and is more resilient to change. A fan of downhill skiing will have difficulty remaining a fan if she experiences a decrease in income and can't afford the equipment, or hurts her knees, or moves somewhere without mountains. Not so the Coca-Cola fan who becomes diabetic! This is a fandom that can weather changes in health, identity, income, location, age, and taste. Fans who can no longer drink Coca-Cola, the bubbly brown beverage, can still collect Coke-themed stuffed animals, make collages out of vintage Coke bottle labels, travel to Coke conventions, or use it to remove grease stains, clean rusty pennies, tenderize steaks, or make their floors nonslip. Coca-Cola is a truly robust fandom.

The most straightforward measure of a person's fandom is easy: time. Measuring fans' social status within a group is often a simple matter of noting how long they spend on activities related to the fan object. If they're always around—making things, doing things, and interacting—then chances are they're superfans. The more time the fans can be encouraged to spend, the more high-level fans there will be. It's no wonder that some Disney social clubs have attendance requirements to make sure that their members stay active and involved.

Group Cohesion Activities

What happened to the Main Street Elite? It's a question to which no one seems to know the complete answer. MSE was one of the very first clubs, and rumor says it once counted more than a hundred active members. And then suddenly, they were gone—it's been months since anyone has seen their trademark vintage-style Mickey patches around the park.

According to one ex-member, the rules for MSE membership had become more and more complicated, and the energy needed to police them may have been too much for the young leadership. Another rumor says they may have had initiation rituals that involved stealing from the park, a practice that got them banned. Or perhaps its members simply lost interest? It's all hearsay and gossip, of course.

"Some of the clubs, you see them walking around the park and they all look like they came out of the same store in the mall, like Hot Topic or whatever. They all look alike, they all have the same vibe, they all have the same supercool man beards, which . . ." Fite pauses for a moment. "Well, I have a supercool man beard too, but they all have this exactly same genre of look and feel," he says. "The clubs that I think are superstringent, with a leader that is ultra-controlling and dictating everything, those clubs aren't around anymore."

The techniques that fan groups use to stay together are known as group cohesion activities. They are the glue that inspires group members to stay involved after the initial contact is made, the actions that help define a fan group and cement the interpersonal relationships that hold it together. It is these activities that a group owner needs to support if the group is to stay viable.

Fans Jostle for Hierarchy

Part of belonging to a group is to place ourselves—our knowledge, tastes, and abilities—on display. To compare ourselves with each other; to be recognized as "good fans" by the only people whose judgment about it matters—fellow fans. Almost all vital fan communities have some sort of structure, overt or subtle, for allowing fans to compete for place within the social hierarchy. Fans need a way to see that they are a community, and what place they occupy within it, and to judge how well they are living up to its cultural norms. This impetus toward mutual approval keeps a fan group unified and focused on its goals. The more that fans emulate their community's idea of success, the more respect they can gain from their fellow fans.

Adult Disney fans are actively discouraged from attending the parks in full costume, lest they be mistaken for cast members. Giving up control over its intellectual property is something to which the Disney corporation is notoriously averse. One result is the phenomenon of "Disneybounding," the activity of putting together outfits that are representative, but not quite literal interpretations, of Disney characters. Tight green jeans, light-green polo shirt, and beige boots evokes Peter Pan. A blue sweater and flowy yellow skirt with a shiny red heart purse is reminiscent of Snow White.

Choosing a minor character to Disneybound as (it's a verb too), like Timothy Mouse from *Dumbo*, takes more skill than a popular one, like Queen Elsa from *Frozen*. To outsiders the result is a cute albeit very colorful ensemble, but to insiders it's an act of membership. Leslie Kay, the fan who originally popularized the concept on her blog, has since gone on to become a bit of an icon within Disney fandom herself. "New Kind of Disney Cosplay Slightly Less Embarrassing Than Original," joked one recent Time.com headline.

Status-building activities within a fandom can take any one of a variety of forms, but with such a visual fan text as Disney, personal displays are a favorite. Disneybounding clothing is just one way to show ever-increasing levels of commitment. When social-club members cover their vests with especially rare or themed pins and buttons, they are making a display of status. Patches showing position within a club, such as the Ace, Jack, or Queen, do the same. Of course, if the pins are expensive enough, they're displaying some very real economic status as well, but by and large these items are a representation of the level of their commitment to their fan object: the long hours waiting in line, the expertise required to track down the very last of a set. A carefully curated collection of pins beats an official Disney "pin trading starter set" any day, even if both cost the same amount of money. These are all items that are meaningless to everyone except the select few who can decipher the code.

As Clay Shirky points out, creating something personal is more appealing than accepting something made by professionals, even if the professionals do it better. An acquaintance might be able to beat a challenging mobile game in a couple of hours, but that doesn't mean we want him to play it on our behalf. We want to take three weeks and beat it ourselves. In the world of costuming, whether for Halloween or among convention attendees, hand-sewn costumes are worth more than store-bought ones even if the mass-produced version is nicer. Some of the patches on the backs of Disney social club vests are incredibly beautiful. Some are not nearly as pretty, and some appear downright amateur. But a hand-drawn patch is often one of the first things a social club member will mention: "One of our own members made this." No one wants a patch that was copy/pasted from clipart. The actual *quality* of the content is less important than the time and effort it took to make it.

Disney has taken note of the Disneybound phenomenon and recently branched out into licensing Disneybound-style clothing—street clothes that are reminiscent of character costumes. The high status that is given to time and creativity within fan groups is something Disney might want to keep in mind. When it comes to this type of prestige, effort trumps money. Fans who try to "buy their way in" to the hierarchy are often ridiculed as wannabes. Smart fan objects know when to keep their hands off their fans' status-seeking activities, interfering only to support them with tools like leaderboards, scorecards, or contests to give the strongest efforts official recognition.

Exchanging Information and Gifts

A water molecule stays bonded together by passing electrons back and forth between its hydrogen and oxygen atoms. Soccer players passing a ball back and forth can never draw farther apart than the strength that their kicks allow. Fan groups are bonded by passing back and forth interpersonal favors, objects, and information. As members build cultural status within a group, they're also building social capital—the networks, cooperation, and trust that bind a group together. Sharing keeps the group intact.

Sometimes the sharing is literal; the buttons dispensed by social clubs are valuable markers of esteem. They wouldn't give those out to just *anyone*. Physical or digital gifts of fan-art commissions, jewelry, fact-finding, or how-tos are also good "passing" materials. So is answering another fan's questions. Or offering sympathy after a breakup. Or clicking "like" on each other's social-media posts. When showing off a Disneybound outfit online, it's good form to link to where others can buy those clothes. It's more than a way to show off personal ability; it's a subtle request for others to try it too.

Acknowledgment and Flattery

People will do for love what they won't do for money, so the saying goes. Sharing activities in a fan group are priceless in the sense that their value can't be quantified. Placing a price tag on the sharing changes the interaction from two fans bonding into a buyer/seller relationship. Many brands have fallen into the trap of encouraging content sharing by offering some type of monetary compensation to Big Name Fans. This runs absolutely counter to the all-important feelings of group accomplishment that result when members make an effort that the whole community will benefit from. It's important to not put a price on love—people do things for status that they'd never consider for a cash prize.

Acknowledgment and flattery are two of the strongest forces keeping group members active. The best type of encouragement gives participants attention and recognition for what they accomplished for themselves, and thanks and approval for what they accomplished for the group. Fans who create the patches for their social club gain personal admiration from other individuals, in the form of compliments and attention for their artistic skill. But they also get the appreciation of their fellow members for doing something good for everyone.

A savvy group leader will find a way to make sure that the creator gets significant social status as well—by being promoted to Queen or Jack in the White Rabbits, for example. It isn't love-bombing; it's the motivating power of encouragement from those higher up in the hierarchy whom we respect.

Punishing Offenders

A group of Rabbits was recently accused of littering while waiting thirty-six hours on a pin-release line. Other social clubs were quick to spread the word. "They said, 'Oh, look at the White Rabbits, they just think they can do whatever they want,'" Fite remembers. The Rabbits immediately apologized to the social-media world at large, and each of the accused members donated $20 to the National Park Foundation. For all that they have labeled themselves the "black sheep of the social clubs," their social norms are downright cour-teous. The fact that Disney social clubs as a whole have, as of yet, drawn no official censure may be attributed to their expertise at self-policing. The contracts, fines, and "serious discussions" by which their top level of hierarchy maintains order may seem a bit melodramatic to an outsider, but they are key to long-term stability.

Although technically fans can fall anywhere on a gradient of group loyalty, in reality they usually self-organize into a core cir-cle of members—superfans—surrounded by a peripheral group of members with more minor involvement. Some superfans gain so much status that they become minor fan objects in their own right. There are always more and more subtle ways for a fan to show off devotion. Superfans are vital to group cohesion. As a group grows, it can become harder and harder to keep it together by force. A moder-ator or owner can inspect each interaction for adherence to the rules and spirit of the fan object, but above a certain population threshold that stops making sense. When groups grow too large for top-down policing, it's up to members to internalize the group's social norms and guard each other from breaking them.

Because superfans are the most steeped in the culture of the group—their very social status depends on it—they're well posi-tioned to act as internal enforcers for the group's social norms. Deciding what is and isn't acceptable. Creating new traditions. Choosing the context of what it means to be a member. For exam-ple, fans of the musician Tom Petty adhere to a careful set of social norms, including religiosity, family, and clean living. Marijuana is an acceptable group discussion topic; heroin is not. Petty's superfans are quick to come down on anyone posting to his fan forums who tries to take the conversation in a more risqué direction, despite the fact that Petty himself is now known to have been at times a heroin addict.

The more alike members of a group are, the more important the tiniest dissimilarity between them seems. Groups divide and divide into smaller subgroups as members look to stake out their individuality. It can get rather heated. Sometimes a group can weather the vitriol and sometimes it can't; superfans help police each other, deciding what is and isn't acceptable behavior before factions become too entrenched. It is vital that superfans have the ability to re-center conversation when internal debate goes too far and ensure that bids for hierarchy fall within the bounds the group has deemed acceptable. Punishing those who violate the internalized rules of the group acts as the glue that holds fan groups together. That isn't to say that there isn't some enjoyment of infighting—keeping defectors in line is fun! This is a concept borrowed from second-wave fandom, as we saw when we discussed the history of fan studies: there's a satisfaction in forcing others to play by our sometimes rather arbitrary rules.

Participating in Ritualized Debate

Of course, sometimes debate itself is a cultural norm. Fans of the young adult series *Twilight* are self-divided into two camps: those who believe the young protagonist Bella should date the attractive and brooding werewolf Jacob, and those who believe that she should date the attractive and brooding vampire Edward. Team Edward and Team Jacob are both active in debating the characters' relative merits as boyfriend material (Edward is more experienced! Jacob is more loving!) and creating memes, art, fanfic, and thousands of blog and social media posts to back up their assertions.

Remember, fans and their fan objects are playing out scripted, make-believe roles. We're pretending that one of these characters is a more deserving boyfriend for Bella, another made-up character. Are the two rivals really going to fight each other for her affection? Do the actors who play these characters in the movie need to be kept apart on the set? Is one of them actually "better" at dating? Should either of these grown men consider a relationship with *any-one* from Twilight's teenaged fan-base? Probably not. But a good community knows when to encourage this sort of ritualized rivalry in a friendly way.

Less than a week after the hangout at the Sonoma Terrace described earlier, a Rabbit will be shamed on Facebook over a rumor that he was gossiping with a cast member about a fellow Rabbit. Friendly though the social clubs may be, they're still human. As in any group, drama is a necessary part of keeping things vibrant and interesting.

"Social systems have two modes—dynamic and dead," notes Shirky. Disagreement within a community can tear a group apart, but drama rarely has the same effect. Metaphorically, a fan group with a lot of infighting, politics, and dramatics is one of the healthiest possible situations. It means people care enough about the community that they're willing fight for it.

There's a Whole Lot of Hugging Going On

Disneyland doesn't seem to mind the social clubs. It's not unusual to see cast members going out of their way to interact with them ("Why did Anakin Skywalker cross the road?" shouted an official park photographer at a gathering of Sons of Anakin members earlier. "To get to the dark side!" Everyone groaned on cue). Online, cast members sometimes complain of line jumping, intimidation, and raucous behavior, and Disney fan forums have their share of outraged season-pass holders, but even the most indignant often acknowledge that plenty of other park visitors do much worse. For the moment, anyway, the social clubs seem to be safe.

The Mad T Party kicks off every Sunday evening next to the Monsters, Inc. Mike & Sulley to the Rescue! ride in Disney California Adventure. It is the subject of much interclub discussion each week: "Are you going to T?" "There'll be girls there!" "I'll be at T later." Of course, there are show times on other days of the week as well, but Sunday is the day when the social clubs all congregate.

On stage, a performer dressed in a punk-inflected Alice in Wonderland outfit is belting out a medley of classic hits. It's a different singer from the woman who portrayed Alice yesterday, but the crowd screams as though they have been following her career for years. Some of them have been camped out, waiting for a spot near the stage, for hours. The performer dances up and down the platform in a careful sequence of punk-style moves. It feels heavily scripted, like a Broadway musical's depiction of a raunchy rock show.

It's easy to feel cynical about Mad T—the faux edginess and carefully choreographed musical theater. But cynicism misses the point: it's not meant to feel real. This is Disney. It's no more ridiculous to cheer for an actor pretending to be a punk singer than it is for an actor pretending to be a princess, and adults need someone to cheer for too. "Real" would be relatively easy, compared to the task of appealing to such a broad audience night after night.

Over by the second dance floor, a member of Mickey's Raiders social club is trading buttons with a member of Tron City Guardians. Members from Live by the Code are mixing and clasping hands over by the backbenches. A Mickey's Raider member is hugging a Mickey's Empire member. A Son of Anakin is hugging another Son of Anakin. There's a whole lot of hugging going on. Across the square, "Just What I Needed" segues into "Spiderwebs."

The White Rabbits have colonized the smoking area over behind the partition at the air hockey tables. They're perched on the planters and blanketing the curbside, meeting up in tight little groups with their back patches turned outward against the night. There are a lot of them. A *lot* of them. And it's dark back here.

"People say, 'They're probably in a gang. They're probably going to be really rude.' They just see a vest," says one White Rabbit. "Modern society might prejudge us, but I think a lot of people are just intimidated. Our tattoos, our shaved heads, they're like, 'Oh he looks scary.' And then you meet him and he's just a big teddy bear. It's like, I'm wearing a red tank top. I'm not that tough." Next to him, a club member with a buzz cut is dancing with a little girl wearing a tutu and fairy wings. They're both hysterical with giggles. It's totally adorable.

As the band winds down with a punked-out version of "When You Wish Upon a Star," everyone migrates to the edge of the cheering crowd. The two-story screen behind the stage shows archival footage of Walt Disney on opening day. The musicians are giving it their all, clawing at their instruments and sweating under their makeup. The audience screams and fist pumps as though the band was a chart-topping supergroup performing their final curtain call. Somewhere in the crowd, a lightsaber waves.

"It's kind of ridiculous isn't it?" laughs Fite. And it is. But it's also fun. Like we're all in on a big ridiculous joke, the entire group of us doing this ridiculous thing together, and that makes it a little wonderful too.

CHAPTER 6

FANS, WHAT ARE THEY GOOD FOR?

He Who Controls _____ Controls the World

From: Karen Ewoks

"I'm getting married on April 27th and we're going to play your game at the reception!"

From: Cards Against Humanity

"Did you know 50% of first marriages end in divorce?"

From: Frank Stickers

"When are you going to be in stock again? Let's be honest. Who is going to go to Staples and print their own cards? Not me. Get your shit together."

From: Cards Against Humanity

"Cards Against Humanity will be back in stock at some point. We could be more specific, but you could have been nicer."

From: Frankton Orifice

"I bought the Bigger Blacker Box, but my Dad sat on it and crushed it! Is there any way I can get a replacement Bigger Blacker Box?"

From: Cards Against Humanity

"In the long run it would be more cost efficient to replace your dad.—Holly."

From: Hamilton B.

"What is the age range for the cards? My 15 year old son is asking for a set, but I'm hedging on it."

From: Cards Against Humanity

"That depends on how bad of a parent you want to be."

From: Dale Chippen

"Would you guys mind responding in an email that just insults me? Is that cool with you? Because that would be really awesome. Love, Dale."

From: Cards Against Humanity

"You're not worth the time.—David."

Shortly after Christmas in 2014, a quarter of a million people opened their mailboxes to find a printed pamphlet with the title "Your Emails Are Bad and You Should Feel Bad." It contained thirty-six pages of emails from customers writing in to the customer-service department at Cards Against Humanity, makers of the card game of the same name, and CAH's responses. The 250,000 recipients had paid $15 each to receive it as part of a "10 Days or Whatever of Kwanzaa" gift box they purchased from CAH. It joined, among other things, a set of comics, a packet of candy that changes the taste of food, a promise to bribe several public officials, and, in their words, "a bunch of stickers that you definitely shouldn't use to vandalize public property—that would be wrong."

CAH's fans—only fans spend $15 to get a box of unrelated junk from a game manufacturer—responded favorably. "Your Emails are

Bad and You Should Feel Bad" currently has 4.3 stars (out of 5) on the online literary review community Goodreads.

The Cards Against Humanity card game comes with two sets of cards: black question cards and white answer cards. The black cards have phrases or sentences that ask a question; the white cards represent potential answers. During each round, the player acting as the judge reads out a black card, and the remaining players use their white cards to pick their best response. It's a game best played with friends who don't mind horrible, horrible vulgarity. A black card reading: "What ended my last relationship?" might receive white cards like "The American dream," "A disappointing birthday party," "Prancing," "A fetus," "White privilege," and "An oversized lollipop." Except there's an almost 100 percent chance that at least one of those cards would refer to sex acts, bodily fluids, or celebrities (along with their sex acts and bodily fluids). Expansion packs are released at regular intervals, adding new cards to the deck and keeping the humor timely and horrible.

Wil Wheaton, actor and host of the *Geek and Sundry* gaming show TableTop, opened his Cards Against Humanity episode with the following warning: "You don't want to watch this episode of TableTop. This episode of TableTop will be offensive to everyone. It will be rude. It will be in exceedingly poor taste, and it will be outrageously profane. If you are sensitive, or offended by . . . anything, we at TableTop encourage you to find one of our other episodes to watch."

Customer inquiries at CAH are answered by a team composed largely of aspiring authors and comedians. In fact, their work is less about customer service and more about creative writing. When customers write in with a question about when items will be back in stock, or a suggestion to make a wolf-themed deck of cards, or a complaint about their missing order, it is official company policy to fix the issue . . . and then immediately mock the asker.

Jenn Bane is the company's community director, which would probably be called head of customer service elsewhere. "Even if they are like the dumbest person you've interacted with, even if everything is their fault, remember that they're a human being, and they're emailing us for a reason. The first thing you do is fix the problem. And then you make fun of them."

The freedom to entertain and amuse in what would traditionally be a dry interaction can be bought only at the price of really really good customer service. A customer who is frightened that a girlfriend's birthday gift might be lost in the mail is not someone to tease. A customer who is relieved that the gift will arrive in time, and who perhaps may be laughing at his or her excessive terror, certainly is.

"We generously give out refunds; we generously send restocks. We'll throw in an extra expansion package because they're having a rough day, or they got broken up with," says Bane. "Just give it. There's clearly a right thing to do, so just do it. There's no standard formatting, and you don't get anything back that says 'You are customer number blah blah blah,'" she explains. "We want to sound not like a corporation. We don't want to sound like you're talking to a robot. We want them to understand that they're talking to an actual human. We'll say, 'We're really sorry,' but instead of saying we're really sorry your order didn't arrive, you might say, 'We're really sorry we fucked up your order.' And people are usually pretty delighted."

CAH is routinely the number one bestseller in Amazon's Toys & Games category. As of late 2016, the core pack had more than 33,000 reviews there, and quite a few of them mimic CAH's signature banter. They've also colonized the "Customer Question and Answers" section. For a customer who wants to know "Why won't Amazon ship this to Canada?" there are dozens of fan responses, including

"Because Canada is too nice for this game" and "Shipping to the new state of 'More North Dakota' will incur a small surcharge. Ay?" Hundreds of customers marked these answers as helpful enough to move them to the top of the answers list. It requires scrolling quite a bit before you'll find the correct response, "Just go to Amazon.ca and order it there."

For Black Friday 2013, the time when many companies attempt to cash in on early holiday purchases with big sales, CAH decided to raise its price for the day from $25 to $30. Max Temkin is one of the game's creators. "We thought people would be angry about it," he remembers. The result was actually a net increase over Black Friday sales from the year before, and an outpouring of good-natured support from both fans and the media. "People liked it. People bought it on Black Friday because they wanted to be part of the joke. They posted their receipts on Tumblr. They really played into it and they were like, 'Oh, this is an incredible opportunity to buy Cards Against Humanity for even more money!' That was really unexpected."

CAH fans value the interactions they have with the company just as much as their copy of the game, whether those interactions come in the form of a customer-service email, a visit with them at a convention, or playing along with a marketing ploy that makes them feel like part of an inside joke. These types of interaction have become part of the Cards experience. On Black Friday, fans were allowed to express their sense of the absurd, support a company they liked, and boast about being a part of something unique, something only a true fan of the game would do.

"What you see in the media, and the coverage, and the social media around it, that's the sort of performance. People like being part of a spectacle like that. It does give everyone the feeling that they're on the inside of an inside joke with us," says Temkin.

Corporate Values vs. Corporate Voice

CAH can get away with an antagonistic publicity stunt because goodwill is at the heart of its business model. It's the type of goodwill that can't be sprinkled on top of a product with savvy marketing or a new catchphrase, or even great customer service. Cards Against Humanity is free. The entire starter card set is available under a Creative Commons license. It can be downloaded from the CAH website as a thirty-one-page PDF along with instructions for printing and storing the cards yourself.

Of course, most customers don't *want* to take an hour to print out thirty-one pages of paper and cut them into paper cards that will disintegrate the first time a beer spills on them. Most are happy to spend $25 (or $30) for a professional version. But offering the cards for free means happier customers in general. Paying that $25 is a choice, not an obligation. It's a lot easier to field complaints about price, or shipping costs, or lost packages when one of the alternatives is always "So don't pay!"

What marketers call "surprise and delight" cannot be crowdsourced. Despite all appearances, CAH's ability to keep its fans on their toes is the result of a carefully orchestrated strategy. It revises the card decks several times a year. The game writers review every card in the deck and decide if it's still relevant. A Britney Spears joke might become a Miley Cyrus joke. There is, intentionally, no change log posted anywhere. The only notification that cards have been updated or replaced is the incremented version number on the back of the box. "As you can imagine, that enrages fans," says Temkin.

In 2015, Cards Against Humanity again ran its holiday subscription service. This time it was called Eight Sensible Gifts for Hanukkah. The booty sent to each participant included a pair of socks, a second pair of socks, a third pair of socks, an investment in the US Treasury Inflation-Protected Securities fund, and an individual subscription to WBEZ, the NPR affiliate in Chicago. For night six, CAH bought everyone at its Chinese factory a week's paid vacation—the gift was the workers' tear-jerking thank you letters and photos. Night seven was a 1962 Picasso lithograph and a survey question: should it be donated to a museum or cut into 150,000 pieces and mailed to subscribers. Night eight was ownership of (a very small piece of) a castle in Ireland.

It takes a special combination of circumstances to make offensiveness a viable marketing strategy, although many try it. Celebrities who are after a bad-boy persona are often advised by their agents to engage in strategic acts of outrageousness. The UK boy band The Wanted was initially instructed to party as hard and publicly as possible to differentiate themselves from rivals One Direction. In Chicago, the infamous Lincoln Park hot-dog stand The Weiner's Circle has created a mystique around its willingness to verbally abuse patrons. Frat-favorite DJ Diplo has been known to use what, for a celebrity courting a different audience, might be considered an unusual level of misogyny. In general, negative-image policies like these often backfire. The Wanted eventually lost the boy-band wars to their younger, more clean-cut musical rivals. And brands that are merely rude are usually put in their place via social-media outrage, boycotts, or petitions.

Organizations often confuse their corporate voice with their corporate philosophy. In the same way that consumers will happily tolerate a monopoly as long as it's benevolent, fans will tolerate, or even enjoy, an abrasive corporate voice as long as they feel that the fan object's motivations are positive. Outrageousness that reflects a bad attitude is distasteful. But outrageousness that hides a heart of gold is fun! CAH has navigated this issue. Its corporate voice may conjure a rude asshole uncle, but CAH is careful to only use it *after* a fan's legitimate complaints and questions have been handled.

Fan management—what to do with a fan group once they have

been won over—is something with which many organizations struggle. Fan loyalty does often quickly lead to increased income for the fan object, a fact that does often seem to justify the immediate time and attention that goes into building the audience. But when it comes to maintaining the relationship, whether the fan group grew organically or was the result of meticulous strategy, many brands end up returning to where they started. That is to say, they treat their fan audience as a group of consumers with particularly attractive buying habits, and nothing more. It's very tempting to remember fan loyalty and forget all of the strings attached.

The most important strategy of fan management requires addressing group cohesion; fan maintenance is the primary concern and any type of monetization comes second.

Hello Brooklyn

"Of course it's personal," read the billboard, white text on a black background, tagged with #HELLOBROOKLYN on the bottom right corner. Next to the tagline was the logo for the Brooklyn Nets, the NBA team shortly slated to move from New Jersey to its new home in the New York City borough of Brooklyn.

If it was meant to be a homecoming, it was already a mixed one. The flashy new Barclays Center, which would house the team, was still under construction, and community reactions to the building were strong on both sides. Enthusiastic fans packed a rally in support outside of Brooklyn Borough Hall, screaming their approval. Meanwhile, the construction site had become the scene of frequent protests as local groups and clergy condemned the loss of housing and jobs, and the creep of gentrification as the borough had become wealthier.

The Nets hadn't been a New York–based team since the 1970s, and at least some Brooklynites didn't necessarily want them back. As one marketer involved in the #HELLOBROOKLYN campaign remembers, "[They were saying] no. Get out of Brooklyn. You're killing our community. People were like, yo, not only do I not care the Brooklyn Nets are coming here, I don't want them here, this is not my team."

The Nets disagreed. "First Home Game Since 1957," read another Brooklyn Nets billboard. (The Brooklyn Dodgers played their last home game that year before moving to California.)

In #HELLOBROOKLYN's version of the story, issues of gentrification were sidestepped. What Brooklynites *truly* cared about was differentiating themselves from the rest of the city. Having a Brooklyn-based basketball team meant no longer having to root for the Knicks, who played in the heart of Manhattan. Other boroughs could have their own teams. The Nets were for Brooklyn.

Nets CEO Brett Yormark, in a statement introducing the #HELLOBROOKLYN advertising campaign, told his future fans, "We are delighted to continue building a connection between Brooklynites and the players on their new home team." Nets chief marketing officer Fred Mangione put it more bluntly in an interview with ESPN. "Our goal is to own Brooklyn," he said.

Months before the move, the Nets released a video acknowledging their future neighborhood's history of playing second fiddle to Manhattan. "We're a friend to the scrappy, the loyal and ready. We've seen spirit and thrills at its very best . . . and at its most trying. We've also been the underdogs, waiting for our chance. And now, Brooklyn, we root for the same cause, because we believe in the same things you do: that neighborhood is family," said the voiceover.

For the Nets to be a true neighborhood team (granted, to a neighborhood of 2.6 million people), it needed a "ritual enemy." Someone or something that all of Brooklyn could hate. We're not like *those guys*, we're like *us*. And people like *us* root for the Nets. In this case, that ritual enemy wasn't another team, it was the anti-Brooklyn—Manhattan. Doubtless the campaign's architects hoped that a cross-borough rivalry would inspire a cross-team rivalry with the New York Knicks.

Dealing with an adversarial fan group was a challenge for the Nets, but certainly not a crippling issue. Long before the first hoop was installed in the arena, the Nets set out to win themselves a fan base to go with their new geography. It took serious advertising dollars to fund their way into the hearts of those Brooklynites who remained reluctant, but all the funding in the world would have been useless without understanding their fan group well enough to choose the right message.

Of course, the Nets are in fact, as of 2016, entirely owned by Russian oligarch Mikhail Prokhorov, who also owns Barclays Center. The Nets belong to Brooklyn only in the sense that some of the borough has become wealthy enough to afford tickets to their games. However, by the time the first Nets-Knicks game came to Brooklyn, the rivalry was in earnest. Official attendance numbers were up 23 percent over their New Jersey numbers. And most important, Nets fans were already leading the NBA in at least one lucrative area: apparel sales. As Brooklynite Ryan Wynn put it at the time, "I don't know what a Brooklyn Nets fan is, all I know is that we're soon to be diehard fans."

Give a Little, Get a Little

It's not impossible to imagine a situation where Brooklynites reacted to the #HELLOBROOKLYN campaign with ridicule, or even parody. Recent history is filled with well-meaning attempts at engagement that were hijacked by mischievous or dissatisfied fans. It's a difficult decision, allowing the public to collaborate on creating a fan object's meaning. Fans in particular have often invested time, energy, and financial resources to understand their fan object better than its initial creators. The concept of handing over brand control to an outside group, whose intentions may or may not align with the owner's, can be terrifying. And yet, despite the danger, fan objects—especially for brands like sports teams (or fashion labels), where so much of the value lies in intangible associations—cannot exist without a strong context. And fans have a wider variety of backgrounds and personal experience to generate that context than any single marketing team.

The 2012 movie *Magic Mike*, a drama about male strippers, was initially marketed as a romantic comedy. A handsome gent in the sex biz finds salvation at the hands of a comely lady and must decide if it's time for more wholesome work. But it soon became obvious that a different audience was excited to support the movie: homosexual men. In a quick about-face, Channing Tatum, the star stripper, appeared on the cover of the gay-oriented *Out* magazine. A *Magic Mike*–themed float appeared in the West Hollywood Gay Pride parade. A new gay-friendly trailer highlighted the sex appeal of a movie that, no matter the plot, does showcase a lot of attractive semi-naked men.

In the early 2000s, carmaker Cadillac saw a similar effect with its Escalade, a luxury SUV originally marketed to suburban parents as a way to transport the team to and from little league. Yet the SUV's ostentatious price, luxury amenities, and ease of modification made it a status symbol for sports stars, hip-hop icons, and other celebrities. Later models became iteratively flashier and more sophisticated. In its heyday in the late 2000s, the Escalade regularly won the not-inconsequential award for the most commonly stolen vehicle in the United States.

The best marketing narratives make associations with a consumer's feelings of self and identity. A good and extremely lucky marketing team might happen upon a narrative that resonates with an audience, such as #HELLOBROOKLYN, all by themselves, but then again they might not.

Of course, another huge advantage of allowing fan groups a say in a brand's meanings is that it helps to give it a veneer of authenticity that would be difficult to generate otherwise. Collaborating with fans in any way can help distance a brand from its original commercial purpose. Deep emotions like playfulness or earnestness, when they can be accomplished without seeming contrived, are both great antidotes to the more mercenary purpose that underpins advertising.

Pabst Blue Ribbon–brand beer relied for many years on a low price tag to remain competitive. It was often the cheapest option on the menu. Yet in the last half decade PBR has become known as the de facto beer of a trendy, urban hipster population. The cause is an entirely fan-created context. PBR's legacy as a cheap, working-class brew helped it gain a reputation as "authentic Americana" among a wealthier population who would otherwise likely purchase something of better quality. Or, to put it less kindly, PBR has become the favorite beer of a privileged subculture that wishes to demonstrate how unpretentious it is. Of course, some relish the irony of the brand. A few might even enjoy the taste, which one reviewer has compared to corn and wet cardboard. But any way the beer is poured, a top-down narrative created by the fan object itself, such as "PBR is a cheap beer," will rarely be as innovative or effective as a bottom-up narrative created by a tuned-in fan base, such as "Drinking PBR shows solidarity with the true American working class."

It is interesting to note that in some New England locations PBR has started losing market share to an unexpected rival, Narragansett. This difficult-to-pronounce lager, purchased in 2004 from Pabst Brewing Company by a private investor, had been around for more than a century and carries a similar in-bar price point. It was once so synonymous with eastern seaboard summers that it was the beer of choice for shark hunter Quint in the classic seventies movie *Jaws*, set in a fictional northeastern town. But by the mid-2000s, its production was down from 2 million barrels annually in the 1960s to just 600 barrels a year.

By 2014, production was back up to nearly 80,000 barrels. Like PBR, the secret weapon in Narragansett's comeback is the allure of authenticity—in this case, a love of authentic local-based heritage brands, served with a side of nostalgia. The brand has capitalized on its comeback by releasing limited-edition Jaws-themed cans. It's definitely a hit with some who believe PBR has become too mainstream.

In the hierarchy of authenticity, the newer, less-known product almost always wins, a truth that holds firm whether the product is an undiscovered old-school beer, an unknown clothing designer, or an off-the-map Chinese restaurant. Authenticity one-upmanship in the indie music community has defined the scene for so long that it has led to the popular tongue-in-cheek catchphrase, "I listen to bands that don't even exist yet."

Remember that fandom is, at heart, externally generated branding. Just like internally generated marketing efforts, fan-created meanings don't need to be based in reality to be effective. Pabst Blue Ribbon beer ceased production in Milwaukee, the blue-collar heartland from which it draws its all-American allure, long before its revival in hipster bars across the nation. It's now owned by a corporate partnership that includes TSG Consumer Partners LLC, a multibillion-dollar private-equity firm based in San Francisco, which has also invested in Famous Amos Cookies, MET-Rx nutritional supplements, Vitaminwater, and Popchips. When it comes to fan objects, what's important is what it means to the potential fan, not what it means to a company's shareholders.

Kickstarting Done Right (and Wrong)

In a few years, it's possible that the area around Barclays Center will have just as many organic cold-pressed-juice bars and yoga studios as Brooklyn's rapidly gentrifying Greenpoint neighborhood just a few miles north.

It is here, in the shell of an old pencil factory, that Kickstarter houses its headquarters. The façade channels old Greenpoint: a blank brick wall with occasional graffiti, the iron windowsills taste-fully rust-covered. In fact, there are few markers hinting this is the home of the most iconic crowdfunding website in the world, not even a painted sign. Inside is all reclaimed wood, antique fixtures, polished concrete floors, and hushed, light-filled loveliness. There's a library straight out of a 1920s murder mystery and a roof garden of local grasses (the guardrail is actually a standing desk). There's a full-sized theater with reclaimed chairs, and an art gallery. In the giant, homey kitchen, near the arcade-style video games, a woman in a vintage sundress passes out salted caramels.

Upstairs in the cavernous workspace, filling the length of one of the long wooden tables that act as desks, sits the Project Liaison team. Their job is to critique and edit potential project pages and help creators set up an attractive campaign. Each of the Kickstarter genres is represented: Art, Comics, and Crafts all the way down through the alphabet to Theater. The team makes sure that every listing has a decent video, a description, and rewards for backers; that the project itself seems legit; and that it all makes sense together. But occasionally they do a lot more.

Kickstarter is a platform: a website. It has no warehouses, stock, or subscriptions. It sells nothing. Its mission, stripped of context, is to provide server space for individuals who want people to give them money, and then to collect that money in return for a fee.

Kickstarter may guide project owners on what type of "thank you" products to gift their backers once a campaign is over, but in general the company wants to be a medium, not a preorder system.

So what is the purpose of such a large team of what, in any other industry, might be called quality-control specialists? They represent a significantly larger presence than the community support team a few rows away, whose job is merely to offer general customer service. In a company with just shy of 140 employees, it's a surprisingly large amount of resources to devote to making sure individual creators are speaking effectively to their audiences.

When Max Temkin and his Cards Against Humanity colleagues approached Kickstarter about hosting the campaign that launched their game into the public eye in 2010, it was not a spur-of-the-moment decision.

The game creators had been designing elaborate stratagems together since first grade. By college, the group found itself hosting sprawling game-themed New Year's parties for friends. With ever-larger crowds to entertain, standbys like Pictionary became impractical. "Cardenfreude" was born. The name didn't last but the game did, and when the party guests returned to their respective universities a month later, they shared it with their friends. By spring break 2009, word of mouth had reached such a fever pitch that Max and one of his co-creators felt moved to launch the now infamous website offering the game for free.

The website drew new users in with the lure of inexpensive fun, but it also, incidentally, collected visitors' email addresses for future contact.

By the time CAH was ready for Kickstarter, it had already attracted a robust audience. Game play had been thoroughly tested through thousands of downloads. And because of the website, it also had reviews from industry giants such as the *Chicago Tribune* and the Onion *A.V. Club*—which should have been impossible for a product that wasn't technically for sale yet. Moreover, Cards already had a relatively huge preexisting buzz. As Max put it in an interview at the time, "Nobody had ever heard of us, so making the entire game available for free was a great marketing tool. Even if someone downloaded the game instead of pledging to our project, they would play with some friends who might pledge."

The rewards for participating in the Kickstarter campaign were simple: back the project, get a professionally printed version of the game. Higher-level backers would get custom cards that could be filled out however they wanted. There were no Cards Against Humanity mugs, key chains, or beer koozies, just the promise of more of the same, printed better. One week into the Kickstarter campaign, a letter went out to all the fans who had previously expressed interest through the original website. It began, "Dear horrible friends. . . ."

The $4,000 goal was surpassed at week two. Further emails were sent out asking for advice on how to use the extra cash, with options such as higher-quality cards and fancier packaging. By the end of the campaign CAH was up to $15,570, at the time a fairly large amount for the platform.

Good crowdfunding campaigns don't just happen. The success of CAH's offering on Kickstarter was the culmination of months of fan interaction and experimentation. With the exception of Kickstarted projects that receive outside support, such as a big media mention, very few are ever successful without the presence of some form of preexisting fan group. It's not that campaigns require a huge number of people who want their product—quite a few people who had already downloaded the free version of Cards by definition had no need for a second one—it's that a core group of preexisting fans is almost always necessary to reach a broader audience.

The Social Part of Social Monetization

Fandom is one of the most effective tools for social monetization—that is to say, using a fan's own friend group as an advocate for money-making activities, especially ones related to marketing. Social networks are extremely efficient at conveying news and information to those they're most likely to impact, as quickly as possible.

The narrower those interests are, the faster and more targeted the messages will be. The release of a new LEGO Jedi Scout Fighter play set might disseminate slowly through an indifferent public, but it will make its way through the Star Wars fan community more quickly, and through the LEGO Star Wars fan community even faster. There is no magic to this—fans are simply more likely to befriend others with similar interests, who want to find out and discuss similar things.

If, as the old marketing adage goes, buyers need to hear about a product seven times before they decide that it's worth checking out, fan communities increase the number of people who hear positive things about the product, and decrease the time it takes for them to do so. It isn't true that social-marketing success always follows the presence of an enthusiastic, well-connected fan group, but it is certainly harder to realize without one. And even then, the group must be properly primed and handled.

Luke Crane's desk at Kickstarter is littered with figurines, card sets, and books—the detritus of dozens of curated Kickstarter projects as well as his own campaigns. His official title is the charmingly generic "Head of Games." His job, in a manner of speaking, is to critique projects for their fan appeal.

"You don't have to have three million fans on Facebook to be successful, but you do have to be tapped in to some kind of community that is familiar with what you represent," explains Crane.

"If somebody comes to me and says, 'I'm just getting started, I have some experience in the industry but I want to raise $200,000,' and I ask them how much [outreach] they've done and they say, 'None,' then I try to very gently nudge them in the direction of maybe you're not ready for Kickstarter yet. Maybe you need to go out into the world with your idea, and show it to people, and build a relationship with a community so that you're not just sitting on Kickstarter drumming your fingers going, 'Where is everybody,' when you launch. You can't just roll out the Kickstarter, slap down a heroic project invention and be like, let's go. Give me all the money."

Crowdfunding is very much about activating a preexisting community. It allows creators to take advantage of original fans as well as the extended network of acquaintances they're likely to entice. This is a completely different strategy from finding an existing fan group and trying to market to it. What makes a person a poker fan, or a fan of a game like *Magic: The Gathering* or Trivial Pursuit, is more personal than a general love of card games. Approaching a community of poker players and trying to convince them to back the Cards Against Humanity Kickstarter would be laughable. "To post for the first time on a community forum with self-promotion is such a delicate thing. Knowing how the community works . . . and being able to get in there and appeal to them and show them that you're one of them, you're making a cool thing, that's key." And that "insider" mindset needs to influence every level of a campaign, not just its promotion.

For example, one common pitfall in crowdfunding campaigns is in choosing the wrong backer rewards—the thank-you gifts that donors receive. Too often, they read like the merchandise booth at a concert: $1 gets a sticker, $5 gets a key chain with a sticker, $15 gets all that *plus* a T-shirt. For an audience of consumers this might make sense: more money equals more stuff. But for a fan, it can cheapen the experience. "Nobody wants a koozie for whatever you're doing," says Crane.

Fans are looking to show their support, not buy some stuff. The wish to be associated with the project creator and be part of something bigger than themselves is a strong one. Backing often comes down to a very emotional, gut-level decision. "We're always, always telling creators: make it a story about who they are and what they're making, and why it's important to them. Appeal to that emotional reaction rather than the transactional one. This process is very much about having a relationship with these people and maintaining that relationship." A Kickstarter to fund a movie must convince backers to spend their cash years before seeing any output, instead of just spending the same amount on a ticket once it has already been made. Both actions support the movie, but the earlier support is much more valuable to the creator.

The best backer rewards are often experiential. A postcard is a terrible reward, but a personalized, signed postcard, with its proxy aura of nearness to the project creator, could be a better one. So is proprietary information, a personal phone call, an in-person invitation, or early access to a product. These rewards symbolize a relationship, a special insider status unavailable to the general population. It's unfortunately also a relationship that can foment feelings of entitlement—it's not unheard of for backers to hassle creators and demand some type of creative control over the project—but in general it's a positive experience for both.

What to Get for the Fan Who Has Everything

Shadowrun is a tabletop role-playing game in which players engage in complex corporate espionage. In the future. A future with elves and orcs and dragons. Eric Mersmann has been playing the game with a group of friends since the mid-nineties, so he was understand-ably excited when Shadowrun Returns, a video-game version from the original creators, went up on Kickstarter. The highest-level backer reward was a private gaming session with one of the game's creators.

"I spent five days going back and forth on whether I should pull the trigger or not [on] that top tier award," he remembers. If he made the pledge, one of the game's original creators would come to his town and act as game master for a Shadowrun game for him and five of his friends. "Of course I knew exactly which five of my friends it would be," he says. "I was just super excited for that opportunity. They said that there were three out of three slots available. I watched the first one go in the first day, and the second one go on the third or fourth day. I hemmed and hawed, and gnashed my teeth, and then I jumped in and took that third spot." The final cost: $10,000.

"People were pretty mystified. From friends of friends, I got reports of indignation that I was spending so much money. It was really funny because the first person who understood was some-body who is not gamer at all, but a huge sports fan. I mentioned that I did this and I was really excited. He was like, 'Oh, yeah, I totally get that,' and I was like, 'Really?' He was like, 'Yeah. If I could sit in box seats at an IU [Indiana University] basketball game with Bobby Knight, I would do that in a second. No matter how much it cost,'" Mersmann recalls.

The phrase "experience economy" refers to the concept that intangible goods such as memories, emotions, and education are fantastically valuable to consumers, more so perhaps than physical products. Premium experiences like this are even more valuable to fans, who may have already tried all of the easily accessible fanlike activities associated with a fan object. It was certainly the case for Mersmann, who has no regrets about the once-in-a-lifetime game he and his friends eventually enjoyed.

"I think that's part of the emotional process of the investment. We all loved the game. We loved our experience playing the game. It was a total high-school-nerd reunion. It was awesome."

The Zach Braff Effect

Fans expect a level of respect in return for their enthusiasm, and rightly so, but it can sometimes be difficult to interpret exactly what form that respect should take—discounts, early access, in-person experiences, limited-edition extras, or other types of swag. Fans are quick to calculate how much monetary value they are willing to assign to their zeal, yet few members of an audience have any concept of the true costs involved in providing and maintaining a fan object.

Says Kickstarter's Luke Crane, "When a backer comes to your project, they look at your goal, and they do a quick calculation in their head: Does that seem right? Can you make this thing with that amount of money? Of course, most of them don't have the knowledge to make a real guess. If they really knew what it cost to make these things, they'd be like, 'Wow, you're not asking for enough money to make that.'" So it sets up this weird dynamic where creators are trying to guess how much backers are willing to pay, and backers are holding creators accountable for a process they don't really understand. When it goes wrong it can be really painful."

During one well-publicized incident, indie rock star Amanda Palmer raised a huge amount of money—just shy of $1.2 million— for a new album on Kickstarter, yet continued to use volunteer musicians in her shows. Fans went mad with condemnation. Surely with so much money she could now afford to pay everyone, despite her pleas that the funds had immediately gone toward the process of making the album. Palmer has since moved her crowdfunding efforts to subscription-based Patreon, perhaps in the quest for more transparency in the relationship between funding and production.

"You can see it in these hilarious and unreasonable demands that fans make. You see fans shouting down people being like, 'How dare you ask for that much money? What are you going to do with all that extra money?'" explains Crane. "We're all like, 'But there's no extra money. I have to make a thing and ship a thing to you. There's zero extra money.'"

Any feeling of being taken advantage of, no matter the grounds for truth, can sour the fan relationship. Call it the "Zach Braff" effect. In 2013, Hollywood star Braff turned to Kickstarter to finance his comedy movie *Wish I Was Here*. He had a large existing fan group from his earlier TV shows and movies, and the goodwill of any number of celebrity friends and costars to help publicize it. His Kickstarter surpassed its $2 million goal within forty-eight hours. Less expected was the huge fan backlash once his numbers got high enough. Braff was already a multimillionaire, and, despite his protestations, many speculated that his net worth might have funded the movie without a need for outside assistance.

Fans want to feel like they have made a difference: something has happened as a result of their love and attention that would not otherwise have occurred. The best Kickstarter rewards show a deep sense of thankfulness and appreciation for a fan's support. If it turns out all that support and effort was wasted, or worse yet, wasn't required in the first place, fans are probably justified in feeling peeved.

The principle holds true for fandoms that will never need to crowdsource, crowdfund, or do anything with the word "crowd" in the title. The fan/fan object relationship is parasocial—it's strictly one-way. Fans feel strongly about the thing they love, but the reverse isn't true, at least at an individual level; it isn't humanly possible for celebrities to learn intimate personal details about every one of their fans. The most valuable fan experiences remove those barriers in the association, flattening it and helping the relationship feel more two-way. Allowing a fan to feel personally responsible for a fan text creation is powerful, but so are activities that can show fans how important they are individually, not just as an aggregate block of enthusiasm.

Building a Better Fan Text

Games and gaming are a common testing ground for different types of fan interactions, perhaps because they are, by their nature, already participatory.

Cards Against Humanity has a "Suggest a Card" area on the front page of its website. "Throughout the history of the company, it's been sort of an adversarial relationship with the 'hard-core' fans, the Cards fandom. They keep pushing us to accommodate fan culture on the game [and] we keep pushing back," says Temkin. "We have tons and tons and tons of suggestions. And they're all terrible and we don't read them."

Whether or not that attitude is just part of its corporate voice, CAH is certainly not alone in its trepidation at embracing fan-created content. Just like allowing fans to collaborate on creating brand meaning, validating fan-created materials has its own dangers.

Content creation is a basic fanlike activity, whether done in the name of self-improvement or as an attempt to forge bonds and gain status within the group. When properly channeled this can lead to the oft-promised rewards of crowdsourcing, like when Frito-Lay–brand snacks asks fans to develop a new flavor of potato chip and has them vote on their favorites. The resulting winner, "Cheesy Garlic Bread," will hopefully be a hit because it reflects what the audience wants to eat. When improperly channeled, it can lead to embarrassment and legal issues, like when Frito-Lay asks fans to develop a new flavor of potato chip and they proceed to bombard the Internet with flavors like "Orange Juice and Toothpaste," "Blood of my enemies," "Sexual Predator," and "Regret." Fandom may come into being when a large enough group of people decides to express a significant emotional response on a shared platform, but some platforms, such as Internet polls, lend themselves to mischief more than others.

Grand Theft Auto is arguably the most popular video game franchise in the world; it certainly ranks near the top of the list. More than a dozen versions have been released in the last fifteen years, and the 2013 version of *Grand Theft Auto V* broke seven different Guinness World Records, including "Most Successful Entertainment Launch of All Time," bringing in $1 billion within the first three days of its release.

During the game, players participate in a number of missions and mini games as they rise through the ranks of a criminal underworld. As an "open world" game, where players are allowed to roam the landscape at will, the cities and suburbs where the action takes place are impossibly dense, with all kinds of hidden nooks and crannies that invite exploration.

With such a lush platform at their disposal, some players choose to go the extra step. As in many similar games, customizing their game play ("modding" it) is as easy as adding a couple extra files to wherever the game is installed on their computers. This has led to a huge online modding community that shares such customizations. Mods range from the completely logical (cars having more realistic refueling requirements; opening up the insides of buildings for player entry) to the interesting (players can hitchhike or try their hand at being a trucker or police officer) to the downright silly (a huge tsunami floods the entire city; giant whales rain down from the sky; that knife is now a dildo; the main character turns into a monkey, kitty, or Spider-Man. Also, lots of flying).

GTA's publisher, Rockstar Games, has always taken a laissez-faire attitude toward its modder community as long as modder efforts are only used for offline, personal play. While the company does not actively support modding—new updates sometimes disable player-created mods accidentally—it certainly doesn't condemn them. In a May 2015 interview, a representative even gave modding tacit approval, stating, "We have always appreciated the creative efforts of the PC modding community and we still fondly remember the awesome zombie invasion mod. . . ."

It's easy to see why: fan-created mods make GTA more valuable overall. They make game play more interesting for the masses and keep expert players involved long after they've finished with the authorized game play, all at no extra expense to the publisher. Instead of sending out cease-and-desist orders—as do some of their counterparts in the music and movie industries—Rockstar has found a way to incorporate its fans' efforts into its own context. The fans get a creative outlet to have fun, show off their coding skills, and earn status within the fan community, and Rockstar gets a new, completely unexpected use for an already existing product. Modding is good for business.

And yet, in April 2015, the headlines on many gaming blogs screamed some variation of this one: "Paid Skyrim Mod Turns Into A Clusterf**k." The video game *The Elder Scrolls V: Skyrim* has a similar visual conceit to Grand Theft: a large, detailed world of towns, fortresses, and natural environments. Unlike Grand Theft, Skyrim's creator, Bethesda Game Studios, and its distributor, Valve, actively encourage modding, even releasing a number of their own creations. So in April they decided to take advantage of their modding community by allowing users to access Mods more easily . . . for a fee.

The debacle that ensued caused one of the fastest about-faces in gaming history. Fan forums and blogs immediately filled with anti-

Valve vitriol, with reactions ranging from outrage to downright aggressiveness. Some modders who chose to participate reported receiving death threats. A number vowed to cease modding rather than relinquish control over their creations. A petition to remove the pay-for-mod system surpassed 100,000 signatures within the first couple of days. By the following week the paid mod system had been shut down, and all purchases refunded.

What went wrong? If fan-created materials are beneficial to a fan object, legitimizing those materials through an official distribution channel should be good policy. After all, fans often see the value and uses of a product better than the creator, and they are better positioned to understand what kind of additions will make it even better.

In Skyrim's case, the issue was partially in the monetization: Valve allocated itself 30 percent of each mod purchase, Bethesda took 45 percent, and only 25 percent went to the creators themselves. Partially, the problem lay in a general fear that this might mean the end of free modding and the vibrant community it had created. And partially there was a feeling of resentment that fan-created materials, traditionally meant to benefit fellow fans, were increasing the bottom line of a for-profit corporation instead. As one commenter put it, "That's what I see here: Bethesda and Valve making money off of the modding community for work that Bethesda should have done in the first place."

Twenty-five percent seems like it's better than 0 percent, but it's human nature to refuse financial transactions that appear unfair. The efforts of any fan willing to give time and energy to making a fan object more valuable are priceless, and any attempt to buy them must be handled very delicately. In a way, putting a cash value on fanlike activities such as content creation can cheapen them.

Sometimes, the best fan management is hands-off: to provide support, encouragement, and maintenance to the fan community, give them the materials they need to develop and show off their love, offer them experiences commensurate with their enthusiasm, keep them informed . . . and then know when to step back and allow human nature to take its course. But that isn't to say that fan groups can't be steered.

The Brooklyn Nets were able to alter the very concept of what it meant to root for their team, converting their status from invading gentrifiers to a symbol of local pride. They carefully investigated what sort of message would speak to the intrinsic desires and wants of their fan group, and were able to overcome a very real and legitimate opposition. Cards Against Humanity has devoted its entire corporate voice to giving fans exactly the type of abrasive customer service they expect, while never making the mistake of *being* abrasive. They understand that their fans don't want that.

Skyrim took something that was working well, a modding tradition that successfully served the fans' quest for self-improvement and status within the community, and, without fully thinking through the implications of its actions, subverted it into a commercial venture. Because it hadn't understood the motivations of its fan group, it made the mistake of assuming the fans would be grateful for any monetary remuneration they received from their modding, no matter how small. The resulting blowup could have been avoided with proper management.

Be deliberate. It's the most important rule when interacting with an existing fan group. Tinkering with something that isn't broken, like the relationship between active fans and their fan object, is an extremely risky business, one that needs a high level of strategy and forethought. There is a very real line between managing fans and taking advantage of them.

CHAPTER 7

AUTHENTICITY

Carrying On Like Mortal Enemies

On the afternoon of May 26, 1987, a New Jersey state trooper doing routine stops on the Garden State Parkway pulled over a rental car carrying two men. The infraction was an open can of St. Pauli Girl beer, part of a six-pack from a nearby convenience store. When the window was rolled down, the trooper smelled marijuana. The driver admitted there were a few joints under his seat.

"Hands on the hood, feet back, and spread 'em," the driver later remembered the trooper saying. Then he radioed for backup. Handcuffing the driver took two pairs of cuffs; he was a *very* big man. The troopers then pulled the passenger from the car and searched his bag. They found a vial of white powder. The passenger was arrested too.

They were taken in separate cars to the police station, where the driver was identified as James Edward Duggan Jr., better known by his professional wrestling identity, "Hacksaw." The passenger's ID said he was named Hossein Khosrow Ali Vaziri, but even the arresting officer recognized the popular World Wrestling Federation character The Iron Sheik. The powder tested positive for cocaine.

But within a few hours Duggan was released, and so was Vaziri, the latter after signing an appearance bond. They returned to their car and continued southbound to Asbury Park, where they were scheduled to beat each other up before a crowd of thousands.

Or at least, that's the story according to Hacksaw. He claims the Iron Sheik had pressured him into a ride when they arrived at the airport together earlier that day. The beers were the Sheik's idea. And Hacksaw hadn't realized that drinking while driving was frowned upon in New Jersey, having just come from the more permissive Louisiana. He felt terrible about it.

Not so, claims the Iron Sheik in a 2013 interview. And after the arrest, he says, Hacksaw simply called his father, who happened to be the chief of police in the city of Glens Falls, one state away, and got them released. They made it to the match in time for its eight p.m. start and put on a great show in which he helped Hacksaw to a spectacular win. Then they got back in the car, bought another six-pack, grabbed some McDonald's, went to a bar, and ended the night partying in a hotel room with some of their female fans.

It's difficult to tell if the chasm between the two versions is a true difference in memory, or just another part of the stage character each performer had spent so long perfecting.

In the theatrical world of professional wrestling, Duggan was a "face," short for baby face, a hero character. The wrestler the audience is supposed to root for. Despite a degree in applied plant biology, Hacksaw, the character he played for the World Wrestling Federation (WWF), had a brawny, patriotic, good-ol'-boy persona. He often entered the ring carrying a two-by-four piece of wood and an American flag.

The Iron Sheik was a "heel"—the character the audience was supposed to root against. Vaziri was an actual Tehran native who had spent time coaching the US Olympic wrestling team before joining the pro wrestling circuit. He had played a number of face characters, but eventually found fame as a heel by adopting a heavy accent, growing an evil mustache, and wearing a costume that looked vaguely Middle Eastern. The character successfully fed off anti-Arab sentiment during the 1979 Iranian Revolution and Iran hostage crisis; his gimmick was to antagonize fans with anti-American taunts before each match. It worked especially well when he was matched up with all-American faces such as Sargent Slaughter, Hulk Hogan, and Hacksaw.

In the spring of 1987, the two characters were supposed to be in the middle of a feud: the Iron Sheik's evil foreigner versus Hacksaw's red-blooded patriot. Just two months earlier they had faced each other in *Wrestlemania III*, a pay-per-view event that broke all previous attendance and revenue records. Several million fans watched the Sheik put his signature camel clutch hold on face character Jim Brunzell, causing Hacksaw to retaliate by smacking the Sheik with his two-by-four. There was what may have been a missed dropkick early in the match by another face against the Sheik, but the Sheik was able to "sell" the move anyway, reacting as though he had been badly hurt by a superior opponent.

For the two characters to now get caught together, in the same car, without some type of in-story plot device to explain it, was trouble.

Hacksaw expected the incident to blow over. He remembers telling his wife when he called that night, "Honey, we got busted today, but I don't think anybody knows."

She called him back the next morning at his hotel. "Jim, everybody knows! The phone's been ringing off the hook here! All your friends have called to check on you, and it's all over the news."

Hacksaw called his father. Then he called Vince McMahon, the WWF's CEO (and sometimes in-story face of WWF management). He was immediately put through. "Jim," said the voice on the other end of the line, "what have you *done* to us?"

By the following week the media were reporting that both actors had been fired for "drug violations." Newspapers around the country crowed. "[They] won't be hitting each other on the head with steel chairs anymore," gloated a column in the *Chicago Sun-Times*. "The 'heroic' Hacksaw and 'villainous' Sheik, who have been carrying on like mortal enemies in arenas across the country, committed the deadly misdeed of being caught having a good old time like a couple of buddies."

At a TV taping in Buffalo on June 2, McMahon issued a furious warning to the remaining wrestlers. He pounded on his podium and exhorted them again and again: mandatory drug testing for cocaine would begin immediately, and faces and heels must absolutely shun each other in public. "This job is bigger than a six-pack and a blow job! Duggan and Sheik will never, ever work for the WWF again!" Of course, it's unclear if the CEO was speaking in or out of character.

The word "kayfabe" describes the pretense that pro wrestling is a sport, not a performance. To maintain kayfabe is to stay in wrestling character at all times, and to insist on the legitimacy of its plot lines and trappings. At the time, kayfabe was the official policy for all WWF wrestlers, even though the choreographed nature of matches was an open secret. "Are those guys really going to kill each other like they claim?" "Is that dude in the mask honestly going to beat up the guy in the cape using a giant clock?" "Did he really just throw him into that rail and then jump on him, or was it staged?" "Is he actually hurt or just pretending?" "Is that real blood?" Without fans asking themselves those questions, even if only subconsciously, perhaps McMahon feared that the willing suspension of disbelief would dissolve.

Modern professional wrestling shares its roots with early traveling-circus sideshows and burlesque. It's a theatrical performance that combines scripted plot elements, improvisation, soliloquy, colorful characters, and over-the-top physical choreography. While there is a real sport called wrestling where the goal is to use grappling and holds to immobilize an opponent, early on enthusiasts learned that it was safer, and more exciting, to turn the wrestling ring into a type of stage where a carefully scripted performance of athleticism could take place. For years, various promotional groups had employed casts of "wrestling performers" to choreograph battles against one another, each group with its own writers, costumes, and championship. When television went mainstream in American households, it was the perfect platform for wrestling's storytelling. Such was the competition for airtime that soon there were only two major promotional organizations left. One of them was the WWF (now the WWE), majority owned by Vince McMahon. By the mid-eighties he had helped to convert wrestling from a circus sideshow into a huge cultural influence.

"Don't they know it's not real?" is the oft-repeated question. Of course the audience knows it's not real. But what of it? Lawrence McBride has spent years examining pro wrestling culture. "It's like sitting around and talking about Santa Claus not being real. Yeah, but that's not the point. It's not fun to sit around and talk about that. It's fun to go to the show and cheer for the wrestler you like."

When audiences see a magic show, it's fun to pretend that the person on stage really is a sorcerer and to gasp at the miraculous feats. It doesn't mean they truly believe that the laws of physics have been suspended. Pretending that the action in the wrestling ring is real is part of the experience.

"The thing about a wrestling show," McBride explains, "[is that] you will go there and everybody in the audience [is] borderline uncomfortable. And they're kind of joking, and they're all cracking wise. 'This is funny. Everybody knows this is fake. This is going to be a joke and we're going to make fun of it.' Then the show starts and every time—*every time*—within five minutes the crowd has gone through this complete change. They are just screaming. They want the good guy to win. They want to see the bad guy get annihilated."

Fans of wrestling will sometimes go to great lengths to proclaim their belief in a fake reality. "They like to say, 'What do you mean, fake? It's not fake.' Everybody has fun saying that," says McBride. "They don't believe that, but everybody loves it." In one recent incident, the notorious heel Triple H stopped in the middle of the show and broke character to go comfort an upset child in the audience. He gave the young fan a hug and ruffled his hair. "Hey, buddy, it's OK," he told the kid. "I'm just playing around."

Wrestling fans who understand what's going on behind the scenes are sometimes called wrestling's Smart Fans or, by some, Internet fans, since the rise of the Internet has contributed so much to their proliferation. Smart Fans appreciate not just the spectacle of wrestling, but the technical, literary, and dramatic challenges that go into staging and performing such an over-the-top theatrical production. They analyze and debate the techniques behind the wrestling choreography. When a performer falls to the ground, Smart Fans look for the tiny blade he's using to cut his forehead to make the damage look more convincing. It's Smart Fans who follow the plot leaks and who know what will happen in each fight. It's Smart Fans who know which feuds are scripted and which ones probably represent real animosity. It's Smart Fans who understand each performer's backstory and the dramatic influences that shape his or her signature moves. As McBride puts it, they are the ones in the crowd saying, "Oh yeah, he's on TV now, but remember when he was working in Alabama and his gimmick was being an evil dentist?"

Smart Fans are such a part of pro wrestling that the sport has developed a number of tongue-in-cheek in-jokes just for them. Throwing an opposing wrestler through a table without massive bodily injury would be a ridiculous, nearly impossible move in real life. So at least once during most pay-per-view wrestling shows, someone gets thrown through the "Spanish Announcers Table," a trick table set up for the purpose of shattering into spectacular splinters while the commentators run for cover. It's a running gag to pretend there is a "safe" table to destroy, rather than allowing wrestlers to throw their opponents through the English Announcers Table (which is, assumedly, more sturdy). Wrestlers sometimes even feign confusion if the Spanish Announcers Table somehow makes it to the end of the match intact.

Which begs the question, if everyone understands that pro wrestling is a show, not a contest, what's in it for the fans?

Henry Jenkins, a legend in modern fan studies, has explored the issue over the last two decades. In the nineties he noted that wrestling gives its primarily male working-class audience an important outlet for storytelling and emotional release. It has all the hallmarks of a good soap opera, a traditionally feminine genre. The characters embody struggles of race, economic disparity, class, and sexuality. The narratives often reflect an attitude of anti-intellectualism; the good guys are simple and masculine, while the bad guys resort to trickery and cheating to win. All of this might feel comforting in a world that increasingly grants more status to brain over brawn.

Today's pro wrestling fans reflect a much wider demographic, and that doesn't even include the large audience of fans who enjoy it ironically. To label it as a "masculine melodrama," as Jenkins did two decades ago, may still be accurate, but that isn't *all* it is.

Wrestlemania!

Bar Nine isn't quite full. At eight p.m. it's still possible to flag a waitress and order wings (twenty minimum) and a Budweiser, although the place is filling up by the second. A part of the bar has been cordoned off with couches and a giant screen showing *Wrestlemania 32*, the once-a-year climax of a number of WWE storylines, seeded throughout the previous months. The bar audience is a mix of men and women, most in black T-shirts. There's a group of well-groomed hipster men sharing a plate of wings toward the front.

On the screen, Shane McMahon is taking on the Undertaker in Hell in a Cell. In a nicely scripted interaction two months ago, Vince McMahon, Shane's real-life father, agreed to give Shane control of the "Monday Night Raw" weekly wrestling programs if Shane could beat the Undertaker, a wrestler with a supernatural-themed gimmick. It may seem like an unlikely plan for long-term corporate business strategy, but in-story it makes complete sense. So far the gentlemen have beaten each other with a wide variety of metal objects (chairs, stairs . . .), and the action is getting tense.

Now Shane is climbing the outside of the chain-link cell wall! Ten feet up. Twenty feet up. "Shane, what are you doing? How much does your legacy mean to you Shane! Not this! Please!" shouts the announcer. "For God's sake, get him down! What the hell is he thinking!"

"My God, is he going to jump?" shouts a hipster in the bar, jumping from his chair.

"No! You can't do this!" yells the announcer. All the group near the front are out of their seats, frantically taking pictures of the screen on their cell phones. The women in the corner are hiding their faces in their hands.

"Dammit, Shane, stop it! Don't do this! No!" the announcer yells.

He jumps! The Undertaker rolls out of the way at the last minute. Shane plummets into the announcer's table, collapsing it into splinters. "For the love of mankind!" shouts the announcer.

"Is he dead? Is he dead?" shouts the hipster.

He's not dead! The bar jumps to its feet shouting its applause.

Soon the match is over. Shane lies ostensibly broken on the mat. "Monday Night Raw" will remain, in-story, the property of Vince McMahon. A medical team, or perhaps a group of actors playing a medical team, rushes across the stage to place Shane on a backboard. But what's this! As the crew hurries him toward the exits, Shane's shaking arm is rising, rising in the air! He's giving the crowd a thumbs up sign! "Wow!" says the announcer. "Wow!"

"Shane is, like, fifty! I can't believe it. I can't believe it," murmurs the hipster.

The action in pro wrestling is scripted, but that's not the same as safe. The hand signals and vocal cues the wrestlers use to subtly broadcast their intended choreography to each other in the ring can't change the fact that it's still quite dangerous. Few long-time wrestlers make it through their careers without at least one or two body-shattering injuries, and deaths are not unheard of. Legendary wrestler Bret Hart writes in his autobiography, "The most important rule of all was to protect my opponent, not myself, because he was putting his trust, his life, in my hands."

The authenticity of wrestling as a spectacle resides not in whether or not it's a sport, but in the veracity of the acting. Sometimes the only way to make something look like it really hurts is to make it hurt. When a wrestler is thrown into a table, even a trick table, trying to land carefully can ruin the whole thing.

"The Smart Fans have this deeper aesthetic sense of, 'Look at this guy, he's bleeding now.' You know that this is a staged event. We know that he willingly did that, and he's doing that for us. It's almost moving, this sort of love for the guys who are willing to injure themselves quite dramatically. They're like a network of people who go out there every month and put their bodies through these incredible performances for the show, as a gift to their fans," says McBride.

All Fans Are Smart Fans

"Cultural dupes" is the phrase that Marxism assigns to consumers who desire an item solely for its context. According to the theory, consumers are like little children: they accept marketing claims at face value. They're not sophisticated enough to realize when they're being fooled. Consumers have no idea that their decisions are being manipulated for profit by those in control, people who wish to distract them from more important issues, like overthrowing the kaiser. In espousing the cultural-dupe theory, Marxism, that most anticlassist of philosophies, perhaps betrays a little latent classism. It is condescending to assume that consumers only feel as they do because they don't know any better. While fans do rely on branding—both internal and external—to inform their allegiances, they're certainly not mindless puppets to it.

All fans are, at some level, Smart Fans. They understand that the objects they care so much about have been carefully constructed to appeal to them. Fandom entails choosing to buy into a context that is, at least partially, always fiction. Darth Vader isn't really trying to take over the universe. The singer Johnny Cash wasn't actually an impoverished and brokenhearted convict cowboy, no matter how many times he sang about it. We know that Oreos decided to launch an organic version of the company's classic sandwich cookie because it saw an unfilled need in the marketplace, not because it suddenly decided that its customers deserved better ingredients.

Even the most hardcore of fans understand that the world will not end if their favorite band breaks up. But it's certainly enjoyable to pretend it will. In early 2015 it was fun to insist, in the most dramatic of terms, that if the singer Zayn Malik left the boy band One Direction, it was the end of the universe, and there was no reason to go on living. Of course, it wasn't, and there was; few people really believed that the laws of physics would be suspended because of the professional choices of any one singer, no matter how dreamy. If the hyperbole found in blogs and social media following his departure had been true, there would have been few survivors.

Almost all fandom involves some form of making believe. In the 1995 novel *City of Dreadful Night* the main character believes that he is being stalked by the spirit of Count Dracula. And yet he grudgingly admits to himself that if he wanted to, he could choose not to believe it. This is probably a feeling familiar to many a fan. Most are aware that the object they have such real, deep feelings for is very rarely, in the strictest WWE sense, real. They understand that they are being "duped" and they find value in playing along.

As long as they are getting something important out of the relationship, fans are subconsciously making the decision, moment by moment, to ignore the inherent commercial reality of their fandom. Authenticity is a fan group's most dangerous Achilles' heel, but when deployed correctly, it makes fans complicit in their own enjoyable self-deception.

Chris and Cliff, Together at Last

In late 2012, State Farm brought together two long-lost twin brothers separated at birth: Chris Paul, the Los Angeles Clippers NBA player, and Cliff Paul, his identical twin brother and State Farm Insurance agent. Chris grew up to be an NBA star, three-time NBA assists leader and respected team player, while Cliff ended up helping his fellow citizens connect with quality insurance coverage.

In a commercial, fans see Cliff being separated from Chris at the hospital, their independent (but seemingly equally happy) childhoods, and their modern-day reconnection. Cliff and Chris pass each other in an elevator and experience a moment of recognition. The announcer explains, "When assisting is in your blood, you know it."

Viewers were enthralled—was Cliff really Chris's long-lost brother? Fans tweeted "I want Cliff to be my agent!" and "How do I hire Cliff Paul?" Sports websites and public forum sites saw message threads popping up with titles like "Is Cliff Paul real?"

By early 2013, Chris and Cliff had fully reconnected, with Chris tweeting out thanks to Cliff for his pregame pep talks. NFL player Drew Brees posted a congratulatory message to the two brothers. TNT basketball analyst Kenny Smith remarked on meeting Cliff in person. Fox sports broadcaster Erin Andrews called it the "year of #twinsanity," thanks to the brothers' reunion. Cliff and Chris appeared together at the 2013 NBA All Star Weekend. By the 2014 event, Cliff himself appeared on stage with entertainer Nick Cannon.

In later spots, Cliff and Chris appeared together teaching their sons—who were exactly the same age—about assisting in their similar roles in their two similar NBAs, the National Basketball Association and the National Bureau of Assists. With each appearance, Cliff Paul's notoriety grew. He amassed tens of thousands of Twitter and Instagram followers and posted daily on both platforms.

Of course, Cliff Paul is very obviously Chris Paul donning a pair of black-plastic-framed glasses. It seems unlikely that many people were truly taken in by the tongue-in-cheek nod to the Clark Kent/ Superman–style transformative powers of eyewear. And in fact no true deception was ever really contemplated: as author Chuck Klosterman pointed out on ESPN radio, "Why do they both have the last name 'Paul'? They were adopted by different families who both had the same last name?" Danger Guerrero, on Uproxx, noted, "Uhhh wouldn't Cliff's birth mother have known she had twins?"

Cliff became a cultural phenomenon nonetheless. He had a Nike Jordan shoe (Chris Paul's shoe, but in Argyle). He made an appearance in NBA 2K14, the 2K Sport's best-selling NBA video game, where the brothers could play one-on-one against each other.

At one Clippers game, attendees held up thousands of Cliff Paul masks in the stands.

But why? Why care so deeply about the "twins," when they were so blatantly and openly the product of a campaign to promote auto and homeowners' insurance to basketball fans?

The character is the creation of the New York–based advertising agency Translation. Marcus Collins, who was involved with the project, believes the attraction came largely because the question of whether or not Cliff Paul was real was engaging. The concept was to keep fans guessing. Hardcore fans know everything about a player—there's no way they would be unaware of a twin. But introducing him as a "long-lost" brother led to a potential gap in knowledge, a gap that introduced the tiniest possibility of reality. Building credibility through on-screen appearances together and tweets from reputable celebrities made the possibility even more real.

Fans were given the ability, the gift, of questioning their take on reality, even if only a little bit. No one ever hid the fact that Cliff was a made-up celebrity—the New York Times ran an article on the "fake twin" campaign before it even launched—but fans enjoyed participating because it was a fun and engaging narrative.

Blurring the line between real and not real, true and made-up, is the purpose of play. It allows us to imagine unlikely scenarios and say, "But what if . . .?" Traditional wrestling and car insurance are both a little boring. But playing with the audience's concept of authenticity distances products from the rules that normally apply. In effect, it frees both objects from their "adult status."

The novelty of a mundane concept suddenly transformed into something new and delightful is a powerful engagement tool. On a neurological level, when humans are confronted with an unexpected change in a familiar pattern, their brains experience a spike in dopamine, the happiness chemical. The more dopamine in our brains, the less we're likely to get hung up on a product's more potentially troubling attributes, such as how much money Vince McMahon is making off each bloody forehead and sprained ankle. Playing with concepts of authenticity decommercializes a product and makes it safe for fans to personally identify with it.

Of course, encouraging an audience to pretend that there's more to a fan object than just its monetary potential can be double-edged. Right now the self-deception serves a happy purpose. Later on, who knows?

The Bobble Hat Crisis

The TV program *Firefly* began airing in September 2002. By the holidays, it had been canceled. Its creator, Joss Whedon, had imagined a seven-year run, but the Fox network had barely shown two-thirds of the first season before pulling the plug.

The show takes place on a renegade starship, its captain and crew lying low after supporting the losing side of a multiplanet civil war. Although their rebellion against the callous bureaucracy may have failed, their spirits remain uncrushed. Now they eke out a vigilante existence at the edges of society through shady (yet moral) activities, still hanging onto their freedom through a mix of wits, resignation, honor, and bloody-mindedness.

Despite its early demise, the show made quite an impression with fans. Whedon, who had already hit it big with shows like *Buffy the Vampire Slayer*, had brought much of his loyal fan group with him, and *Firefly*'s Space Western premise brought in new devotees. After the cancellation, fans mounted an intense lobbying campaign to convince Fox to change its mind. They raised money and wrote postcards. Fox was unrepentant, and no other network wanted to buy it. *Firefly*, it seemed, was gone for good.

Yet for years the fandom lived on. Fans dubbed themselves

"Browncoats" after the nickname for the losing side of the show's central military conflict, and spread the word. Message boards, social groups, and websites multiplied too quickly to count. Fans raised money for charity and created fan films and documentaries. The first run of the DVD of the series sold out within twenty-four hours of its preorder announcement.

In 2006, Universal Pictures decided to fund the feature-length movie *Serenity*, which brought back the cast for a storyline based on what would have been the series' second season. The movie was a financial wash, making just $39 million gross ticket sales against an estimated production cost of exactly that amount, but the fans didn't seem to mind. By definition, *Firefly* fandom appeals to people who love a good lost cause. As *Entertainment Weekly* put it, "Martyrdom has only enhanced its legend."

Firefly fizzled a little post-*Serenity*. Then, in 2012, Fox seemed to remember its long-ignored investment.

In the show, crew member Jayne Cobb is a muscly tough guy who, in one unaired episode, unexpectedly shows his softer side when his mother sends him a silly hand-knitted hat. It's orange. It has earflaps and a bobble. For years, Browncoats had been knitting their own versions to wear to conventions, meet-ups, or, occasionally, even outside. The hat had become an important tribal marking to help them identify fellow enthusiasts. Because the episode was never aired during the initial broadcast, only serious fans understood the symbolism.

Like the crew they admired, a number of Browncoats scraped by through the marginal commerce of selling hats to each other. At one time, a search for "Jayne hat" on the handicrafts website Etsy turned up dozens of entries. eBay had even more. Even Whedon weighed in on the cottage industry in knitwear, explaining the love of Jayne's hat at Comic-Con: "[It's] the fact that it's got that homemade feel, because people can make it themselves. Also, it's very flattering."

At the beginning of 2012, Fox licensed the hat design to Ripple Junction, an apparel company, which began mass production of Jayne hats. It sold them to the large-scale e-retailer ThinkGeek. Its version was both nicer and, for the most part, less expensive than any of the handmade hats available.

Shortly thereafter, the listings for homemade hats began disappearing from Etsy. The timing was certainly suspicious—fans asked, was Etsy following through on requests from Fox or Ripple Junction about the unsanctioned headwear? Soon it was confirmed, as store after store received notices from Etsy informing them that Fox's intellectual-property director had demanded the removal of their products. The notice also included a warning not to discuss the situation with others. "Are You A Firefly Fan Who Makes Jayne Hats? Watch Out, Fox Is Coming For You," warned a headline in The Mary Sue, a popular geek website.

Did Fox have the right to capitalize on a property that had so unexpectedly ballooned in value? Certainly. And it also had the right to stop others from doing so. Yet what ensued was an uproar that might seem disproportionate to the cause.

Fox had misunderstood the motivations of its audience. Fan activity had kept *Firefly* relevant throughout Fox's decade-long neglect, and it was fan interest that had turned the Jayne hat into an iconic symbol. Some of the Etsy hats were destined for babies. Or chemotherapy patients. The craftspeople who found themselves targeted and penalized often knitted their hats from a place of love.

"I hope you are proud of yourselves," wrote fan-store *Firefly* Cargo Bay on Facebook in a post that received more than 1,000 likes within a day. "I personally think you suck for even thinking of licensing the jayne hat. You. Just. Dont. Get. It." Another fan complained: "They can be legally, morally, and ethically in the right and still have this stink to high heaven." Even Adam Baldwin, the actor who had played Jayne so many years earlier, weighed in on Twitter, joking, "All Your 'Jayne' Hats Are Belong To Us!"

Most sellers, fearing legal action, removed the listings from their stores. The remainder renamed them with tongue firmly in cheek, branding them with headlines like "See Spot Run With Not Jane Hat," "Ma's Earflap Hat," and "Controversial Hat With A Backstory."

By early April, the outrage showed no sign of slowing. As a major retailer of the hat, a heavily criticized ThinkGeek felt the need to defend itself. "We just wanted you to know that Think-Geek had nothing to do with the C&D notices," it pleaded on its company blog. Criticism continued. Shortly thereafter, ThinkGeek wrote a long entreaty to placate their fans, starting: "Browncoats, we hear your concerns. . . ." ThinkGeek had nothing to do with the legal notices, they said, but to assuage the outrage, the company opted to donate its profits from the sales of the hat to a *Firefly*-based charity called Can't Stop the Serenity for as long as they stocked the hats.

It was a drastic step; ThinkGeek had helped to develop the hat with Ripple Junction. To forgo their profits on the Jayne hat effectively voided months of work. Yet, this financial hara-kiri may be all that saved ThinkGeek from more serious repercussions had the condemnation continued to snowball.

By targeting Browncoat hat sellers, Fox committed two major sins in the eyes of fans: They violated one of the fan group's most cherished cultural norms, the ideal of the plucky misfit holding its own against a heartless bureaucracy. And they also violated the group's social hierarchy. They were penalizing their very top-tier fans for, effectively, being overly loyal.

Although none of this was directly ThinkGeek's fault, doubtless the website hoped that humbling itself would appease the brown-coated masses. After all, they still had another two dozen *Firefly*-themed products in stock to sell to them.

Loyalty to the Message, Not the Medium

Fandom results from a tenuous bargain. Fans choose to buy into a premise only as long as it serves their needs. They actively decide if, and how far, they're willing to be duped.

All fandom involves a willing suspension of disbelief. But no matter the level of loyalty a fan expresses for a fan object, the true loyalty lies with the concepts the object represents. These are two completely separate allegiances. Fans are willing to remain loyal to the thing they love only so long as they are not forced to confront its true commercial nature.

Even with a rich and well-developed context, few brands can brush off details that directly oppose the narrative they represent. When a chasm opens up between the values a fan object claims to embody, and the values of the fan object as a commercial entity, the balance is upset.

Firefly fans felt positively about the television show, a set of episodes with attractive actors, nice special effects, and witty repartee. But in the end they connected with the show's theme of self-determination. Their emotional response was to its "victory of the underdog"–themed stories. As long as both content and philosophy were harnessed toward the same goal, fans were happy. But as soon as the two were in opposition, fans were quick to call foul. All fans are, at some level, Smart Fans. They can tell the difference between their two loyalties.

This tacit compromise underlies the outrage that occurs when a "feel-good" brand is accused of misconduct. Allegations of poor working conditions in factories owned by context-heavy brands such as Nike or Apple hit us hard, while the same allegation at, say, a paper mill or a copper piping factory might not. Both Nike and Apple go to great lengths to cultivate an aura of excitement, self-improvement, and wealth. There is something inherently inauthentic about juxtaposing those feelings with reports of impoverished or underage laborers.

Authenticity is the glue that allows fans and fan-object owners, two actors with potentially conflicting motivations, to unite toward a single cause. Brands that attempt to co-opt an existing fan group's practices without taking on the core values of the group as well are doomed to controversy.

It is possible that no mass-marketed version of the Jayne hat would ever have sat well with *Firefly* fans, regardless of how delicately the marketing had been handled. Lip service rarely works because fans have made the most important investment possible: their personal sense of self. What might seem to the fan-object owner like a harmless commercial play can in fact affront a fan's very identity.

Multiple fan objects can give someone the same sense of self, and it's trivial for a fan group to jump ship to another fan object when betrayed. Every allegation of poor labor standards at a Nike factory is a boon for other fitness-lifestyle manufacturers, even those who aren't necessarily designing sportswear. It is not hard to imagine many a Browncoat in the wake of the hat debacle deciding that Star Wars, with its similar narrative of space-aged rebellion and adventure, was more their style.

#DoingItWrong

Marketers who are more used to one-way communications may forget that, when a fan group has been insulted, it's a far deeper issue than just antagonizing a customer. Fail a customer and she probably just chooses not to buy again. Insulting a fan group is a personal affront. Fans have the motivation, time, and social capital to fight back.

Audience engagement, encouraging users to participate in brand-related activities, is a magic box that, the theory goes, somehow transforms enthusiasm into dollars. Of course, in real life, it depends on the type of engagement and what it's being used for.

"Use this hashtag on Twitter (or Instagram, or Tumblr, or Facebook) to share your stories about . . ." is such a common refrain that few marketers bother to ask what's in it for the fans. Like authentic fan practices, the "use this hashtag" method relies on a fanlike activity the audience is already doing: sharing their opinions, participating in the context about a brand, and socializing with each other. Yet these marketing campaigns use an authentic fan practice for an inauthentic purpose. It's a rare brand that anticipates making changes to its product or marketing as a result of customer tweets.

Most campaigns of this type are an attempt to turn fans into billboards. A self-aware brand may highlight the "best" stories it receives, thereby giving the participants status within the fan group, but even such half-hearted marketer responsiveness is rare. In general, the interaction serves no one but the brand owner. Like Jayne's hat, a real fan practice has been co-opted for corporate use. Target the wrong audience of participants, and they will get angry.

The fast-food giant McDonald's is a brand badly in need of popular support in the United States. Even its most committed fans may refer to it as a secret vice or guilty pleasure. Falling sales, a volatile stock price, and the rise of healthier alternatives have forced the burger seller to scramble. A positive tweet from a respected friend could remind people that McDonald's hamburgers are still around, and that lots of people do still eat them.

In 2012 the brand launched the hashtag #McDStories on Twitter. Even the most health-conscious among us might still have fond memories of attending a McDonald's-themed birthday party as a child, or scarfing a McDonald's burger with teammates after middle-school soccer practice. Each 140-character-long story posted by a happy fan to Twitter would propagate to that fan's friend group and perhaps beyond. Just the action of "coming out of the closet" as a McDonald's fan might influence others to try the food again.

The problem with inviting audience members to use their personal social networks for corporate exposure is that there's no way to control what is in fact exposed. In this case more audience members semed to want to share unhappy McDonald's stories than happy ones. Tweets ranged from the cautionary ("Dude, I used to work at McDonald's. The #McDStories I could tell would raise your hair") to the downright direct ("One time I walked into McDonald's and I could smell Type 2 diabetes floating in the air and I threw up. #McDStories"). McDonald's pulled their paid promotion of the hashtag within two hours, but, alas, the jeers took months to vanish. As Forbes put it, "Twitter has the audience with the most sensitive B.S. meter of any popular platform."

Of course, any organization might attempt to push its own agenda on its audience, only to realize that the audience has a very different one. In 2014, the New York Police Department tried to polish its image with some hashtag outreach. #MyNYPD was supposed to act as a label for happy photos involving New York's finest. Their audience disagreed, flooding the hashtag with graphic pictures of recent police brutality and violence. The reaction wasn't totally unexpected, particularly because taking pictures of the NYPD was one of the very offenses that had, in some highly publicized cases, apparently been considered arrest-worthy.

To experience an authentic fan relationship, a fan object must acknowledge the real user experience and motivations of its fans, not the corporate fantasy of what that experience should be. Fans need to be understood, even in situations where there is no chance of catering to them. It is impossible to "sprinkle some authenticity" on a marketing technique.

Fandom at its best is a story of fan/fan-object collaboration, not co-option. A brand owner should adopt the perspective of a fellow fan, working together with his fan group to develop and support something they both feel deeply about. It doesn't necessarily require in-depth ethnographic studies or complicated crowdsourcing platforms to discern how fans feel. Both of these techniques run the risk of "othering" fans, treating them like some exotic tribe who need to be carefully examined, labeled, and categorized.

Feeding Us Our Memories

One tactic might be to simply hire some fans and let them drive the interaction policy themselves. But an even better one would be for creators to work toward creating a fan object that they do, in fact, sincerely love and understand in a fanlike way. While that level of authenticity is rare, it's still probably the best way to truly empathize with the real fan experience. Strategy that comes from a place of true enthusiasm and affection beats an outsider's facsimile of it every time.

Like many transplants to New York City, Sarita Ekya and her husband Caesar spent their first few months living in their East Village sublet eating their way through the neighborhood.

"I was like, wouldn't it be great if there was a place that did mac and cheese? There has to be one of those," Sarita remembers saying. "Lo and behold, we started Googling around, and we're like, 'What? There's no place that just does mac and cheese?' We really fell in love with the idea."

S'MAC, or Sarita's Macaroni and Cheese, does one thing. Granted, it does a dozen variations of that one thing. In the early days, the line often went out the door of their New York City East Village location all the way down the block to Second Avenue. The restaurant would sometimes run out of food halfway through the evening.

Besides being filling and inexpensive, mac and cheese as a meal taps into a rich vein of cultural nostalgia. Whether it's the blue Kraft box of macaroni or a favorite aunt's secret recipe, the dish is thick with personal memories for many people. Strangers who have no intention of ever visiting the shop sometimes write Sarita to describe how much they love macaroni and cheese. "It's a little bit intimidating. It's a food that's in their mind, or in their heart, or in their body. You have to live up to this expectation. It's not easy," says Sarita.

A few blocks to the east of S'MAC lies Melt Shop, one location in a growing chain of grilled-cheese restaurants. Its origin story is not quite as whimsical, but just as effective, as its comfort-food compatriot: entrepreneur Spencer Rubin and his then-boss were working at a real estate development firm while they spent their free time brainstorming new business ideas. Melt Shop was born.

Because grilled cheese mines authentic childhood nostalgia, Melt Shop too ended up benefiting from simple happy childhood memories. Familiarity is key to the concept. "I think that's why we're seeing a resurgence of all these familiar concepts in new forms," Rubin says. "We always strive to create cool ideas with unique twists, but always keeping approachability in mind. We don't want people to walk through our door and say, 'Ah, that place is too fancy for me,' or 'Ah, that place is out of my reach.'"

All fandom, be it for a celebrity, activity, piece of content, or brand, has a strong element of nostalgia. The very definition of fandom involves activities that allow the fan to relive a pleasurable memory or association. Nostalgia plays a bigger role in some fandoms than in others—it's arguably the primary driver of brand fandoms such as Polaroid instant film and Surge soda, but in other cases it is one among many purposes. Fans might watch baseball because they love the game, but they also might want to feel close to a family tradition, or enjoy critiquing the athleticism of the game, or comparing different stadiums' hot dogs.

Fans understand the difference between a respectful attempt to invoke memories of childhood comforts and a cheap attempt to appropriate those same memories. The very nature of many large-scale fast-food chains often necessitates a militant level of secrecy in their ingredients, motivations, and practices, not to mention a complicated layer of corporate bureaucracy to organize the whole thing. It's no wonder fans react so badly when those same corporations demand to know their customers' most cherished thoughts and recollections.

The best way to handle nostalgia is to be completely up front about its intent. In fan situations, transparency very often leads to trust. It's certainly not the only method, but for the vast majority of fan objects, the better fans' understanding of the thing they love, the closer they can feel to it.

The End of Kayfabe

On February 10, 1989, WWF representatives testified to the New Jersey Senate that pro wrestling was "an activity in which participants struggle hand-in-hand primarily for the purpose of providing entertainment to spectators rather than conducting a bona fide athletic contest."

In acknowledging the open secret, pro wrestling was finally choosing to be transparent about its use of artifice. They would never again be able to claim that wrestling was a sport, not a show. At the same time they would also be freed from many of the regulations that govern true sporting events, requirements to which they'd formerly paid expensive lip service. Sports are heavily regulated. Theater is not. Gone would be the extra fees on WWF television appearances; gone were the prematch physicals and state-licensed referees. A generation later, modern cynics analyzing the effect of deregulation have raised another point: athletes have to be free of performance-enhancing drugs; actors don't. It's difficult to know in hindsight what effect the 1989 testimony and subsequent deregulation had on any potential steroid inquiry, but, regardless, it would be fully four more years before there was a large-scale probe into their use in pro wrestling.

It was the beginning of a new golden age for pro wrestling; the nineties saw it become more popular than ever. Just two years after firing two of his top performers over "drug violations," Vince McMahon had created a new wrestling, one that was even more in tune with the over-the-top athletic theater fans cared about. The fake veneer of competition was gone. The golden era of kayfabe was drawing to a close.

In 1996, Kevin Nash, a heel who wrestled as "Diesel," and face Scott Hall, aka Razor Ramon, were in the process of leaving the WWF. It was an emotional time for those who had followed the two popular characters' careers. On May 9, in Madison Square Garden, Diesel was wrestling his friend, the face Shawn Michaels, in a steel-cage match for what might be their last-ever event together.

Diesel was down, lying on the mat. Michaels stood over him in triumph. Then Razor Ramon entered the ring and hugged Michaels. At first it seemed that he was congratulating his fellow face on his victory. But no, here came Paul Michael Levesque, the dastardly heel who would soon become Triple H, also entering the ring, and he was hugging Razor Ramon too! And then Diesel, who only moments before had been writhing on the mat in agony, stood up and hugged everyone.

The four wrestlers—faces and heels—turned to each other and engaged in what can only be termed an emotional group embrace, heads together, arms tight around each other's bulging shoulders. This was no lonely car stopped by chance on an interstate. It was a deliberate break in character. They were friends, friends who would miss each other, and they wanted the audience to know it. They clasped hands and raised their arms in the air for a final curtain call, all four of them, faces and heels, together, as the crowd cheered and screamed.

CHAPTER 8

WHEN FANDOM GOES WRONG

When fans revolt, it's not pretty. Feelings of fandom are deeply tied into a fan's personal identity, and it's easy for the brand owner to accidentally ignore, trivialize, or modify something that sits at the heart of fan feelings. It is a rare fan object indeed that doesn't make the occasional misstep and suffer the inevitable wrath of its previously adoring audience. Sometimes such uprisings can be avoided or defused. Sometimes it's more important not to avoid or defuse them at all.

Fan revolts often emerge out of seemingly small actions taken by the fan-object owner. Frequently, the corporate management team doesn't realize what it's done, nor does it understand where the subsequent backlash comes from. But every change within a fandom requires the fans to reevaluate if the new values of their fan object still match their own. When the pope issues a new decree about church policy, it changes what it means to be a Catholic for people around the world. When a political party decides to update its stance on an important issue in order to court a new demographic, it changes what it means to be a member of that party for its existing constituents. If people don't like it, they must decide if they wish to go along with the change, advocate for its reversal, or abandon the fandom altogether.

Fans are not always right. Brand owners frequently have business imperatives that conflict with the change-averse nature of their fandom, and unpopular decisions sometimes address legitimate business concerns. Without such decisions, the fan object might cease to exist. Legal departments need to protect an organization's intellectual property, research and development departments need to expand into new fields and products, and marketing departments need to attract new customers if a business is to grow. Some of the best brand decisions have reduced an existing fan base but in time created a much wider new one.

Having fans feels good. Having fans is fun, and it's validating and empowering. But ultimately, there is a dark side of fan management, a side that's about recognizing what could cause a fan revolt, preparing for the backlash, deciding if it's worth it, and responding as authentically as possible.

"I Died a Little Inside Today"

Bill Samuels Jr. and his son Rob had a problem. Their family business was seeing skyrocketing sales, and they couldn't begin to keep up with demand. For most other products this issue would lead to temporary shortages while production ramped up, but in the liquor business it's more complicated. It takes roughly six years to age a barrel of Maker's Mark bourbon, the Samuels family's famous whiskey (or whisky, as they prefer to spell it). That means when Maker's Mark misestimates demand, it takes six years to readjust their supply.

On March 15, 2012, a heavily debated US–Korea Free Trade

Agreement had gone into effect, ending tariffs on most goods flowing between the two countries. Opponents on both sides decried
the deal—US producers complained that it didn't do enough for
US exports of beef and steel, and Koreans worried that it would
hurt domestic agriculture. Massive anti-FTA rallies rocked South
Korea, with at least one protester setting himself on fire. Nevertheless, the US accepted it in October 2011, and Korea followed suit a
month later.

Suddenly, untariffed American booze flooded into South Korea.
Vodka, rum, and gin all saw upticks in consumption, but the arguable winner was bourbon-style whiskey.

Bourbon is the American liquor. Ninety-five percent of the
entire global bourbon supply comes from Kentucky. The United
States Senate has declared it "America's Native Spirit." Western-
style liquors like bourbon have become increasingly popular in
Korea as a booming economy gives consumers a taste for affordable
luxury. It's expensive enough to be a status symbol, but not expensive enough to exclude the middle class. The Distilled Spirits Coun-
cil, a trade group representing US-based liquors, had spent years
and millions of dollars lobbying for the trade agreement, and they
had prevailed. Bourbon leaving the US bound for Korea had once
carried a 20 percent tax. Soon it would effectively carry none.

The FTA came in the middle of a rapid rise in the fortunes of
American whiskey makers. In Japan, an appetite for highballs
had boosted whiskey imports. In Hong Kong, magazines ran suggestions about which bars to find exotic whiskeys in and which
mixologists made the best Old Fashioned and Manhattan. "In the
liquor industry, one of the only things hotter than Kentucky bourbon is super-expensive Kentucky bourbon," quipped Bloomberg
Business.

In theory, as one of Kentucky's most established bourbons,

Maker's Mark's brown square bottle with the hand-dipped red wax seal was perfectly positioned to benefit from the new Asian markets, especially in Korea, where whiskey was already the hard liquor of choice.

Brand lore has it that the current version of Maker's Mark was invented in the 1950s, when Bill Samuels Sr. baked whiskey ingredients into loaves of bread to find the perfect grain combination. The winning loaf, an unusual mix of red winter wheat, corn, and malted barley, went on to become the beverage as it is today: a bourbon with a good balance and a medium body, with a taste of spice, caramel, vanilla, cherries, citrus, and nuttiness. To bring out those flavors, each barrel is aged for five and a half to seven years, to taste. A tasting panel, including the master distiller, has to decide that the bourbon is ready for the world before it can be sold.

Therein lay the problem. Given the average maturation time for a barrel, the distiller must guess what demand will be like more than half a decade in the future. A wrong guess now means there will be too much or too little supply when the batch is ready later. Usually, they're spot on. Occasionally they miss, like when the *Wall Street Journal* ran a surprise front-page article about Maker's Mark back in 1980, unexpectedly boosting sales well beyond their supply. But the new surge in overseas interest was unlike anything they had seen before. Had Maker's Mark been able to predict the explosion of demand in Asia, perhaps it could have increased its stocks in time. As it was, if it failed to make a splash in Asian markets during the window of opportunity, other brands would beat the company to it.

Facing the specter of the kind of shortages that can cause irreparable damage to a brand, Maker's Mark had two options. The first was to raise prices, something they were loath to do because it might place its product out of reach of the very audience it was courting.

The second solution was to stretch its existing supply. Or, in layman's terms, to water it down.

All bourbon has water added to it at various times in its life cycle. Maker's Mark proposed to add a little more. Formerly, Maker's Mark bourbon was 90 proof, or 45 percent alcohol. The new recipe would add enough water to reduce the alcohol content by 6.7 percent, down to 84 proof. The additional volume would allow the existing supply to stretch for an extra four years, enough time to begin ramping up production to meet the new demand. At the very least, it would give the distiller a chance to retain its competitive edge against bourbons whose shorter maturation process left them better equipped to enter the new markets.

Maker's Mark calls its biggest fans "Ambassadors," and offers them a loyalty program with special merchandise and advance announcements about new products. They can get their name on a barrel of bourbon. It's these fans that Maker's Mark first decided to inform about the recipe update. After all, if transparency increases trust, being as honest as possible with fans was surely the best policy.

The email went out on a Saturday. In it, Rob Samuels, the CEO, and Bill Samuels Jr., son of the man who had created the 1950s baked-bread recipe, explained the situation: the demand for Maker's Mark bourbon had exploded beyond their expectations, and they were in danger of running out. They promised that, except for the updated alcohol content, the rest of the process would remain unchanged, and the taste would be identical. "In other words, we've made sure we didn't screw up your whisky," they wrote.

The news site *Quartz* ran a short piece on the new recipe on its website. A few tweets were posted on Twitter. The world held its breath. And then, shortly after seven thirty p.m., like an angry, drunken wave, the Internet rose up and broke upon Maker's Mark with outrage. In their own words:

"SHAME on you Maker's Mark for doing this."

"Some bonehead Accountant must have come up with this greedy scheme at the expense of quality!!!!"

"Only a Commie Liberal would think that watering down a product so that more customers gets [sic] less is the right path."

"Shame on you Maker's! Who cares of [sic] some Frenchmen or other terrorist can't enjoy our sweet American nectar!?"

"I knew this stuff was going to start happening once the younger generation took the helm."

"Criminally stupid idea."

"Hearing this has cut me to the heart."

"This is an absolute travesty."

"I hereby resign as a Maker's Ambassador. I have bought my last bottle."

"I died a little inside today."

"Don't worry Marker's Mark—there will be less demand now!"

"Idiots."

Before long the feedback had turned into a kind of gleeful indignation, as though the audience enjoyed having something to get good and angry about. And these were Maker's Mark's superfans! The fans who had invested money in Maker's Mark collections. The fans who wore Maker's Mark logos, and attended Maker's Mark tastings, and extolled the virtues of Maker's Mark to nonbelievers. The fans who could normally be expected to defend Maker's Mark, or at least give it the benefit of the doubt.

Fandom thrives on the fun and excitement of feeling like we are part of an entity that's bigger than ourselves, but that entity doesn't have to be something nice. Angry mobs are also a lot of fun, at least for those on the inside. As one commentator joked,

"Our fans have made us one of the best-selling bourbons of all time. To say 'thank you,' we're gonna . . . water it down! No no, really, you don't have to thank us . . . Um, where did you get all those torches and pitchforks from?"

By the next day, the new brew had been dubbed "Maker's Watermark," and what was supposed to be a minor recipe tweak had catalyzed a rebellion. Maker's Mark's Facebook page spiraled into gleeful carnage. Hundreds of blogs voiced their vitriol. The twitterverse was in revolt. Mainstream media took full advantage of the easy website traffic, with headlines like "Less Potent Maker's Mark Not Going Down Smoothly In Kentucky." Forum after forum filled with advice about which new bourbon brands to try now that Maker's Mark was disgraced. Fans derailed the conversation at a Maker's Mark corporate event being held at a steakhouse in Indiana. "Let's just say they didn't hold back," remembered Rob Samuels later.

Anger turned into hostility, which in turn shaded into ugliness as only the Internet can. Both of the letter signers' email addresses were publicly posted to encourage harassment. The Maker's Mark offices were deluged with emails and phone calls. "Enjoy your bankruptcy proceedings, Maker's Mark. The Age of the Customer has begun, and we're tired of being crapped on by corporate thugs," snarled one so-called fan on Facebook.

Bewildered by the unexpected pushback, Rob and Bill Samuels tried to explain themselves in an interview with *Quartz*, the news outlet that had broken the news. We honestly have no choice, they explained. You won't be able to tell the difference. Really. The explanation only seemed to stoke the flames ("Now you're saying we don't have any taste?"). The new blend had become such a nexus of emotion that appeals to logic were almost beside the point.

The following Sunday, Maker's Mark, dazed from a week of abuse and hostility, wrote to say they were capitulating to fan demands. Even though they thought reducing the alcohol content of Maker's Mark was the right thing to do, they wrote, "this is your brand—and you told us in large numbers to change our decision. You spoke. We listened. And we're sincerely sorry we let you down."

Customers Are Always Right. Fans Aren't.

It is terrifying to be on the receiving end of fan anger. It's all the more so because fandom uses the language of extremes. This band is THE BEST BAND THAT EVER EXISTED EVER. That other rival band is PURE EVIL AND TOTAL CRAP. Nothing compares to the outrage of a fan group that has decided to get good and mad for a while.

It's fun to get angry. It's fun to, for example, compare a slight alteration in the recipe of a beloved beverage with Nazism. In fact, equating something to Nazism on the Internet is so common it has been given its own adage: Godwin's Law. The hyperbole of it adds to the silliness, and the more seriously we claim to take it, the more fun it is. But few fans truly believed a minor decrease in the alcohol content of a mid-tier bourbon was the moral equivalent of the violent deaths of 60 million people.

All of fandom is, on some level, about pretending. It's about making a choice to buy into the immaterial, ephemeral context surrounding a fan object. Sensationalism is practically built in. But when playing make-believe about a fan object, it's easy to forget that we are playing make-believe games with real pieces. Real people, real business decisions, and real lives are involved.

The nature of fandom means there will always be tension

between business imperatives and fan desires because a single object is being used by two very different groups of people for two very different purposes. Owners require the object to make a profit or else their ability to maintain it suffers. Fans require the object to be dependable so they can build fanlike activities around it.

Ordering a Maker's, neat, in a bar gives off a different set of signals than ordering an inexpensive shot of Old Crow, and a very different set of signals than ordering a Bud Light. If Maker's Mark is suddenly "worth less," at least to those in the know, fans look like suckers for having been so devoted. It's no wonder fans take any affront so personally. Their outrage reflects a feeling of personal betrayal above and beyond the reality of the change.

Fan communities wobble all the time, and 99 percent of the time they eventually self-correct. Star Wars fans decide that even though they hated the prequels, there's probably no need to burn down George Lucas's Skywalker Ranch. The members of a losing political party decide they actually *wouldn't* prefer to move to Canada. But it can be difficult to tell when the line between griping and true outrage has been crossed.

Makers' Mark competitor Jack Daniel's meets the technical requirements to be a bourbon, although the company prefers to advertise it only as a Tennessee whiskey. And Jack has a similarly rabid fan base. Between 1987 and 2002, Jack Daniel's lowered the proof of its core product from 90 to 86, and, then, finally to 80 to avoid excise taxes and bring down production costs. A few magazines noticed the change, and there was even a small petition about it, but Jack Daniel's held firm. The world soon forgot there had ever been a different recipe, and sales were higher than ever.

At what cost did Maker's Mark appease its fan base? Was there any way this minuscule recipe change might have made less of a splash?

Maker's Mark comes off the still at 130 proof, which means that, with a final alcohol content of 90 proof, it has already been significantly watered down during the aging process. If a high alcohol content was truly its main selling point, argued food critic Jason Wilson, these fans should have long ago graduated to one of the many higher alcohol bourbons already in existence, like the 107-proof Weller Antique or the 120-proof version of Knob Creek. For that matter, only a tiny portion of bourbon fans drink their alcohol neat. The rest add ice, soda, water, simple syrup, bitters, or juice. The second a single ice cube touches the bourbon, it's already lower proof than any proposed change.

One thing is certain: Maker's Mark itself turned the recipe change into an issue at the start, by looping their "Ambassadors" into the discussion. Fans take the word of their fan objects seriously. If the issue was significant enough to merit a special email, it was probably significant enough to get angry about. If Maker's Mark hadn't tried so hard to explain itself to fans, it's possible the update might have gone unnoticed.

Fandom is inherently conservative. It is the nature of fandom to resist innovation, even when it might be for the better. Fans have a close connection to their fan object, and they can be expected to fight against anything that might change the meaning of that connection. Even—and this is important—if no actual physical change has taken place. Many bourbon experts agree that Maker's Mark probably would have tasted exactly the same, or possibly even better, because a higher alcohol content actually dulls taste buds.

While marketers take the old adage "the customer is always right" to its extreme, academic Stephen Brown argues that in reality "[T]he customer is always right wing—conservative, reactionary, stuck-in-the-mud. . . . They resist change. They inhibit innovation. They want more of the same. They not only venerate the object of their desire, they entomb it in aspic forever and ever, amen."

In some ways it's easier to build fanlike activities around a fan object that is no longer alive. It's easier to collect a full music catalog for a band that's not constantly adding new albums. It's easier to memorize all the quotes from characters in a movie that never has a sequel. A fan object with a completed fan text will never change, never betray a trust, never disappoint. Plenty of fans would rather see their fan object dead than dishonored.

By the time Maker's Mark announced it was reversing its bourbon recipe decision, the fan furor had already started to die down. Tweets had peaked the previous Tuesday. By the following Sunday, when the second email went out, discourse was almost back to pre-announcement levels. "They under-reacted to social media at first, then freaked, then maybe over-reacted," tweeted media commentator Jay Rosen at the time. It's very possible that, had Maker's Mark waited a few more days, the outrage might have blown over.

In an ironic twist, the company had its highest grossing quarter ever. Not as a thank-you for retracting their decision, but because fans had scrambled to buy out what they thought would be the last 90-proof bottles. The few 84-proof bottles that were released are expected to become valuable collector's items.

The Tyranny of the Vocal Minority

When a group rebels, it may seem to the fan-object owner that every last fan is threatening them. Social media swell with angry posts, corporate email boxes flood with ranting letters. Mainstream media write human-interest pieces, almost always with terrible puns in their headlines. Petitions circulate calling for a boycott unless the brand immediately meets fan demands. But often, after the commotion is over, it turns out that the fan rebellion was smaller than it seemed. How is it that a very small group of fans with a minority viewpoint can seem like a huge group of people on the Internet?

Kristina Lerman and a team of computer scientists at the University of Southern California have been trying to find out. They call it the Majority Illusion. In June 2015 they released a paper explaining how it works. Say we have a network of friends. Most of those friends have a couple of other connections, about the same number as we do, but a few "connectors" will have vastly more. If a friend with the usual reach shares a picture of a cat, the number of people who receive the picture will be low. If those people then share it with their own social networks, the chances of overlap will also be low. But if someone with a high number of connections shares it, everyone in the network will receive the picture at once. Anyone they share it with is likely to have seen it already, giving the illusion that everyone in the entire world is suddenly really into cats.

The effect is that social networks, especially digital ones where content travels freely, make it easy to trick people into feeling as though the majority of people share an opinion. Even if, in reality, it's only shared by a small, well-connected group.

For example, studies suggest that teens are more likely to assume that the majority of their friends consume more alcohol than they actually do. It's an illusion: the kinds of teens who get invited to wild parties are by definition more likely to have larger groups of friends to do the inviting. They fill their immediate social network, a network that's much larger than average, with pictures of booze, and suddenly it appears that everyone must be drinking. The effect famously shows up in politics, making extremist views seem more prevalent than they actually are. Explained Lerman in an interview, "As many as 60–70 percent of nodes will have a majority active neighbors, even when only 20 percent of the nodes are active."

The majority illusion implies that fans who complain the loudest are often the ones it is most important to ignore. Fans almost always have sophisticated platforms in place to express themselves, but the nature of these platforms means that sometimes only those with the strongest, often negative, viewpoints get heard.

This phenomenon was noted by another set of marketing professors writing in the *MIT Sloan Management Review* in 2011 as they observed the rise of online discussion spaces such as forums and product reviews. While large portions of the population read online reviews before buying a product, significantly fewer customers leave reviews. Generally, reviewers need to feel strongly, either positively or negatively, to share their opinion about something. People with moderate opinions are less likely to bother leaving a product review or to see the need to join in an online conversation about it. Discussions like this have a built-in selection bias.

Compounding the issue, psychological studies have found that the majority of opinions that come from self-proclaimed experts in an area, such as fans, often trend negative. "More involved customers skew their ratings downward to stand out," explained the researchers. It is much safer to disapprove of something than to risk our reputations by backing an unproven product or idea. The study found that forums where there were both strong positive and negative feelings about a product tended to turn completely negative, and to do so more quickly than groups with customers who had more moderate opinions. It was true even if both groups had the same opinion on average.

Superfans are the definition of an involved audience that has strong opinions and a platform on which to express them. Once sentiment about a topic is trending one way or another, other customers tend to pile on the winning side. A flood of negative comments about a fan object may hide the fact that only a portion of fans hold a negative opinion. It's very easy for a small group of strong-feeling people to overwhelm a discussion and skew the conversation. Those with more moderate opinions are pushed to the side by the vocal minority.

Maker's Mark executives may have felt like the entire world had suddenly turned on them, but in reality the outrage likely represented the views of a much smaller percentage of fans.

Handling a Fan Rebellion

When a fan rebellion occurs it needs to be dealt with swiftly, before extremists can intimidate more level-headed fans into silence. That doesn't mean deleting negative posts or trying to pretend the issue doesn't exist, nor does it mean capitulating to fan demands. It means acknowledging their concerns, letting fans know their opinions are heard and respected, and offering solutions fast to help mitigate the issue.

The process requires a bit of delicacy and a lot of understanding. Fan demands and opinions need to be taken seriously, but not literally. Those demands are an important marker of how a fan object is perceived, but they may not represent what's best for a brand. Finding solutions for dealing with demands, ways to satisfy the vocal minority without sacrificing the integrity of the object itself, is of paramount importance.

Often, understanding fan demands is about interpreting what the fans are actually requesting, not what they think they're requesting. "Don't give people what they want, give them what they need," geek icon Joss Whedon famously said. "What they want is for Sam and Diane to get together. . . . Don't give it to them. Trust me. . . . They need things to go wrong, they need the tension. Things have to go wrong, bad things have to happen." An audience demanding a certain relationship pairing might actually be asking for more romance in the storyline. An audience that is demanding that a product be colored purple might really be asking for it to look friendlier.

Fans of Whedon's own TV show *Buffy the Vampire Slayer* demanded a pairing of the show's two main characters, Buffy, and her gentle love-interest vampire, Angel. So the writers wrote in a single night of bliss . . . before turning Angel into a psychopathic killer. The retail equivalent of this is to offer limited runs of something—superfans can feel empowered to track down the item they demanded, while the rest of the fandom will be unaffected. Offering a special experience to contest winners, offering a one-time screening—these are methods of taking fan demands seriously without allowing the fan object as a whole to be sidetracked.

Why Can't Spider-Man Be Gay?

The Sony Pictures hack of 2014 contained any amount of titillating gossip. The script for the new James Bond movie was leaked, as were a number of unreleased movies. Salary details showed that female stars were routinely paid less than male ones. Executives referred to Angelina Jolie as a spoiled brat and made racist comments about Barack Obama. No one came away looking very good.

One document immediately caught the public attention—at least, the attention of comics fans. A licensing contract between Sony Pictures and comics giant Marvel laid out all the required traits for Peter Parker (and his secret identity, Spider-Man). Peter Parker does not torture or smoke. He does not kill except in self-defense. He gets his powers from a spider bite. He grew up in New York City. He was raised by his aunt and uncle. He must be male. He must be heterosexual. He must be white.

"But of course Spider-Man is a hetero white guy," a fan might protest. "I've seen the movies and read the comics and he is definitely white." It's easy to forget these are made-up characters, subject to the whims of whoever happens to be writing about them at the time. Superheroes in-story regularly change shape, powers, time periods, and dimensions—compared to that, a change in race or sexuality is a relatively easy plot point.

Of course, there are real situations where maintaining a set of characteristics is important to the story. Black Panther would, at the very least, need a name change if he were suddenly Swedish. But there is no in-story purpose for Spider-Man to be white. For that matter, spider bites don't have a gender preference. And as for being heterosexual, there's no reason that Spider-Man's version of New York City couldn't contain a range of love interests to suit any sexuality. It might even make it more realistic. As one headline put it at the time of the leak, "Spider-Man is contractually obligated to be boring at parties."

The comics industry has historically come under fire for featuring straight white male characters at the expense of anyone else. There are relatively few examples in comics prior to the early 2000s where female and minority characters weren't either villains, or where they didn't end up getting brutalized so that the main character had a motivation to do some righteous butt-kicking. "Black dude dies first" is the name of a media trope going back to the seventies, and killing off female characters in horrible, often sexual ways, is such a common plot device that it's been given a name: fridging, after a ludicrous 1994 comic where Green Lantern discovers that his girlfriend has been murdered and stuffed into a refrigerator. As commentator Andrew Wheeler puts it, "If Marvel makes *Thor 3* before it makes Black Panther, it will have made *ten* movies headlined by blond white men named Chris before it makes *one* movie headlined by someone who isn't even white. (They can cast a black actor named Chris. That's totally OK.)"

It wasn't always that way, especially not for the industry's female readership. In the 1930s and '40s, all types of comics—humor, horror, superhero, and romance—were popular, with some estimates clocking readers in at about 90 percent of American adolescents regardless of gender. The comics-heavy magazine *Calling All Girls* claimed a distribution of more than half a million—a huge number for a World War II–era population.

In the late forties, a psychiatrist named Fredric Wertham began publishing articles and giving talks with names like "Horror in the Nursery" and "The Psychopathy of Comic Books," culminating in *Seduction of the Innocent*, a manifesto in which he claimed that comic books lead to evils such as theft, drug use, homosexuality, sexual fetishes, communism, and general mayhem. "I think Hitler was a beginner compared to the comic-book industry," he testified at a US Senate Subcommittee Hearing on Juvenile Delinquency, in one of the first applications of Godwin's Law. His research was deeply flawed and much of it was outright fraudulent (not to mention, to a modern eye, a bit silly). Nevertheless, the moral panic that followed saw parents' groups across the country demanding the removal of comics from pharmacies and bookstores. A number of towns held comic-book burnings.

By 1954, the Comics Code Authority had been created to enforce a blandly unobjectionable moral code across the comic-book industry. The terrified publishers were already defending themselves by discontinuing many of their more edgy titles and modifying others so there could be no misunderstanding about their virtuous intent. Heroes became more manly and patriotic; heroines became more docile. The Wonder Woman of the 1940s fights Nazis. But by the sixties, although she continued to be "wonderful," it wasn't abnormal to see storylines with titles like "Wonder Woman's Surprise Honeymoon," in which the heroine's prospective bridegroom obsesses about her potential lack of cooking skills.

As comic-book storylines became less friendly to female interests, many female readers moved on to other forms of media. Comics distribution disappeared from mainstream outlets, replaced by specialty comic-book stores that served the now heavily male audience. The new outlets were decidedly masculine, a quality that drove away yet more female readers.

Kelly Sue DeConnick, writer on the popular *Captain Marvel* superhero comic book series, grew up on an overseas military base. With limited access to American television, the selection of superhero comics at the base's bookstore was an important link to life back home. But by the early eighties, DeConnick and her fellow female fans found themselves unintentional casualties of the age of specialty comics stores. "There are some really fantastic, really progressive, welcoming comic book stores, where people don't smell like pot and wear sweatpants," she says. "But for quite a while, those stores were in the minority."

By the time big-budget superhero movies began rolling out in the nineties, it was difficult to imagine a significant female audience for them. Ex post facto excuses abounded: Girls didn't care enough about licensed toys. Girls didn't spend enough on media. Or one common defense: girls aren't visual enough (which ignored the success of the fashion and magazine industries). Few people imagined that perhaps girls were nervous about being seen going to movies like that, or that they weren't interested in another lazily written lady murder. "Women are not drawn to things that are actively insulting to them," observes DeConnick.

In the nineties, manga—Japanese comics with a wide array of storylines—hit the United States mainstream. With less cultural baggage, they were welcomed by conventional bookstores. "Women and girls started buying manga at $10 a pop. Those books were flying off the shelves. Those books were keeping bookstores in malls open. If you think about that for a moment, Japanese comics have to be read back-to-front, and right-to-left. It was literally easier for these girls to learn to read backwards than it was for them to find their way into American comics," says DeConnick.

At the same time, the Internet allowed women to find like-minded fans and declare their fandom in safe, supportive spaces. Freed from the necessity of physical comic-book stores, women and girls began buying online comics in hordes. Suddenly, it was very clear that women did like comics after all. For decades, the comic-book industry had been ignoring a huge audience, an audience that was keen to spend money.

Fandom Myopia

The tyranny of the vocal minority is powerful enough to bully a liquor company into making a potentially disastrous business decision, but the effects can be much subtler. Many brands fall into the trap of catering to one fan group to the exclusion of other potential consumers. It's a mistake to believe that a fan group's opinions and demands always reflect those of the general public. As Stephen Brown puts it: "Fans, furthermore, are atypical. True, they talk an awful lot; they really, really love the product; and they are nothing if not proactively evangelistic. But they are also self-selected. They are not representative, not even remotely. Their enthusiastically put views are hopelessly distorted, albeit hopelessly distorted in a direction marketers find congenial. Isn't it great to gather eager followers? Isn't it wonderful to co-create with our oh-so-articulate customers, as the marketing textbooks recommend? Aren't we the bees' knees of branding? The answer, in a nutshell, is NO."

By the time the comics industry remembered that all kinds of people love comics, the predilections of one very specific demographic had skewed the industry: dark, gritty, masculine. It's

important to note that there was nothing wrong with this per se—
many comics from this period are amazing, thoughtful works of art
despite their reduced audience appeal. But from a purely money-
making point of view, limiting their variety was a mistake.

There is nothing altruistic about allowing women and minori-
ties a place in comic books. "They're companies. They're companies
that have to make a profit. If they're doing the right thing and maybe
not leaving some money on the table, great, everybody wins. But
to be sure, it comes down to the notion that, 'wait, women spend
money too?'" says DeConnick.

Elsewhere in the world, in places with fewer historical barriers
to readership, graphically based books were able to grab significantly more market share. Although the specific cultural causality
is difficult to trace, it's tough to argue with the numbers: in 2014, the
Japanese manga market reached 281 billion yen (or about US $2.7
billion). In the United States and Canada that number was a mere
$935 million. Japan, with only about a third of the total population,
still managed to sell nearly three times the amount of comic books.

Catering to a single, limited fan group may seem attractive
because angering the core audience can backfire so spectacularly. As
the single-audience model relaxes its stranglehold on the industry,
the reaction from the traditional comics fan base has been mixed.
It's still not uncommon for journalists and artists who advocate for
diversity in comics to receive harassment or threats. Nevertheless,
Thor is currently female. Batwoman is presently bisexual. Ms. Marvel is Muslim-American. Even Archie Comics has a married gay
couple. Miles Morales, Marvel's Spider-Man of African-American
and Puerto Rican descent, met with outrage from mainstream comics fans when he first appeared in print in 2011. Peter Parker wasn't
gone for good; he reappeared again within three years of his death,
so the Caucasian Spider-Man was in no way imperiled. Still, many

fans remained incredulous and angry. Change in a fan object is difficult, and changing the meaning of the fan object is hardest of all. Yet, years later, the Miles Morales character is still popular.

Taking Over Burberry

A person who is hungry has one problem; a person who isn't hungry has a thousand problems, so the saying goes. A fan object without fans usually has only one goal: creating fans who are motivated enough to "verb" on behalf of the brand. But once the enthusiasm pours in, then what? Creating a fan group is, in a way, the easy part, because it's the part that's most controllable. Fan groups backlash against their fan object and pigeonhole it to cater to their very specific wants. Fan-created content, rituals, and other activities can be so good that it becomes unclear which are intended to be canon and which are not, causing legal excitement on all sides.

The more context a fan object has, the more likely the fan community is to take on a life of its own. Fans of Madonna have widely been credited with being instrumental in the advent of third-wave feminism. Superman, with his refugee status and valuable skills, is regularly brought up in immigration debates. Labor-rights advocates, debt-relief campaigners, and politicos from the left and the right often use imagery from the Star Wars movies. It's common for fans to collude in supporting issues related to their fan object—for example, to bring back a canceled television series (or roll back a hated recipe change).

Underlining these issues lies the problem of hijacking, a phenomenon that has received a lot of attention in recent years. Fans, by definition, repurpose a fan object for personal use, but that doesn't mean the fan-object owner will always like the use to which the object is put.

Esurance, an Internet-centric insurance company, has a mascot named Erin, a pink-haired spy in a cat suit who tracks down secret insurance deals. Or at least they used to. Erin was a victim of her own success, developing a vocal fan base who created stories and pictures (many of them X-rated) on her behalf. At the height of her popularity, googling Esurance Erin without Safe Search turned on was *extremely* not safe for work.

A corporate mascot should be recognizable and memorable, but so much depends on what it is being remembered for. British high-fashion brand Burberry became infamous in the early 2000s when its signature checkered plaid design was adopted by the working-class youth population in England derisively referred to as "chavs." The pattern had previously been used discreetly, as the liner in raincoats and scarves. Chavs used it in everything—hats, pants, skirts, and doggy beds. The American equivalent might be if Brooks Brothers clothing suddenly became immensely fashionable at NASCAR events.

The new fans were unwelcome ones for Burberry. Pubs banned Burberry clothing from their premises; the rich were mortified. As one commentator put it, "Quite a lot of people thought that Burberry would be worn by the person who mugged them." It has taken Burberry over a decade to reclaim ownership over what is still known in many places as "Chav Check."

Why Can't We All Just Get Along?

Hijacking is such a terrifying phenomenon that the smallest possibility is often enough to send brand owners running to their legal departments. Overreactions to completely innocent, or even helpful, fan behavior are a common cause for a fandom to rebel. Many a fan meltdown could have been avoided by a deep breath and five minutes of introspection on the part of the fan object.

In 2014, IKEA, the Swedish-based global furniture company, sent a cease-and-desist letter to a blogger by the name of Jules Yap. Yap ran the extremely popular website IKEAhackers.net, which helped people "hack" IKEA furniture into new, creative, and unexpected designs. The site was already almost a decade old when IKEA's lawyers demanded that Yap hand over the URL.

When fans act in unexpected, uncontrollable ways, such as using the brand name for their own purposes, the proactive solution is often the same as IKEA's—to file a legal claim to protect intellectual property. It isn't a wrong thing to do per se—the legal side of brand management is a serious business—but US trademark and copyright regulations aren't especially helpful when it comes to managing fan expectations.

"I don't have an issue with them protecting their trademark but I think they could have handled it better," Yap told the *Washington Post*. "I am a person, not a corporation. A blogger who obviously is on their side." Fans don't need to be treated with kid gloves, but they do need to be treated differently than people who are trying to make a quick buck. Sending a cease-and-desist to someone squatting on a domain name like IKEA-furniture.com makes sense. In the case of a blogger running a fan site, even one making money off the site, a polite letter opening a conversation might be a better option. Yap's lawyer was able to negotiate a deal with IKEA allowing her to continue operating the site in a noncommercial fashion, without on-site advertising to support her efforts. As soon as the agreement was made public, fans of the site exploded.

Cory Doctorow, an author and co-editor of *Boing Boing*, tore into IKEA: "Ikea's C&D is, as a matter of law, steaming bullshit. There's no trademark violation here—the use of Ikea's name is purely factual. The fact that money changes hands on Ikeahackers (which Ikea's lawyers seem most upset about) has no bearing on the trademark analysis. There is no chance of confusion or dilution from Ikeahackers' use of the mark. This is pure bullying, an attempt at censorship. . . ."

Less than a week after Yap went public, IKEA was forced to backpedal. "We want to clarify that we deeply regret the situation at hand with IKEAhackers," IKEA told a reporter at Yahoo. Yap was invited to visit the company's home offices, and, in a meeting with the CEO—the CEO!—of Inter IKEA Systems B.V., they ultimately forged an agreement allowing Yap to continuing operating the site, ads and all.

"Yay! Pop the lingonberry juice," Yap wrote.

It was a "routine procedure in defense of trademarks, activated following improper use of the Nutella trademark within the fan page"—that's what Ferrero, the manufacturer of the hazelnut-chocolate spread Nutella, claimed when they found themselves in a similar situation in 2013.

Nutella's American Facebook page now has 31 million fans, but for many years, Nutella was a relative unknown in the United States. As an American expat living in Italy in 2007, Sara Rosso, a Nutella super-fan, was struck with the lack of attention Nutella received across the Atlantic. "Why weren't they eating this chocolaty elixir globally?" she asked in a retrospective in 2016. Nutella had almost no online mar-keting presence in English, and the few Americans who knew about it had to seek it out in specialty grocery stores.

Rosso wanted to evangelize about the gooey spread she loved on a grand scale. Her solution was the creation of World Nutella Day, and a blog to get the word out. It fast became a focal point for food bloggers to send their recipes, songs, poems, videos, and other odes to Nutella. The value to Ferrero was significant; Google searches for Nutella show an ever-steady increase over time, with spikes each February around the holiday, which takes place on the fifth. By early 2012, Rosso and her co-host Michelle Fabio had even published *The*

Unofficial Guide to Nutella, which they claim as the first English-language book on the topic.

The result of Rosso's efforts was a cease-and-desist order from Ferrero's legal team, demanding she immediately stop using "the Nutella name, logo or likeness." Rosso was shocked. "This is something I did as a fan," she explained to the *Huffington Post* at the time. "I have a full-time job; I'm not trying to make a business out of this."

"Cease & desist? How bout I cease & desist buying Ferrero products?!?" wrote fan Dave. Allison, another fan, returned a recently purchased carton to the grocery store. "When they asked me why I returned it I told them about the cease & desist and they said I was not the first person to do this," she wrote. Mainstream American media, which had happily covered World Nutella Day events for years, jumped on an easy story. Ferrero representatives called Rosso a few days later to back down, allowing the site to continue as it had.

It's hard to tell what would have happened had Nutella continued with their cease-and-desist. Had the outrage been restricted to superfans, the impact on Ferrero's bottom line would have been limited. But once it became known to the larger audience, and press outlets picked it up, it became clear that Ferrero had created a public-relations disaster. Their actions made them look like bullies, and self-defeating ones at that. Their explanation, that their own legal department had issued the order without consulting anyone, made them seem soulless and out of touch.

A few minutes of thought and deliberate planning about how to handle situations when fans overstep their bounds would have avoided a huge amount of ill will. Doctorow, today an advocate for copyright and trademark legal reform, points out what is obvious to everyone except, it appears, corporate lawyers: "You can get the same benefit from offering a royalty-free license as you get from threatening a lawsuit."

Organizations would do well to first try replacing the cease-and-desist approach to fan management with one that brings fans into the fold. If the organization is largely happy with the fan's activities, it always has the option of making the fan's activity official. Sometimes giving fans permission to use the trademark, with proper controls and oversight, lets everyone win. If that seems too daring for corporate counsel to accept, there's always the old fallback: good old-fashioned disclaimers. They might seem boring in a world where threatening cease-and-desist orders are the norm, but they do get the job done. Asking a fan group to make it clear that they aren't affiliated with or funded by, or have anything at all to do with, the company may make a lot of concerns go away.

Fear is a terrible reason to lash out at the people who love something. And fear also robs the brand owners of the fruits of their labors. Just a few years after their legal kerfuffle, Rosso willingly—and happily—transferred ownership of the now considerably valuable World Nutella Day to the Ferrero Group. She didn't even ask for compensation (just a donation to the World Food Programme). Choosing to work with, rather than against, their superfan paid off in the long run.

#DoingItRight

When a fan group truly has an axe to grind, there is no good way to head it off. Techniques of appeasement, such as giving something and then taking it away, will only further fuel an "us vs. them" mentality. Fighting for a cause is exciting and romantic, and it's even more true when one side does indeed have the moral high ground.

It's important to note that, in many cases, simply acquiescing to fan demands isn't foolproof either. Despite all of their knowledge, fans don't know what's best for their fan object. They only know what's best for its audience. Often the two are the same, but occasionally they're not. When a brand placates its fan group by giving in to a demand, everyone will feel really excited and powerful and good about what they've done together . . . briefly. Then the fans will lose interest and move on to other exciting issues, while the fan object tries to cope with the long-term consequences of its decision.

In situations where fan dictates simply can't be met, the best course of action for fan-object owners might be to humanize the situation. To remind fans that there are real human people involved, that they and the fans are all on the same side, that they understand the fans' concerns, and to explain why they've made their decision. It's important for people to be reminded that both sides of the discussion are made up of fellow fans, wanting to do what's best for their shared passion.

If fans are able to view the fan-object owner as another member of their fan group instead of a corporate overlord, there's much less to fear from transparency. As Don Tapscott and Anthony D. Williams put it in their book *Wikinomics*, "If you trust your customers, you don't have to control them." Fan groups may wobble, but they do tend to right themselves in the end. If an organization has instilled the right social norms into its superfans, it should be able to explain itself as best it can and allow the community to handle it from there. That's what it's there for.

Of course as Maker's Mark proves, that's not always the case. Sometimes transparency creates trust, but sometimes transparency shatters the thin veneer of authenticity that allows fans to forget that the thing they love is also a commercial product.

The best course in every potentially explosive situation is to think carefully about what that transparency is going to reveal. Owners should decide if it aligns with what they know about their fans' feelings and motivations. It requires being deliberate. It means considering who these fans are, where they sit within their fan group's hierarchy, what aspect of their identity is caught up in the fan object, and what they feel they're getting out of their fanlike activities.

Will this transparency make fans feel like insiders? Or will it make them feel betrayed *by* the insiders?

Fan groups have a natural life cycle. As fans hit new stages in their lives they will rotate in and out of different fan groups, attaching themselves to new objects that better serve their new needs. This is okay. Fans are wonderful, and inspiring, and enriching, and enraging. When they decide to leave a fan group because their fan object has changed over time, as it must, it's natural to feel personally rejected. It's easy for fan-object owners to get caught up in a spiral: Could we have fixed things? Were they being unreasonable? If only we hadn't done that one thing maybe they'd still love us. Breakups are always hard. It's all right to hide under the metaphorical covers with a pint of ice cream until the feelings go away.

But it's important to remember this too shall pass. There will be new fans, fans who *are* a perfect fit. Fans who will find in the same fan object the answer to their questions about self-identity, and community, and rebellion, and ideology.

These are fans who will complete their first serious fanlike activity, and who will rush on to the next one full of the enthusiasm at their brush with something that makes them feel like a better version of themselves. Or something that told the world about who they wanted to be. Or maybe just something that was a lot of fun. And perhaps they will write excitedly in their diary that night, as Alice Drake did so long ago, "I never tho't I would do that!"

AFTERWORD

Zoe Fraade-Blanar

Dealing with a fan group, a fan group you like and respect, is wonderful and terrible and heartbreaking and rewarding, and it's dramatic as hell. The fans giveth and they taketh away. I once spent a morning defusing a massive fan meltdown about a low supply of in-stock Corgis, only to discover a flattering piece of fan fiction about myself an hour later (wildly inaccurate, but still, flattering). That kind of thing stays with you.

When we release something the fans are into, their excitement is an instant high. We refresh the social media obsessively, reading each comment out loud and debating every piece of feedback. When we release something they don't like and the outrage pours in, sometimes I just want to say, "Jeez guys, we're doing the best we can! Stop being so darn mean to us; seriously, they're only stuffed animals!"

And then I'll get a note like this: "I honestly can't express deeply enough how Crabby saved my life. He's been there for me to relentlessly squish and hold on to throughout the absolute hardest times while I've been in the hospitals, recovery centre, etc. and he continues to be there while I fight and push through the daily struggles and pain. Having him has done so much for me and it's all because he even existed due to Squishable and the lucky chance that I was the one to adopt him."

And suddenly we feel horrible for not trying hard enough. When a superfan takes an unannounced hiatus, we've more than once scanned the news in her hometown to make sure that nothing unexpected has happened. We obsess about them, and make things for them, and try to please them, and feel like total and complete losers when we don't. And in return, they've given us a business.

Things were simpler when we first started up in 2007. Boxes of Squishables filled the living room of our one-bedroom apartment, and I would draw frogs and flowers on each precious package before we carried it downstairs and over to the FedEx store two blocks away. The trick was to really wedge them under your armpits so the boxes on the top balanced out.

As we grew, we started noticing mystifying goings-on among some of our customers. Squishable-themed profiles like Mortimer the Mini Snail, AnonyMoose, Ambassador Bushybottom von Fuzzybutt, and the League of Extraordinary Squishiness popped up online. These customers drew pictures. They took photos. They drew pictures on their photos. They answered questions for newcomers before we even noticed them. They invented Squishable jargon to refer to their collections (a Lem is a Limited Edition Mini!). They made an unofficial "Trading Post" for swapping used Squishables, and started a Squishable book club. And what we couldn't fathom was, some of them didn't even own a Squishable.

As our business got bigger, some of the fans made cross-country pilgrimages to see our offices. They signed petitions to get us into conventions and toy stores. They took vacations to visit each other, and sent presents of baked goods and artwork and handmade jewelry. They raised money for charity. A lot of it. One set of fans created a formal committee to convince us to bring back a retired Squishable design, a Squishable Devil Bear. Their group had outreach campaigns. And hand-pressed buttons. We were convinced.

They told us when a product was right and when it was wrong, and they encouraged us to release things we never would have considered. "A Kitsune? What is that? A Japanese multitailed fox? Really? Well, all right, I guess we're releasing it . . . oh, and now we're completely sold out."

If the Shiba Inu debacle of 2012 happened today, we would toss a second style through production without a thought. It's been years since we've needed to budget on a style-by-style basis; these days, we can afford to be benevolent. When fans erupted with anger over the "happy-style" eyes on a mini crab design, we were able to run off a second batch with more tragic-looking eyes within a month. The happy-eyed crabs have since turned into a collectors' item, which we feel a little smug about.

That wasn't always the case, and it may not be again. Fandom evolves as the platforms that support it evolve. Already, Facebook's ever-changing algorithm and interface mean we're having very different interactions with present-day fans than even a year ago. Perhaps soon we'll be using something different entirely.

And the fans themselves change too. Early fans who found us in middle school have long since graduated from college. Some are still with us, with collections that fill entire rooms and storage facilities, and in at least one case, a whole extra apartment. And some have moved on. We mourn them. "I wonder what happened to that girl who made that aquatic-Squishable–themed fan page. She was so talented. I miss her photos of narwhals stuck in trees," we'll say.

And we'll feel nostalgic for a moment. And then we'll get back to work, because we have *this* year's Halloween party to plan, and fan designs to critique, and fan tweets to reply to, and fan emails to read. One lady writes to tell us that if we make a Squishable Pug, she will, like, literally tell ALL her friends, and they will TOTALLY buy a billion billion of them, I'm totally not even exaggerating you guys. She says.

Now, fan mail is not a contractually binding document; there's the tiniest possibility that maybe, just maybe, she might be speaking from a place of enthusiasm rather than fiscal certainty. Dog-lovers—we have been bitten by them before. But then again, fans come up with some brilliant ideas.

A Pug? Well, all right, sure. Let's give it a go.

ACKNOWLEDGMENTS

Superfandom is the culmination of years of experimentation, bloody-minded stubbornness, and angst-ridden nights. We would like to thank the following folks who have helped guide (and occasionally prod) us through the process:

This book happened because Clay Shirky was willing to sit down and discuss our ideas over sushi. Without his encouragement, support, and advice from the very first day, it would not have occurred.

Many thanks to our agent, Zoë Pagnamenta, and her colleague Alison Lewis at the Zoë Pagnamenta Agency, as well as Sally Holloway at Felicity Bryan Associates in the UK.

Brendan Curry, our editor, his colleague Nathaniel Dennett, and everyone at W. W. Norton who has been so supportive throughout the process, as well as Clare Grist Taylor and Louisa Dunnigan at Profile Books.

Our first-draft readers Ann Heimberger Jernow, Natalya Minkovsky, and Christopher Santulli, and our final-draft readers Katherine Dillion, Maddy Novich, Thomas Robertson, and Russell Pinke.

The many experts in academia, industry, fandom, and beyond who took the time to inform this book: Beatriz Alvarado, Daniel Amrhein, Jenn Bane, Charbel Barakat, Katie Batza, Eileen Bellomo ("Snooky"), Tish Bellomo, Christian Bladt, Christopher Bonanos, Richard Boursy, Amber Bruens, Jay Bushman, Daniel Cavicchi, Christopher Cleary, Marcus Collins, Ian Condry, Jack Conte, Luke Crane, Kelly Sue DeConnick, Paul DeGeorge, Jesse DeStasio, Guillaume Devigne, John Dimatos, Joost van Dreunen, Sarita Ekya, Jake Fite, Missie L. Fite, Kate Frambach, David Gallagher, Michael Goldmacher, Jonathan Hsy, Doug Jacobson, Florian Kaps, John Keefe, Mary-Kay Lombino, Lawrence McBride, Eric Mersmann, David Park, Dov Quint, Virginia Roberts, James Robinson, Jon Rosenberg, Spencer Rubin, Christian Rudder, Casey Saffron, Elena Salcedo, Sean Sheridan, Erik Smith, Oskar Smolokowski, Max Temkin, Robert J. Thompson, Trent Vanegas, Aaron W., Anna Wilson, and everyone who chose to remain anonymous.

Our research assistants, Jordan Bowles and Sarah Jewett.

Zoe's colleagues at New York University's ITP Graduate Program, including: George Agudow, Katherine Dillion, Shawn Van Every, Nancy Hechinger, Tom Igoe, Dan O'Sullivan, Marianne Petit, Daniel Rozin, Daniel Shiffman, Midori Yasuda, Marina Zurkow, and, of course, Clay, as well as Jay Rosen at the New York University Arthur L. Carter Journalism Institute. A special thank you to Red Burns (in memoriam) for her leadership, inspiration, and good humor.

Aaron's mentors in the History and the Writing Seminars departments at Johns Hopkins University, including Lou Galambos, Dale Keiger, and Joanne Cavanaugh Simpson.

Thank you to all the students who have shaped and contributed to our classes over the years, and in particular the students of *Fandom: Popular Subcultures in a Digital Age* at ITP and Studio 20 at the NYU Journalism Institute.

Thank you to the entire team at Squishable, both past and present: Elizabeth Barnes, Sam Cooper, Brian Cross, Charles Donefer, Anastasia Holl, Eric Holland, Pat Hughes, Beth Roberts, Christopher Santulli, Rishika Singh, Debbie Stair, Scott Watson, Melissa Gonnella, Russell Pinke, Kendra Wells, and every intern who did so much to keep us up-to-date.

Our families, especially Maxine Fraade, George Blanar, and Laura Fraade-Blanar; Laurie Hamilton; Robert Glazer, Susan Cliett, and Kristi Glazer; and our friends who put up with us.

A very special thank you to Archer. Though he won't be able to read this for many years, his patience during this process will be spoken of with hushed tones and reverence for eons to come.

Finally, this book exists first and foremost because of the million-strong Squishable Nation. You are our reason for waking up in the morning, our best teachers. Your kindness and support, your creativity, and your willingness to give back to each other and to us are a constant source of wonder. For ten years you have inspired us, amazed us, and occasionally terrified us, and for that we will forever be grateful. To every Squishable superfan, may your snurfles forever be fuzzy.

NOTES

Preface

vii **On Facebook:** All quotes from fans and team members on Facebook are from Squishable.com, Inc.'s Facebook fan page, https://www .facebook.com/squishabledotcom (10/29/2012–10/30/2012).

ix **Suddenly, angry comments filled our Kickstarter:** This and all other Squishable Shiba Inu Kickstarter references and notes are from Squishable.com, Inc., Update #9, Goodness! It's a Shiba Inu Squishable! https://www.kickstarter.com/projects/squishable/ goodness-its-a-shiba-inu-squishable/posts/345203 (11/8/2012); and https://www.kickstarter.com/projects/squishable/goodness-its -a-shiba-inu-squishable/.

xi **internal chat client:** All quotes by Squishable Team members on our internal chat client from Transcript, Squishable.com Corporate Chat Client at squishable.hipchat.com (10/29/2012-10/30/2012).

Introduction: Welcome to the Fandom Singularity

1 **"I never tho't I would do that!":** All quotations and details of Alice Drake's tour from Alice Drake, *Travel diary of Alice Drake* (1896–1900). Handwritten ms. at Gilmore Music Library, Yale University.

We originally found Drake's story in Daniel Cavicchi, "Loving Music: Listeners, Entertainments, and the Origins of Music Fandom in Nineteenth-Century America," In *Fandom: Identities and Communities in a Mediated World*, by Jonathan Gray, Cornel Sandvoss, and C. Lee Harrington (New York: New York University Press, 2007), 234–49. See Cavicchi's article and his book, *Listening and Longing: Music Lovers in the Age of Barnum* (Middletown, CT: Wesleyan University Press, 2011) for a detailed overview of the compatriots of Alice Drake who made similar undertakings.

4   **Musicomania, an excessive and uncontrollable love:** Cavicchi, "Loving Music," 234–49.

4   **might have contented themselves:** Interview with Daniel Cavicchi by Zoe Fraade-Blanar and Aaron Glazer (12/15/2014).

4   **the growth of cities meant vast new concert halls:** Daniel Cavicchi, "Fandom Before 'Fan': Shaping the History of Enthusiastic Audiences," *Reception: Texts, Readers, Audiences*, History, vol. 6, no. 1 (2014): 52–72.

5   **"well that's great, but we want more":** Ibid.

5   **forsook their gentlemen callers:** Cavicchi, "Loving Music," 234–49.

5   **"The concert room was crowded" . . . "We saw bonnets torn off":** Cavicchi, "Loving Music," 234–49.

6   **unbridled emotions:** James Kennaway, *Bad Vibrations: The History of the Idea of Music as a Cause of Disease* (Surrey, England: Ashgate, 2012).

7   **Kii Peninsula of Japan is still crisscrossed:** UNESCO World Heritage Center, "Sacred Sites and Pilgrimage Routes in the Kii Mountain Range," http://whc.unesco.org/en/list/1142 (n.d., accessed 9/3/2016).

7   **Margery Kempe is known today:** Most of the information about Margery Kempe is from *The Book of Margery Kemp* (fifteenth century; New York: Penguin Classics, 2004); Gail McMurray Gibson, *The Theater of Devotion: East Anglian Drama and Society in the Late Middle Ages* (Chicago: University of Chicago Press, 1989).

7   **novel-length tome:** Kempe, *The Book of Margery Kemp.*

8   **saturated with religious imagery:** Gibson, *The Theater of Devotion.*

8   **Franciscan nuns had tried it:** Ibid.

8   **"a reckless man" . . . "many enemies":** Kempe, *The Book of Margery Kemp,* 98, 158, 175.

8   **"casual house arrest":** Gibson, *The Theater of Devotion.*

9   **also prephonograph:** Interview with Daniel Cavicchi by Zoe Fraade-Blanar and Aaron Glazer (12/15/2014).

9   **throughout recorded history:** Cavicchi, "Loving Music," 234–49.

11   **predictable buying habits:** M. Hills, *Fan Cultures* (New York: Routledge, 2002), 29.

12   **opened for Lady Gaga:** Lady Gaga, Twitter post, https://twitter.com/ladygaga/status/456207861832380416 (4/15/2014).

12   **commercials for Toyota:** B. Ashcraft, "Whose Promoting Google Chrome in Japan? Why, a Virtual Idol," *Kotaku,* http:// kotaku .com/5877099/whose-promoting-google-chrome-in-japan-why-a-virtual-idol (1/18/2012); B. Ashcraft, "A Truly Bizarre Domino's Pizza Commercial," *Kotaku,* http://kotaku.com/5989097/this -dominos-pizza-commercial-is-truly-bizarre (3/7/2013); Y. Koh, "Toyota's New U.S. Saleswoman: Virtual Idol Hatsune Miku," *Wall Street Journal* (5/10/2011), http://blogs.wsj.com/japanrealtime/2011/05/10/ toyotas-new-u-s-saleswoman-virtual-idol-hatsune-miku/.

12   **has long turquoise pigtails:** Crypton Future Media, "Hatsune Miku and Piapro Characters," Piapro.net, http://piapro.net/intl/en_ character.html (n.d., accessed 9/5/2015).

12   **mascot for a vocal synthesizer:** James Verini, "How Virtual Pop Star Hatusne Miku Blew Up In Japan," *Wired,* http://www.wired.com/ 2012/10/mf-japan-pop-star-hatsune-miku/ (10/19/2012).

13   **"you make the music":** Interview with Ian Condry by Zoe Fraade-Blanar and Aaron Glazer (12/21/2014).

14   **"surprised by the speed and scale":** Email interview with Guillaume Devigne (US/EU Marketing, Crypton Future Media) by Zoe Fraade-Blanar and Aaron Glazer (9/17/2014).

14   **company adopted an unexpected policy:** Ibid.

14   **coincided with a crackdown on copyrighted videos:** Interview with Ian Condry by Zoe Fraade-Blanar and Aaron Glazer (9/21/2014).

14   **eleventh-most-visited website:** http://www.alexa.com/topsites/countries/JP (9/25/2016).

14   **a record label called KARENT:** Email Interview with Guillaume Devigne by Zoe Fraade-Blanar and Aaron Glazer (7/26/2016).

15   **36,000 of her most devoted fans:** Crypton Future Media, "Hatsune Miku Expo 2016 North America Tour Report" (n.d.).

15   **wave green light sticks:** "Colors," Unofficial Cheering Guide for Vocaloids, http://chant.mikumiku.org/doku.php?id=basics:colors (9/11/2014).

15   **trappings of a concert:** "Hatsune Miku Expo 2016 North America," Journeys, concert at Hammerstein Ballroom, New York (5/28/2016).

15   **"It was the vibe":** Kelly Faircloth, "I Went to a Hatsune Miku Concert and It Was Fucking Amazing," *Jezebel,* http://jezebel.com/i-went-to-a-hatsune-miku-concert-and-it-was-fucking-ama-1648557083 (10/21/2014).

15   **"very serious and deep issues":** Interview with Ian Condry by Zoe Fraade-Blanar and Aaron Glazer (12/21/2014).

16   **"a close and familiar figure":** Email Interview with Guillaume Devigne by Zoe Fraade-Blanar and Aaron Glazer (12/17/2014).

16   **"not going to turn into Miley Cyrus":** Verini, "How Virtual Pop Star Hatsune Miku Blew Up In Japan."

16   **"It's like being on Willie Nelson's bus":** *Sharing the World,* produced by *The Late Show with David Letterman,* performed by Hatsune Miku (10/9/2014); Brian Ashcraft, "Virtual Idol Hatsune Miku Dazzled on *David Letterman,*" *Kotaku,* http://kotaku.com/virtual-idol-hatsune-miku-dazzled-on-david-letterman-1644187820 (10/9/2014).

17   **"You must not distort":** Creative Commons, "Attribution-Non-Commercial 3.0 Unported," https://creativecommons.org/licenses/by-nc/3.0/legalcode (accessed 9/3/2016).

17   **"in a sexual context":** Crypton Future Media, *For Creators,* http://piapro.net/intl/en_for_creators.html (accessed 9/5/2015).

17   **animated softcore:** https://www.youtube.com/watch?v=qcc4cm
     a5gDs (3/8/2014).

     Chapter 1: Fandom Is a Verb

21   **In the Presence of the Oracle:** Descriptions, background infor-
     mation and "man on the street" quotations, unless otherwise cited,
     from the 2016 Berkshire Hathaway Annual Meeting in Omaha,
     Nebraska, attended by Zoe Fraade-Blanar and Aaron Glazer
     (4/30/2016).

22   **altered version of the song "YMCA":** E. Holm, Moneybeat, *Wall
     Street Journal*; "Recap: The 2014 Berkshire Hathaway Annual Meet-
     ing," http://blogs.wsj.com/moneybeat/2014/05/03/live-blog-the
     -2014-berkshire-hathaway-annual-meeting/.

22   **tens of thousands of people:** David Earl, KETV, "Berkshire meet-
     ing attendance took a hit, thanks to live stream," http://www.ketv
     .com/news/berkshire-meeting-attendance-took-a-hit-thanks-to
     -live-stream/39318232 (5/2/2016).

23   **moved its corporate shareholder meeting:** "Shareholders Stand
     By Disney's Board," *Los Angeles Times*, http://articles.latimes.com/
     1998/feb/25/business/fi-22703 (2/25/1998).

23   **"on Craigslist and eBay for $5":** *Bloomberg News*, "Buffett Sells Passes
     to Beat Scalpers," http://www.nytimes.com/2004/04/17/business/
     buffett-sells-passes-to-beat-scalpers.html (4/17/2004); J. Ping, "eBay:
     Berkshire Hathaway 2009 Annual Meeting Tickets for $5," MyMon-
     eyBlog, http://www.mymoneyblog.com/ebay-berkshire-hathaway
     -2009-annual-meeting-tickets-for-5.html (4/16/09).

23   **"it never occurred to me" and other quotes by Christian Russo:**
     Interviews with Christian Russo (pseudonym) by Zoe Fraade-Bla-
     nar and Aaron Glazer (2014).

23   **closer to 40,000:** Holm, Moneybeat.

24   **shareholders themselves:** M. J. De La Merced, "Berkshire Hatha-
     way's 2014 Shareholder Meeting," *New York Times*, http://dealbook
     .nytimes.com/2014/05/03/live-blog-berkshire-hathaways-2014
     -shareholder-meeting/ (5/3/2014); Holm, Moneybeat.

24 **"America is doing extraordinarily well"**: De La Merced, "Berkshire Hathaway's 2014 Shareholder Meeting."

24 **"I think he handled it very well"**: De La Merced, "Berkshire Hathaway's 2014 Shareholder Meeting.

24 **"doesn't get paid by the word"**: Motley Fool Staff, *The Motley Fool*, "2014 Berkshire Hathaway Annual Q&A With Warren Buffett and Charlie Munger," http://www.fool.com/investing/general/2014/05/21/2014-berkshire-hathaway-annual-qa-with-warren-buff.aspx (5/21/2014).

24 **"I'm already part of the problem"**: Interview with unnamed banker by Zoe Fraade-Blanar at the 2016 Berkshire Hathaway Annual Meeting (4/30/2016).

24 **"Here there are no empty seats"**: Interview with unnamed attendee by Zoe Fraade-Blanar at the 2016 Berkshire Hathaway Annual Meeting (4/30/2016).

25 **"Warren and Charlie we love you!"**: Overheard by Aaron Glazer at the 2016 Berkshire Hathaway Annual Meeting (4/30/2016).

25 **"It's always like this"**: Interview with unnamed See's Candies employee by Zoe Fraade-Blanar at the 2016 Berkshire Hathaway Annual Meeting (4/30/2016).

25 **"This is what he eats?"**: Overheard by Zoe Fraade-Blanar at the 2016 Berkshire Hathaway Annual Meeting (4/30/2016).

26 **"My dad bought it for me last year"**: Interview with unnamed teenage attendee by Zoe Fraade-Blanar at the 2016 Berkshire Hathaway Annual Meeting (4/30/2016).

26 **"Last year, you did your part"**: Warren Buffett, "Berkshire Hathaway Inc. 2013 Letter to Shareholders," http://www.berkshirehathaway.com/letters/2013ltr.pdf, 22 (2/28/2014).

26 **tune of $40 million**: Buffett, Ibid.

27 **T-bone, cooked rare, a double portion of hash browns, and a Cherry Coke**: L. Lopen, "Inside the Legendary Omaha Steakhouse That Warren Buffett Takes Over One Day Every Year," http://www.businessinsider.com/gorats-warren-buffett-steakhouse-2013-5 (5/3/2013).

27   **"Only sissies get the small one":** Buffett, "Berkshire Hathaway Inc. 2013 Letter to Shareholders," 21.

27   **Twenty-six loose diamonds:** Borsheims Press Release, "Warren Buffett Sells 6 Buffett-Signed Diamonds, Other Jewelry at Borsheims," http://borsheimsbrk.com/3152/warren-buffett-sells-6-buffett-signed-diamonds-other-jewelry-at-borsheims (5/4/2014).

27   **exhibition match:** *A good point at 2014 Berkshire Ping Pong Party*, https://www.youtube.com/watch?v=wja-rQduOtM (5/5/2014).

28   **"This is a family affair":** Interview with family of attendees from Chicago by Zoe Fraade-Blanar at the 2016 Berkshire Hathaway Annual Meeting (4/30/2016).

28   **"Susie goes there":** Ibid.

28   **"Are you rich?":** Interview with Tommy by Zoe Fraade-Blanar at the 2016 Berkshire Hathaway Annual Meeting. (4/30/2016).

29   **almost certainly be denied:** See, for example, Eric Holm, "Meet the Man Behind Berkshire's Latest (Doomed) Dividend Push," *Wall Street Journal*, http://blogs.wsj.com/moneybeat/2014/05/02/meet-the-man-behind-berkshires-latest-doomed-dividend-push/ (5/2/2014).

30   **to buy still more:** A. Cripple, "Warren Buffett Fans Explain Why They're Keeping the Faith," http://www.cnbc.com/id/28342496 (12/23/2008).

30   **giant Dairy Queen spoon:** "Warren Buffett Signs Giant Red Dairy Queen Spoon to Be Auctioned on eBay for Charity," http://www.businesswire.com/news/home/20100721006102/en/Warren-Buffett-Signs-Giant-Red-Dairy-Queen (7/21/2010).

30   **The Battle for Washington Square Park:** Description and all "man on the street" quotes, unless otherwise cited, from the Lightsaber Battle NYC 2014 attended by Zoe Fraade-Blanar and Aaron Glazer (8/9/2014).

30   **Facebook event page:** https://www.facebook.com/events/491340 464345362/ (8/9/2014).

31   **top ten movies of 2015:** http://www.boxofficemojo.com/yearly/chart/?view2=worldwide&yr=2015&p=.htm. (9/5/2016).

31   **Disney's $4 billion acquisition:** See D. Leonard, "How Disney Bought Lucasfilm—and Its Plans for 'Star Wars,'" *Bloomberg Business*, http://www.bloomberg.com/bw/articles/2013-03-07/how -disney-bought-lucasfilm-and-its-plans-for-star-wars (3/7/13).

31   **17,000 characters listed in the *Holocron*:** http://www.npr.org/2013/ 07/16/202368713/use-the-books-fans-star-wars-franchise-thrives-in -print (7/16/2013).

33   **flocking to DeLorean car shows:** http://www.deloreancarshow.com/ (n.d., accessed 9/5/2016); http://www.deloreanconvention.com/ (n.d., accessed 9/5/2016).

33   **annual visitors to the Guinness Storehouse:** Nicola Anderson, "Guinness Storehouse country's main tourist draw," *The Independent* (Ireland), http://www.independent.ie/life/travel/travel-news/ guinness-storehouse-countrys-main-tourist-draw-30876732.html (2/1/2015).

34   **natural urges toward self-expression and interaction:** D. Tapscott and A. D. Williams, *Wikinomics: How Mass Collaboration Changes Everything* (New York: Portfolio, 2010).

34   **a performance needs an audience:** M. Hills, *Fan Cultures* (New York: Routledge, 2002), xi.

35   **three stars on Yelp:** https://www.yelp.com/biz/gorats-steak-house -omaha (accessed 9/25/2016).

35   **fandom tends toward in-person interactions:** Interview with Thomas Robertson by Zoe Fraade-Blanar (5/29/2013).

36   **Creative works by amateurs:** C. Shirky, *Cognitive Surplus: Creativity and Generosity in a Connected Age* (New York: Penguin Press, 2010), 83–84.

36   **title sequence for Season 8:** S. Kelley, "Doctor Who fan who inspired series 8's opening title sequence: 'I had to pinch myself,'" *RadioTimes*, http://www.radiotimes.com/news/2014-08-23/doctor -who-fan-who-inspired-series-8s-opening-title-sequence-i-had-to -pinch-myself (8/23/2014).

38   **Our bodies are a canvas:** Hills, *Fan Cultures,* 23.

39   **$2.5 billion spent on costumes:** "NRF: 157 Million Americans Will

Celebrate Halloween This Year," Press Release, https://nrf.com/media/press-releases/nrf-157-million-americans-will-celebrate-halloween-this-year (9/23/15).

39   **goes toward licensed properties:** N. Spector, "Most popular Halloween costumes of 2015 from eBay, Pinterest and Polyvore data," http://www.today.com/money/most-popular-halloween-costumes-2015-ebay-pinterest-polyvore-data-t49606 (10/28/2015).

39   **Google Frightgeist:** https://frightgeist.withgoogle.com/ (accessed 12/18/2016).

39   **Flo the Progressive Girl:** Progressive, "Dress Like Flo," http://at.progressive.com/fun-and-entertainment/dress-like-flo (12/9/2015).

39   **Bieber fans sometimes organize "buyouts":** A. Chen, Gawker, "The Unstoppable Rampage of the Belibers," http://gawker.com/5864603/the-unstoppable-rampage-of-the-beliebers (12/2/2011). For a recent example, see https://www.thestar.com/entertainment/music/2015/11/12/justin-bieber-fans-planning-buyout-of-his-new-album-on-saturday-donating-surplus-to-charity.html (11/12/2015).

41   **2013 study of Bud Light fans:** "Case Study | ROI/Sales: Bud Light," http://www.facebook-successstories.com/bud-light/ (2013); T. Wasserman, Mashable, "Bud Light Offers Proof That Facebook Ads Work," http://mashable.com/2013/04/30/bud-light-facebook-ads/ (4/30/2013).

42   **$1.56 billion purely on advertising:** E. J. Schultz, "A-B InBev Ends an Era of In-house Media," *AdAge*, http://adage.com/article/agency-news/a-b-inbev-ends-era-house-media/294971/ (9/15/2014).

43   **"all of those instruments":** J. Firecloud, http://antiquiet.com/interviews/2008/08/breaking-ground-with-jack-conte/ (8/4/2008).

43   **"Art became fundamentally tied to commerce":** Telephone interview with Jack Conte about Patreon by Zoe Fraade-Blanar and Aaron Glazer (8/18/2014).

44   **"support an artist":** Ibid.

44   **over a million active pledges:** Graphtreon.com, *Patreon Statistics*, https://graphtreon.com/patreon-stats (7/19/16).

44   **"listeners like you":** See http://www.npr.org/about-npr/178660742/public-radio-finances (n.d., accessed 9/25/2016).

45   **"I don't really wear T-shirts"**: Interview with J. Rosenberg about
     Patreon and *Scenes from a Multiverse* by Zoe Fraade-Blanar and
     Aaron Glazer (8/14/2014).

45   **$3,094 a month through Patreon**: Jon Rosenberg's Patreon,
     https://www.patreon.com/jonrosenberg (accessed 7/19/2016).

46   **"VFX school on a budget"**: Corridor Digital's Patreon, https://www
     .patreon.com/corridordigital (accessed 8/24/2014).

46   **"Operation Kiddie Freedom"**: Jon Rosenberg's Patreon.

46   **"When I hit $7,000"**: Jack Conte's Patreon, https://www.patreon
     .com/jackconte (accessed 8/24/2014).

46   **"self-identified crew of people"**: Telephone interview with Jack
     Conte.

46   **"seeing a plate on the wall"**: Telephone interview with Jack Conte.

47   **"Being a patron denotes some type of relationship"**: Telephone
     interview with Jack Conte.

Chapter 2: The Rise of Commercial Fandom

49   **It was early in 2011**: Quotes from Erik Smith, aka Dr. Franken-
     roid, are from a number of interviews and emails: telephone inter-
     view with Erik Smith by Zoe Fraade-Blanar and Aaron Glazer
     (1/20/2015 and 5/17/2016); email correspondence with Erik Smith,
     2015–2016.

50   **ceasing production of instant film**: P. J. Lyons, http://thelede
     .blogs.nytimes.com/2008/02/08/polaroid-abandons-instant
     -photography/?_r=0 (2/8/2008); telephone interview with Mary-
     Kay Lombino by Zoe Fraade-Blanar and Aaron Glazer (1/22/2015).

51   **consumer camera production had already ended**: C. Dentch,
     "Polaroid to Exit Instant Film as Demand Goes Digital," http://www
     .bloomberg.com/apps/news?pid=newsarchive&sid=apS0e2r9t
     J7M&refer=us (2/8/2008).

51   **financial difficulties**: D. Phelps, "Polaroid is latest Petters firm to
     file Chapter 11," *Star Tribune* (12/19/2008).

51   **online petition**: A. Kellogg, http://www.gopetition.com/petitions/
     save-polaroid-film/signatures.html (accessed 9/25/2016).

51   "always be a place for Polaroids": A. T. Union, "Polaroid fans hope film won't go way of vinyl," *Kitchener-Waterloo (Ontario) Record* (3/6/2008).

52   "Digital cameras are boring": T. Teeman, "End of the reel for the chic and cheerful Polaroid," *(London) Times* (2/15/2008).

52   "no negatives and no digital file": Interview with C. Bonanos by Zoe Fraade-Blanar (1/21/2015).

53   3.5 times the forecasted rate: S. Bradley, "On for young and old: devotees snap up Polaroid stocks," *Sydney (Australia) Sun Herald* (6/29/2008), 33.

53   "make our film categories last": Dentch, "Polaroid to Exit Instant Film as Demand Goes Digital."

53   Florian Kaps was an instant-photography enthusiast: M. Wright, "The Impossible Project: Bringing back Polaroid," *Wired UK* (11/4/2009).

53   shutter the factory: T. Bradshaw, "Bringing back Polaroid's instant film," *FT Magazine* (8/14/2009), http://www.ft.com/cms/s/0/ 6c82e490-87a2-11de-9280-00144feabdco.html?siteedition=intl #slideo.

53   lamented the coming loss: M. Wright, "The Impossible Project."

54   lease the now-defunct factory: C. Doughtery, "Polaroid Lovers Try to Revive Its Instant Film," *New York Times*, http://www.nytimes.com/2009/05/26/technology/26polaroid.html (5/25/2009).

54   "very crazy supply chain": Telephone interview with Oskar Smolokowski by Aaron Glazer and Zoe Fraade-Blanar (12/12/2014).

54   "pod of white chemistry": Interview with C. Bonanos.

54   two years for the Impossible Project to launch: Telephone interview with Oskar Smolokowski by Aaron Glazer and Zoe Fraade-Blanar (12/12/2014).

55   Impossible called them "Pioneers": Ibid.

55   "preserving this beautiful medium": Ibid.

55   "actually a little bit harder": Ibid.

55   3,000 early Pioneers: Ibid.

56   "an Impossible photograph": Ibid.

56   **"pretty much lost everything"**: Telephone interview with Erik Smith (1/20/2015).

56   **"like the great Dr. Frankenstein"**: Ibid.

57   **"Impossible Status"**: Impossible's rules were posted at https://shop .the-impossible-project.com/pioneer/. The site is no longer acces- sible, but can be found at https://web.archive.org/web/2015072815 1248/https://shop.the-impossible-project.com/pioneer/ (accessed 7/28/2015).

57   **"This was my opportunity"**: Telephone interview with Erik Smith.

57   **"this Polaroid fool"**: Ibid.

58   **"Photography is so much"**: Ibid.

58   **"I needed something in my life"**: Ibid.

58   **bankrupt in late 2008**: Phelps, "Polaroid is latest Petters firm to file Chapter 11."

59   **holding company for the intellectual property**: Dale Kurschner, "Polaroid is ready for its closeup: how the iconic company is remak- ing itself for the 21st century," https://www.minnpost.com/twin-cit- ies-business/2015/04/polaroid-ready-its-closeup-how-iconic -company-remaking-itself-21st-cent (4/3/2015).

59   **"The spectrum draws people in"**: Interview with Dov Quint at The Polaroid Fotobar, Las Vegas, NV, by Aaron Glazer (7/1/2015).

59   **manufactured by a range of secondary factories**: Ross Rubin, "And The Brand Played On: How Tech Icons Polaroid And RCA Live On Through Licensing," *Fast Company*, https://www.fast company.com/3060449/and-the-brand-played-on-how-yesterdays -tech-icons-live-on-through-licensing-deals (6/8/2016).

60   **" 'That's so retro' "**: Interview with Dov Quint.

60   **eighty-second on the CoreBrand Brand Power Rankings**: Core- Brand, LLC, "CoreBand 100 Brand Power Ranking" (2011).

60   **"no longer a mass-market product"**: M. Wright, "The Impossible Project."

60   **"Small World Machines"**: J. Moye, http://www.coca-colacompany .com/stories/happiness-without-borders/ (5/13/2013).

61   **units of Coke sold**: C. Champagne, http://www.fastcocreate.com/

1683001/how-coca-cola-used-vending-machines-to-try-and-unite
-the-people-of-india-and-pakistan (5/30/2013).

62 **tempting to call them ancillary:** H. Jenkins, "Afterword: The
Future of Fandom," in Jonathan Gray, Cornel Sandvoss, and C.
Lee Harrington, *Fandom: Identities and Communities in a Mediated
World* (New York: NYU Press, 2007), 357–364.

63 **context makes these commercial products relevant:** B. Solis, *The
End of Business As Usual: Rewire the Way You Work To Succeed in the
Consumer Revolution* (New York: Wiley, 2011), 46.

63 **inspires others to do the same:** C. Shirky, *Cognitive Surplus: Creativity and Generosity in a Connected Age* (New York: Penguin Press. 2010).

63 **"human pseudo-events":** D. Boorstin, *The Image: A Guide to Pseudo-
Events in America* (New York: Vintage, 1992); Hills, *Fan Cultures.*

64 **"social lubricant":** J. Heilemann, "All Europeans Are Not Alike,"
New Yorker (4/28/1997): 175.

64 **"Old Spice means quality":** Vintage 1957 Animated & Live Old
Spice Commercial, https://www.youtube.com/watch?v=x42mG-
pIwCgg (motion picture, n.d.).

65 **"Smell Like a Man, Man":** Case Study: Old Spice Response Campaign, http://www.dandad.org/en/old-spice-response-campaign/
(n.d., accessed 9/25/2016); https://www.pg.com/en_US/downloads/
innovation/factsheet_OldSpice.pdf (n.d., accessed 9/25/2016).

65 **"What about *next* year?":** T. Wasserman, "How Old Spice Revived
a Campaign That No One Wanted to Touch," http://mashable.com/
2011/11/01/old-spice-campaign/ (11/1/2011).

66 **engagement patterns:** R. Walker, *Buying In: What We Buy and Who
We Are.* (New York: Random House, 2010), xv.

66 **more likely than past generations to look for information:** J.
Fromm, C. Lindell, and L. Decker, "American Millennials: Decipher-
ing the Enigma Generation," http://barkley.s3.amazonaws.com/
barkleyus/AmericanMillennials.pdf (2011).

66 **Thirty-four percent of millennials:** Goldman Sachs, "Millennials:
Coming of Age," http://www.goldmansachs.com/our-thinking/
pages/millennials/ (n.d.).

67   **attach a narrative:** Walker, *Buying In*, 8.

67   **the PDC-2000:** Polaroid Annual Report 1996, http://www.bitmedia
      .com/ar96/commercial.html (1997).

67   **"Feed the rush":** D. Barboza, "Caffeinated Drinks Catering to
      Excitable Boys and Girls," *New York Times* (8/22/1997).

68   **"go and get a Surge":** Telephone interview with Sean Sheridan by
      Zoe Fraade-Blanar and Aaron Glazer (1/8/2015).

68   **"can or a bottle, or a two-liter or ten two-liters of Surge":** Ibid.

68   **"it causes students to talk more and misbehave":** P. Dodds,
      "School bans Surge, says caffeine-packed drink makes students too
      hyper," *Associated Press* (4/11/1997).

68   **"buying it out everywhere I went":** Telephone interview with Sean
      Sheridan.

69   **Surge Movement Facebook page:** https://www.facebook.com/
      surgemovement/ (n.d., accessed 9/25/2016).

69   **"wasn't really one of leadership":** Telephone interview with Sean
      Sheridan.

70   **"Stop being a negative nancy":** https://www.facebook.com/surge
      movement/photos/a.153479818094993.29215.147561302020178/
      351655908277382/?type=3&theater (3/4/2013).

70   **"We should get a billboard":** Telephone interview with Sean Sheridan.

70   **Indiegogo was underway:** https://www.indiegogo.com/projects/
      billboard-for-surge-soda#/ (accessed 9/25/2016).

70   **"Dear Coke":** V. Guerra, "Coke's 90's Drink Surge Revives After A
      Long Campaign For The Coca-Cola Company," *Food World News*,
      http://www.foodworldnews.com/articles/6044/20140916/coke
      -90s-drink-surge-surge-coca-cola-the-coca-cola-company-90s
      -surge-movement.htm (9/16/2014).

70   **"Surging days":** Telephone interview with Sean Sheridan.

71   **"last Friday of the month already":** Ibid.

71   **"We got our occasional troll":** Ibid.

71   **Surge returned:** S. Maheshwari, "Coca-Cola is Bringing Surge
      Back," https://www.buzzfeed.com/sapna/coca-cola-is-bringing-
      surge-back (9/15/2014).

71 **personal email:** J. Moye, http://www.coca-colacompany.com/
stories/meet-the-three-guys-behind-the-movement-to-bring-back
-surge/ (9/18/2014).

71 **" 'Don't tease me' ":** Telephone interview with Sean Sheridan.

72 **"biggest throwback Thursday":** Guerra, "Coke's 90's Drink
Surge Revives After A Long Campaign For The Coca-Cola
Company."

72 **"echo boom" generation:** J. Doherty, "On the Rise," http://www
.barrons.com/articles/SB50001424052748703889404578440972842742076
(4/29/2013).

72 **Fowler's time in office:** P. J. Boyer, "Under Fowler, FCC treated as
Commerce," http://www.nytimes.com/1987/01/19/arts/under-fowler
-fcc-treated-tv-as-commerce.html (1/19/1987).

73 **create the figurines concurrently:** R. Lobb (director), *Turtle Power:
The Definitive History of the Teenage Mutant Ninja Turtles* (motion
picture, 2014).

73 **Saturday-morning cartoons are no longer:** G. Sullivan, https://www
.washingtonpost.com/news/morning-mix/wp/2014/09/30/saturday
-morning-cartoons-are-no-more/ (9/30/2014).

75 **Digital networks lower the discovery cost:** Shirky, *Cognitive Surplus,* 88.

78 **suddenly a comfortably upper-middle-class position:** Though
it's from an earlier era, for a discussion on professions and class in
American see P. Fussell, *Class: A Guide Through the American Status
System* (New York: Touchstone, 1992).

79 **"I'm the guy to blame for running out":** J. Laxen, "Surge makes a local
comeback," http://www.sctimes.com/story/life/food/2015/10/06/
surge-makes-local-comeback/73396572/ (10/6/2015).

Chapter 3: From Convention to Conventional

81 **"We Have a Place for You Here":** Details on the background
and history of the Renaissance Faire, unless otherwise cited, are
from American Studies professor Rachel Lee Rubin's incredibly
detailed study of Rennie culture: *Well Met: Renaissance Faires and*

The American Counterculture (New York: New York University Press, 2014).

81 **"I was very shy"**: D. Jacobson (director), *Faire: An American Renaissance*, https://vimeo.com/ondemand/faire (motion picture, 2014).

82 **groovy new project**: K. Patterson, http://fairehistory.org/faire-found ers.html (7/19/2016); Z. Stewart, "Hear Ye, Hear Ye: 'tis Faire Time," http://articles.latimes.com/1987-04-19/entertainment/ca-1684_1_ hear-ye (4/19/1987).

82 **unusual curriculum**: "The Original Renaissance Pleasure Faire," http://freethinkerspub.yuku.com/topic/11652#.V1MZZPkrKYk (5/10/2013).

82 **as a fundraiser**: K. T. Korol-Evans, *Renaissance Festivals: Merrying the Past and Present* (Jefferson, NC: McFarland, 2009).

83 **uniquely American phenomenon**: Rubin has an excellent discussion of this, noting much of what makes the Renaissance festival exciting is "traditional to the Renaissance festival, rather than the Renaissance," Rubin, *Well Met*, 2.

83 **smoked turkey legs**: Ibid.

84 **women to go braless**: Ibid., 19–21.

84 **"heady experience"**: Ibid., 225.

84 **"when I put on this costume"**: E. Gilbert, "Knight Fever," *Spin* (12/1996): 100–108.

84 **Early faire sexuality**: See Rubin, *Well Met*, 208–11.

85 **faire supported careers**: Rubin, *Well Met*.

85 **Penn and Teller**: P. Jillette, "39 years ago today, Teller and I did our first show together at the Minnesota Renaissance Festival," https://twitter .com/pennjillette/status/501804681853956096 (8/19/2014).

85 **Flying Karamazov Brothers**: http://www.fkb.com/history.php (accessed 9/16/2016).

85 *Faire Free Press*: Rubin, *Well Met*, 38–39.

85 **"come Sunday night"**: Jacobson (director), *Faire: An American Renaissance*.

86 **"You could be something"**: Ibid.

86   **"you are a misfit"**: Telephone interview with Doug Jacobson by Zoe
      Fraade-Blanar and Aaron Glazer (1/7/2015).

86   **first-wave, second-wave, and third-wave interpretations**: For
      a great overview of the academic development of fan studies, see
      "Introduction: Why Study Fans?" in *Fandom: Identities and Com-
      munities in a Mediated World*, by Jonathan Gray, Cornel Sandvoss,
      and C. Lee Harrington (New York: New York University Press,
      2007), 9–10.

86   **fandom as a place where marginalized members**: Henry Jenkins
      popularized this theory in his seminal essay "Star Trek Rerun,
      Reread, Rewritten: Fan Writing as Textual Poaching," originally
      published in 1988, and his later book *Textual Poachers: Television
      Fans and Participatory Culture* (New York: Routledge, 1992). In a
      later reprint of the article, he argues that the research is outdated:
      "over the past decade and a half, everything I described here has
      changed." See Jenkins, "Star Trek Rerun, Reread, Rewritten," in
      Jenkins, *Fans, Bloggers, and Gamers* (New York: NYU Press, 2006).

87   **more than 6,000 people**: E. Gross and M. Altman, *The Fifty-Year
      Mission: The Complete, Uncensored, Unauthorized Oral History of
      Star Trek: The First 25 Years* (New York: St. Martin's Press, 2016), 247.

87   **"Vulcan ideals of tolerance"**: Star Trek Convention NYC 1973,
      https://www.youtube.com/watch?v=EkgoLZJWg5c.

87   **any range of subcultures**: Jenkins, "Star Trek Rerun, Reread,
      Rewritten," 42.

87   **"badges of pride"**: "Slagman," http://www.metafilter.com/31238/
      iPods-Pro-and-Con (2/9/2004).

88   **"Think Different"**: http://lowendmac.com/2013/think-different
      -ad-campaign-restored-apples-reputation/ (4/9/2007).

88   **progressive heroes**: "Steve Jobs thought different," *CBS News*,
      http://www.cbsnews.com/news/steve-jobs-thought-different/
      (10/5/2011).

88   **"The misfits"**: Apple "Think Different" advertisement (10/2/1997),
      https://www.youtube.com/watch?v=nmwXdGm89Tk.

89   **Patterson faced major political challenges**: Rubin, *Well Met*, 56–58.

89 **"Dragon!":** Rubin, *Well Met*, 64.

89 **High-class taste:** M. Maffesoli, "The linking value of subcultural capital: constructing the Stockholm Brat enclave," in Bernard Cova, Robert Kozinets, and Avi Shankar, *Consumer Tribes* (New York: Routledge, 2007), 96.

90 **Insane Clown Posse:** B. McCollum, "Merch masters," *Detroit Free Press* (10/25/2009), K6.

90 **popular culture is scandalous:** M. Hills, *Fan Cultures* (New York: Routledge, 2002), 9.

90 **excluded from formal culture:** P. Nancarrow, and C. Nancarrow, "Hunting for Cool Tribes," in Cova, Kozinets, and Shankar, *Consumer Tribes*, 132.

90 **outsiders scratch value:** Hills, *Fan Cultures*, 59.

90 **fandom as a form of rebellion:** Jenkins, "Star Trek Rerun, Reread, Rewritten," 42.

90 **I can make my own utopia:** See Jenkins, *Textual Poachers*.

91 **"Sloats":** Gilbert, "Knight Fever," 100–108.

91 **"cut the soles off your shoes and join the circus":** Jacobson (director), *Faire: An American Renaissance*.

91 **"odd outfits acting weird":** Rubin, *Well Met*.

92 **expanded to a wider audience:** J. A. Gross, "The Festival Gap: Comparing Organizers' Perceptions of Visitors to a Survey of Visitors at the Carolina Renaissance Fest" (master's thesis, East Carolina University, 2006).

92 **opened to a flood of cheap Chinese imports:** Telephone interview with Doug Jacobson.

92 **Corporate sponsorships:** Royal Faires, "Our Sponsors," The Carolina Renaissance Festival and Artisan Marketplace, http://www.carolina.renfestinfo.com/ (10/30/2015); Royal Faires, "The Festival," The Annual Arizona Renaissance Festival & Artisan Marketplace, http://www.royalfaires.com/arizona/ (10/30/2015).

92 **"now, it's a business":** Rubin, *Well Met*, 52.

92 **"'I'm not valuable anymore'":** Telephone interview with Doug Jacobson.

92   **closing because of profitability concerns:** Jacobson (director),
      Faire: An American Renaissance.

93   **"kill their savior":** Telephone interview with Doug Jacobson.

93   **nearly 70,000 attendees:** J. Kane, "Burning Man, bigger? Atten-
      dance may grow," *Reno Gazette-Journal,* http://www.rgj.com/story/
      life/2015/04/20/burning-man-asking-blm-population-increase/
      26101069/ (4/20/2015).

93   **"Don't interfere":** A. Fortunati, "Utopia, Social Sculpture, and Burning
      Man," in L. Gilmore and M. Van Proyen, *AfterBurn: Reflections on Burn-
      ing Man* (Albuquerue: University of New Mexico Press, 2005), 156.

93   **commerce-free:** http://burningman.org/event/preparation/faq/#
      General_Information (9/17/2016).

94   **give away or barter:** Fortunati, A. "Utopia, Social Sculpture, and
      Burning Man," 158–159.

94   **"One-Up One Another":** N. Bilton, "At Burning Man, the Tech
      Elite One-Up One Another," *New York Times* (8/20/2014).

94   **Getting there is not cheap:** T. Anderson, "How to enjoy Burning Man
      without burning your cash," *CNBC,* http://www.cnbc.com/2016/
      08/25/how-to-enjoy-burning-man-without-burning-your-cash.
      html (8/26/16).

95   **RV rentals:** M. Corona, "Burning Man brings business to Reno RV
      renters," *Reno Gazette-Journal,* http://www.rgj.com/story/life/arts/
      burning-man/2014/08/23/burning-man-brings-business-reno-rv
      -renters/14515321/ (8/23/2014).

95   **Burning Man census:** "Socioeconomic Diversity and Trends," https://
      blackrockcitycensus.wordpress.com/2015/05/08/socioeconomic
      -diversity-and-trends/ (5/8/2015). The Burning Man Census data has
      since moved to: http://journal.burningman.org/census/.

95   **"eat drugs in search of the next greatest app":** Bilton, "At Burning
      Man, the Tech Elite One-Up One Another."

95   **turnkey camp was even vandalized:** D. Gayle, "Luxury camp at
      Burning Man festival targeted by 'hooligans,'" *The Guardian,* https://
      www.theguardian.com/culture/2016/sep/05/luxury-camp-at-burn
      ing-man-festival-targeted-by-hooligans (9/2/2016).

96 **"fandom as societal re-creation"**: For a discussion on third-wave fandom, see Gray, Sandvoss, and Harrington, "Introduction: Why Study Fans?," 6.

96 **re-create the mainstream system**: Hills, *Fan Cultures*, 46.

96 **"Sparkle Ponies"**: S. Burris, http://www.rawstory.com/2016/08/disgusted-burners-slam-wealthy-sparkle-ponies-who-are-taking-luxury-helicopter-rides-to-burning-man/ (8/30/2016).

97 **"geeks and misfits"**: Jacobson (director), *Faire: An American Renaissance*.

97 **"assumed to be a hooker"**: Telephone interview with Tish and Eileen "Snooky" Bellomo by Zoe Fraade-Blanar (1/14/2015).

98 **"stripper stores"**: Ibid.

98 **"go-go boots"**: Ibid.

99 **$250 from a family member**: C. L. Adams, "The Martha Stewart of Punk Rock?" http://www.bloomberg.com/bw/stories/2007-08-08/the-martha-stewart-of-punk-rock-businessweek-business-news-stock-market-and-financial-advice (8/8/2007).

99 **opened a punk-clothing boutique**: https://www.manicpanic.com/ourhistory (9/18/2016).

99 **"only sell stuff that we would wear"**: Interview with Eileen "Snooky" Bellomo at Licensing Expo by Zoe Fraade-Blanar (6/19/2013).

99 **"Johnny Thunders"**: Telephone interview with Tish and Eileen "Snooky" Bellomo.

99 **hair dye from England**: M. Ulto (director), *Manic Panic 30th Anniversary,* https://www.youtube.com/watch?v=G4R1NkAA3jk (motion picture, 2007).

99 **making pilgrimages**: Telephone interview with Tish and Eileen "Snooky" Bellomo; Ulto (director), *Manic Panic 30th Anniversary*.

99 **"had hardly anything to sell"**: Telephone interview with Tish and Eileen "Snooky" Bellomo.

100 **Members of the B-52s . . . Cyndi Lauper and The Ramones**: Ulto (director), *Manic Panic 30th Anniversary*.

100 **"like a clubhouse"**: Telephone interview with Tish and Eileen "Snooky" Bellomo.

100 "emotional and teary": Ibid.

100 "the feel-good hair dye": Ibid.

100 corporation behind Manic Panic: Adams, "The Martha Stewart of Punk Rock?"

100 "little scary": Telephone interview with Tish and Eileen "Snooky" Bellomo.

100 "took her mind off of her problems": Ibid.

101 "wanted to take a picture": Ibid.

101 "love my hair pink": Ibid.

102 third-wave fandom: Gray, Sandvoss, and Harrington, "Introduction: Why Study Fans?," 9–10.

103 specific set of tribal colors: Nancarrow and Nancarrow, "Hunting for Cool Tribes," 130.

103 which symbols represent which class: R. Pearson, "Bachies, Bardies, Trekkies, and Sherlockians," in Gray, Sandvoss, and Harrington, Fandom, 98–109.

103 price at one time was $3,134: S. Yara, "The Most Expensive Jeans," http://www.forbes.com/2005/11/29/most-expensive-jeans-cx_sy_1130feat_ls.html (11/30/2005).

103 "Negative frequency-dependent preferences and variation in male facial hair": Z. J. Janif, R. C. Brooks, and B. J. Dixson, "Negative frequency-dependent preferences and variation in male facial hair," Biology Letters (4/16/2014).

106 highest-grossing animated film: http://www.boxofficemojo.com/alltime/world/ (accessed 9/26/2016).

106 petitioned their chamber of commerce: Rubin, Well Met, 62.

107 "Dear Friends": M. R. Bloomberg, Letter to Manic Panic (7/7/2007).

Chapter 4: Wearing Our Fandoms on Our Sleeves

109 Frida Kahlo is giving away margaritas: All descriptions, interviews, and "man on the street" quotes from the Licensing Expo, including the Frida Kahlo booth, are from visit to the Licensing Expo 2014, Las Vegas, NV, by Zoe Fraade-Blanar and Aaron Glazer (June 17–19, 2014)

and visit to the Licensing Expo 2013, Las Vegas, NV, by Zoe Fraade-Blanar and Aaron Glazer (June 18–20, 2013).

109   "Tequila!": http://www.dpsons.com/fridakahlotequila/ (4/25/2016).

110   **Frida Kahlo was a complicated figure:** See Hayden Herrera, *Frida: A Biography of Frida Kahlo* (New York: Harper Perennial, 2002); *The Diary of Frida Kahlo: An Intimate Self-Portrait* (New York: Abrams, 2005).

110   **"She was very much into aromatherapy":** A. Alexander, http://www.drugstorenews.com/article/frida-kahlo-skin-care-line-now -available-natural-skin-care (11/19/2007).

112   **bringing in $543 million gross worldwide:** http://www.boxoffice mojo.com/movies/?id=despicableme.htm (accessed 9/18/2016).

112   **"It feels like everybody has a Spider-Man T-shirt" and all other quotes by Jesse DeStasio:** Telephone interview with Jesse DeStasio by Zoe Fraade-Blanar and Aaron Glazer (10/27/2016).

114   **$2.5 billion:** A. Busch, " 'Minions' Lines Up Biggest Promo Push In Uni's History With McDonald's And More," http://deadline.com/ 2015/07/minions-promotional-push-biggest-in-studio-history-1201 471603/ (7/8/2015).

115   **Coca-Cola, with $1.3 billion:** http://www.retail-merchandiser.com/ reports/retail-reports/1754-the-coca-cola-company (6/2/2014).

116   **"we'll continue to reach more people":** "Gwyneth Paltrow Wows Licensing Expo," *Global License!* (6/19/2013).

116   **top-grossing licensor:** Top 150 Global Licensors. *Global License!*, (5/2015), T3–T47.

117   **"End of the World Pope":** Exhibited at the 2013 Licensing Expo.

118   **postulates a fandom autobiography:** M. Hills, *Fan Cultures* (New York: Routledge, 2002), 82.

119   *Casino Royale:* Ian Fleming, *Casino Royale* (London: Jonathan Cape, 1953).

119   *eats an avocado:* Avocados were a delicacy rarely seen, to the point that two major supermarket chains later waged a P.R. battle over who actually brought them to Britain first. See M. Delgado, "Sainsbury,

M&S … and the great ad-vocado war," http://www.dailymail.co.uk/
femail/food/article-1186938/Avocado-wars-M-S-Sainsburys-battle
-introduced-fruit-first.html (5/25/2009).

119 **"was to the beleaguered nation a salve":** See S. Winder, *The Man
Who Saved Britain: A Personal Journey into the Disturbing World of
James Bond* (New York: Picador, 2007).

120 **"at least we'd retained our sense of style":** W. Cook, "Novel man,"
http://www.newstatesman.com/node/160075 (6/28/2004).

120 **reviving effect Ian Fleming's creation had on British culture:**
Winder, *The Man Who Saved Britain.*

121 *Labyrinth* **and** *Labyrinth* **crossover pieces of fan fiction:** https://
www.fanfiction.net/movie/Labyrinth/ (accessed 9/18/2016).

121 **"British Empire was at its apex":** Cook, "Novel man."

121 **"vast shift from Imperial state to European state":** Winder, *The
Man Who Saved Britain.*

122 **advantages of sports fandom membership:** For a deeper dive into
the topic, see Wann's dozen-plus co-authored articles studying the
psychological impact of being a sports fan.

122 **155 university students in Kentucky:** D. L. Wann and S. Pierce,
"The Relationship between Sport Team Identification and
Social Well-being: Additional Evidence Supporting the Team
Identification–Social Psychological Health Model," *North Ameri-
can Journal of Psychology* (2005): 117–24.

122 **"the extent to which the fan views the team as an extension of
his or herself":** D. Wann, "Understanding the Positive Social
Psychological Benefits of Sport Team Identification: The Team
Identification–Social Psychology Health Model," *Group Dynamics:
Theory, Research and Practice* (2006), vol. 10, no. 4: 272–96.

123 **"feeling of camaraderie":** Ibid.

124 **huge tactical advantages:** H. J. Schau and A. M. Muñiz, "Temper-
ance and Religiosity in a Non-marginal, Non-stigmatized Brand
Community," in Bernard Cova, Robert Kozinets, and Avi Shankar,
Consumer Tribes (New York: Routledge, 2007), 144–62.

124 **transcendence in conformity:** Ibid., 1–26.

125   **"want to be one of the nonconformists":** "Raisins," Episode 14, Season 7, *South Park*, written and directed by Trey Parker (12/10/2013).

125   **two very different motivations:** R. Walker, *Buying In: What We Buy and Who We Are* (New York: Random House, 2010), xv.

125   **unique and special:** Walker, *Buying In*, 22.

125   **experiment with new philosophies:** Hills, *Fan Cultures*, 82.

126   **Chocolate slavery:** See, for example: "Tracing the bitter truth of chocolate and child labour," *BBC Panorama*, http://news.bbc .co.uk/panorama/hi/front_page/newsid_8583000/8583499.stm (3/24/2010); D. McKenzie and B. Swails, "Child slavery and chocolate: All too easy to find," *CNN*, http://thecnnfreedomproject .blogs.cnn.com/2012/01/19/child-slavery-and-chocolate-all-too -easy-to-find/ (1/19/2012); Brian O'Keefe, "Bitter Sweets," *Fortune*, http://fortune.com/big-chocolate-child-labor/ (3/1/2016).

127   **a $100 billion industry:** Marketsandmarkets Press Release, "Global Chocolate Market worth $98.3 billion by 2016," http://www.markets andmarkets.com/PressReleases/global-chocolate-market.asp (n.d.); J. A. Morris, "A taste of the future: the trends that could transform the chocolate industry," https://www.kpmg.com/Global/en/Issues AndInsights/ArticlesPublications/Documents/taste-of-the-future .pdf (6/2014).

127   **Harry Potter Alliance:** For an academic perspective on the HPA as a movement, see H. Jenkins, " 'Cultural acupuncture': Fan activism and the Harry Potter Alliance," *Transformative Works and Cultures* 10 (2012), http://journal.transformativeworks.org/index.php/twc/ article/view/305/259.

127   **"Not in Harry's Name":** Campaign details, unless otherwise cited, are from the Harry Potter Alliance's recounting of the story, at The Harry Potter Alliance, "Not in Harry's Name: A History," *Storify*, https://storify.com/TheHPAlliance/nihn-a-history (2015); and A. Rosenberg, "How 'Harry Potter' fans won a four-year fight against child slavery," *Washington Post*, https://www.washingtonpost.com/ news/act-four/wp/2015/01/13/how-harry-potter-fans-won-a-four -year-fight-against-child-slavery/ (1/13/2015).

127   **Snapewives:** Z. Alderton, " 'Snapewives' and 'Snapeism': A Fiction-Based Religion within the Harry Potter Fandom," http://www.mdpi.com/2077-1444/5/1/219/htm (3/3/2014).

127   **Harry and the Potters:** http://harryandthepotters.com/ (accessed 9/26/2016).

128   **"now it's time to become one":** Granger Leadership Alliance & Harry Potter Alliance, http://grangerleadershipacademy.com/ (n.d., accessed 3/31/2016).

128   **"not specific to one issue":** Telephone interview with Paul DeGeorge by Zoe Fraade-Blanar and Aaron Glazer (12/14/2014).

128   **"Albus Dumbledore asked us to choose":** A. Hoyos, "Harry Potter Chocolate Gets an 'F' in Human Rights," *Andpop*, http://www.andpop.com/2013/02/21/harry-potter-chocolate-gets-an-f-in-human-rights/ (2/21/2013).

129   **"collective voice of the Harry Potter Alliance":** J. Berger, "Letter to Andrew Slack and the Harry Potter Alliance," https://storify.com/TheHPAlliance/nihn-a-history (accessed 12/22/2014).

129   **"WE WON!":** http://www.thehpalliance.org/success_stories (n.d., accessed 9/16/2016).

129   **"Do you like the Smiths":** D. Hill, " 'Heaven Knows I'm Miserable Now,' " A Night of Smiths Music and Speed Dating TOMORROW Night at the Black Rabbit Bar," Dave Hill's Internet Explosion, http://davehillonline.com/blog/2010/02/heaven-knows-im-miserable-now-a-night-of-smiths-music-and-speed-dating-tomorrow-night-at-the-black-rabbit-bar/ (2/2/2010).

129   **forty-nine seconds:** H. Nicholson, http://www.dailymail.co.uk/travel/article-1213316/Alton-Towers-launches-worlds-fastest-speed-dating-event-rollercoaster.html (9/14/2009).

130   **tattooed:** J. Carlson, "Single Smiths Fans of the World Unite . . . in Brooklyn," http://gothamist.com/2009/01/30/smiths_speed_dating.php (1/30/2009).

130   **unapologetically hipster:** A. Martin, "Speed-Dating with Morrissey," *New York*, http://nymag.com/daily/intelligencer/2009/01/smiths_speed_dating_it_seemed.html (1/30/2009).

130   **crossed two rivers:** B. Parker, "Smiths and Singles in Greenpoint Fit Like Hand in Glove," *Gothamist,* http://gothamist
.com/2009/04/16/smiths_and_singles_in_greenpoint_fi.php#
photo-1 (4/19/2009).

130   **series of personality quizzes and questions:** Interview with Christian
Rudder, co-founder of OKCupid, by Zoe Fraade-Blanar (1/14/2015).

130   **Engine42, Circuiter, Unicornlvr, THEDOCTORW, Watcher75,
IDeeJay, Hightek34:** Profile descriptions based on profiles viewed
at www.okcupid.com. All profile names and identifiable details have
been anonymized.

131   **"shorthand to announce":** Interview with Christian Rudder.

131   **just under a minute reviewing a dating profile:** "How to Catch
Your Valentine's Eye: Online Dating Eye-Tracking Study Reveals
That Men Look, Women Read," http://www.businesswire.com/
news/home/20120207006032/en/Tobii-Technology-AB-Catch
-Valentine%E2%80%99s-Eye-Online (1/7/2012).

132   **declare and maintain position within a group:** M. Maffesoli, "The
linking value of subcultural capital: constructing the Stockholm
Brat enclave," in Cova, Kozinets, and Shankar, *Consumer Tribes*;
and Nancarrow and Nancarrow, "Hunting for cool tribes," in Cova,
Kozinets, and Shankar, *Consumer Tribes*, 129–42.

132   **pick the products:** Maffesoli, "The linking value of subcultural capital," 95.

133   **"lively, playful disposition":** J. Austen, *Pride and Prejudice* (New
York: Penguin Classics, 2003).

133   **"obsessive dollhouse pleasure":** D. Carr, "24-Hour Newspaper
People," *New York Times* (1/15/2007).

134   **"the more specific you are, the better off you'll be":** Interview with
Christian Rudder.

134   **"make sure that it's your foot though":** Ibid.

134   **a World Champion player:** A. Bereznak, http://gizmodo.com/
5833787/my-brief-okcupid-affair-with-a-world-champion-magic-the
-gathering-player (8/29/2011).

135   **"There's a code that you're relaying":** Telephone interview

with Virginia Roberts by Zoe Fraade-Blanar and Aaron Glazer (1/15/2015). Roberts's website is at theheartographer.com.

136   **"There's always money in the banana stand"**: "Top Banana," *Arrested Development* (aired 11/9/2003).

136   **"your actual words are worth . . . almost nothing"**: C. Rudder, http://blog.okcupid.com/index.php/we-experiment-on-human -beings/ (7/28/2014).

136   **Cosmic-space:** Profile descriptions based on profiles at www.okcupid .com.

Chapter 5: Membership and Status in the Happiest Place on Earth

139   **Down the Rabbit-Hole:** All quotes and on-the-ground reporting, unless otherwise cited, are from interviews with members of the White Rabbits, the Sons of Anakin, and Mickey's Empire during a visit to Disneyland and Disney's California Adventure by Zoe Fraade-Blanar (9/18–20/2015). Some interviews have been anon-ymized or represented by the interviewee's first name or initial at the interviewees' request.

140   **Disney-themed social clubs:** For a good overview of Disneyland Social Clubs, see C. Lam, "The Very Merry Un-Gangs of Disney-land," *OC Weekly*, http://www.ocweekly.com/2014-02-27/news/ disneyland-california-adventure-social-clubs/ (2/27/2014); and C. Van Meter, "The Punks of Disneyland," http://www.vice.com/ en_ca/read/the-punks-of-the-magic-kingdom (3/11/2014).

140   **"plainclothes undercover Disney FBI/CIA dude"**: Phone inter-view with Jake Fite by Zoe Fraade-Blanar (7/28/2015).

141   **"Everything is managed"**: Ibid.

142   **"Dapper Day"**: L. Lecaro, http://www.laweekly.com/arts/a-guide -to-disneylands-unofficial-dress-up-days-5402663 (2/27/2015).

143   **more than three hundred:** http://www.scsofdisney.com/unofficial -list-of-official-social-clubs.html (n.d., accessed 9/26/2016).

143   **pins give off a complicated set of signals:** Telephone interview with Elena Salcedo of Mickey's Empire by Zoe Fraade-Blanar and Aaron Glazer (8/3/2015).

144 **part of the Sons of Anakins' outfit:** *The Cut,* http://sonsofanakinsc .com/?page_id=117 (n.d.).

145 **"They would always talk about Disney":** Telephone interview with Elena Salcedo.

145 **"'seeing if I could hang out'":** Ibid.

146 **"ride the Pirates of the Caribbean":** Ibid.

146 **Club 33:** Description from visit to Disneyland's Club 33 by Zoe Fraade-Blanar (9/19/2015).

147 **membership includes A-listers:** P. Forbes, "Inside Club 33, Disneyland's $10,000 Dining Club," http://www.eater.com/2013/1/28/ 6489395/inside-club-33-disneylands-10000-per-year-dining-club (1/28/2013).

147 **life-timer was recently banned:** J. Pimentel, "After his Club 33 membership is revoked, Lake Forest man sues Disney," *Orange County Register,* http://www.ocregister.com/articles/ club-668224-membership-disney.html (6/23/2015).

147 **"when we first started coming":** Telephone interview with Jake and Melissa (Missie) Fite by Zoe Fraade-Blanar (10/26/2016).

148 **"little intimidated by us":** Ibid.

148 **"feels kind of smarmy":** Interview with Trent Vanegas by Zoe Fraade-Blanar (9/18–20/2015).

149 **"punishment consists of probation":** Email with Trent Vanegas by Zoe Fraade-Blanar (10/5/2015).

149 **"never been instances":** Telephone interview with Trent Vanegas by Zoe Fraade-Blanar (8/4/2015).

150 **"If we have a hierarchy":** Telephone interview with Jake Fite by Zoe Fraade-Blanar (7/28/2015).

150 **"It's hard to find friends":** Telephone interview with Aaron W. by Zoe Fraade-Blanar and Aaron Glazer (8/28/2015).

152 **Someone hangs out with a group of people:** D. Park, S. Deshpande, B. Cova, and S. Pace, "Seeking community through battle: understanding the meaning of consumption processes for warhammer gamers' communities across borders," in Bernard Cova, Robert Kozinets, and Avi Shankar, *Consumer Tribes* (New York: Routledge, 2007), 212–23.

153   **an instant connection:** M. Hills, *Fan Cultures* (New York: Rout-
        ledge, 2002), 6–7.

153   **incubation period:** R. Henry and M. Caldwell, "Imprinting, incu-
        bation and intensification: factors contributing to fan club forma-
        tion and continuance," in Cova, Kozinets, and Shankar, *Consumer
        Tribes*, 165–73, 168.

154   **"tales of the miraculous":** H. J. Schau and A. M. Muñiz, "Temper-
        ance and Religiosity in a Non-marginal, Non-stigmatized Brand
        Community," in Cova, Kozinets, and Shankar, *Consumer Tribes*,
        144–62.

154   **grownup rules are suspended:** Cova, Kozinets, and Shankar,
        "Tribes, Inc: The New World of Tribalism," in Cova, Kozinets, and
        Shankar, *Consumer Tribes*, 1–26.

155   **"long time to finally grow":** Telephone interview with Jake Fite.

156   **self-sufficiency will take a while:** C. Shirky, *Cognitive Surplus: Cre-
        ativity and Generosity in a Connected Age* (New York: Penguin Press,
        2010), 163.

156   **diverse ways to participate:** Shirky, *Cognitive Surplus*, 200.

157   **too much for the young leadership:** As Clay Shirky argues: "Orga-
        nizing groups into an effective whole is so brutally difficult that, past
        a certain scale, it requires professional management," in Shirky, *Cog-
        nitive Surplus*, 83.

157   **"all came out of the same store":** Telephone interview with Jake
        Fite.

158   **cement the interpersonal relationships:** M. Maffesoli, "The link-
        ing value of subcultural capital," in Cova, Kozinets, and Shankar,
        Consumer Tribes.

158   **on display:** Maffesoli, "Tribal Aesthetic," in Cova, Kozinets, and
        Shankar, *Consumer Tribes*, 27–34.

158   **more respect they can gain:** Maffesoli, "The linking value of sub-
        cultural capital," 96.

158   **"Disneybounding":** D. Bevil, "Outfits show boundless love of
        Disney—Fans' styles are homage to characters without being out-
        right costume," *Orlando Sentinel* (5/19/2015), A1.

158 **Leslie Kay:** http://disneybound.co/LeslieKay (n.d., accessed 9/26/2016).

159 **"New Kind of Disney Cosplay":** B. Tuttle, "New Kind of Disney Cosplay Slightly Less Embarrassing Than Original," http://time.com/money/3888425/disneybounding-trend/ (5/19/2015).

159 **creating something personal is more appealing:** Shirky, *Cognitive Surplus,* 78.

160 **branched out into licensing Disneybound-style clothing:** L. Liddane, "Can't dress up at Disneyland? Streetwear meets Disney in 'Disneybound' style," *Orange County Register,* http:/www.ocregister.com/articles/disneybound-633983-disney-character.html (9/6/2014).

160 **building social capital:** R. Kozinets, "Inno-tribes: Star Trek as Wikimedia," in Cova, Kozinets, and Shankar, *Consumer Tribes,* 206–8.

160 **subtle request for others to try it:** Ibid., 19.

161 **do for love:** Shirky, *Cognitive Surplus,* 72.

161 **Acknowledgment and flattery:** Ibid., 81

162 **" 'do whatever they want' ":** Telephone interview with Jake Fite.

162 **become minor fan objects in their own right:** C. Otnes, and P. Maclaran, "The consumption of cultural heritage among a British Royal Family brand tribe," in Cova, Kozinets, and Shankar, *Consumer Tribes,* 51–66.

162 **vital to group cohesion:** Shirky, *Cognitive Surplus,* 198.

162 **adhere to a careful set of social norms:** Schau and Muñiz, "Temperance and Religiosity in a Non-marginal, Non-stigmatized Brand Community," 144–62.

163 **the tiniest dissimilarity:** Freud called this the narcissism of small differences. S. Freud and J. Strachey, *Civilization and Its Discontents* (1930; New York: W. W. Norton, 2010).

163 **keeping defectors in line is fun:** Shirky, *Cognitive Surplus,* 108

164 **"Social systems have two modes":** Ibid., 197.

164 **cast members sometimes complain:** See D. Nasserian, "Insignt [*sic*] Into Disney Social Clubs: The Main Street Elite," http://www.disneygeekery.com/2013/10/04/insignt-disney-social-clubs-main-street-elite/ (10/4/2013); C. Van Meter, "The Punks of Disney-

land," http://www.vice.com/en_ca/read/the-punks-of-the-magic
-kingdom (3/11/2014); and P. C. Vasquez, http://www.ozy.com/fast
-forward/gangs-of-disneyland/6646 (3/8/2014).

166 **"kind of ridiculous"**: Interview with Jake Fite by Zoe Fraade
-Blanar (9/20/2015).

Chapter 6: Fans, What Are They Good For?

167 **He Who Controls:** All email quotes from J. Bane, et al., *Your Emails
Are Bad and You Should Feel Bad* (Chicago: Cards Against Humanity, 2014).

168 **"10 Days or Whatever of Kwanzaa":** See https://www.holidaybullshit
.com/ (9/19/2016); R. Katz, https://www.puregeekery.net/2014/12/
29/10-days-whatever-kwanzaa-day-whatever/ (12/29/2014).

168 **"a bunch of stickers":** Day 2, https://www.holidaybullshit.com/
(accessed 9/19/2016).

169 **Goodreads:** http://www.goodreads.com/book/show/24488744
-your-emails-are-bad-and-you-should-feel-bad (accessed 3/26/2016).

169 **"You don't want to watch this episode of TableTop":** Geek and
Sundry, Cards Against Humanity: Aisha Tyler, Laina Morris, & Ali
Spagnola Join Wil on TableTop S03E10, https://www.youtube.com/
watch?v=QCEqUn7If44 (3/19/2015).

170 **"remember that they're a human being":** Telephone interview with
Jenn Bane, community manager for Cards Against Humanity, by
Zoe Fraade-Blanar and Aaron Glazer (1/10/2015).

170 **"generously give out refunds":** Ibid.

170 **more than 33,000 reviews:** https://www.amazon.com/Cards-Against
-Humanity-LLC-CAHUS/dp/B004S8F7QM (accessed 9/26/2016).

170 **"Why won't Amazon ship this to Canada?":** Amazon, retrieved from
Cards Against Humanity, http://www.amazon.com/wont-Amazon
-ship-this-Canada/forum/Fx209LQY89OFTF8/Tx1A4YFQT
GH3GW9/1/ref=cm_cd_al_psf_al_pg1?_encoding=UTF8&asin=
B004S8F7QM (10/22/2013).

171 **"We thought people would be angry about it":** Telephone interview
with Max Temkin by Zoe Fraade-Blanar and Aaron Glazer (2/5/2015).

171   **"on the inside of an inside joke":** Ibid.

172   **Cards Against Humanity is free:** https://cardsagainsthumanity
      .com (accessed 9/20/2016).

172   **"that enrages fans":** Telephone interview with Max Temkin.

172   **Eight Sensible Gifts:** https://www.eightsensiblegifts.com (accessed
      9/20/2016); J. Cook, http://mrsjennifercook.com/2015/12/24/8
      -sensible-gifts-cards-against-humanity/ (12/24/2015).

173   **party as hard and publicly:** L. Widdicombe, "Teen Titan: The
      man who made Justin Bieber," http://www.newyorker.com/maga
      zine/2012/09/03/teen-titan (9/3/2012).

173   **verbally abuse patrons:** K. Pang, http://www.chicagotribune
      .com/dining/ct-the-wiener-circle-chicago-obscenity-laced-hot-dog
      -stand-sold-20150918-story.html (9/18/2015).

173   **unusual level of misogyny:** J. Gordon and A. Phillips, "Diplo
      Criticized for Stealing GIF, Accused of Misogyny, Gets in Twit-
      ter Fight With Portishead's Geoff Barrow," http://pitchfork.com/
      news/58441-diplo-criticized-for-stealing-gif-accused-of-misogyny
      -gets-in-twitter-fight-with-portisheads-geoff-barrow/ (2/12/2015); C.
      Coplan, http://consequenceofsound.net/2015/02/diplo-stole-some
      ones-gif-artwork-responds-with-misogynistic-insults/ (2/12/2015).

173   **tolerate a monopoly as long as it's benevolent:** P. Temi and L.
      Galambos, *The Fall of the Bell System: A Study in Prices and Politics*
      (Cambridge: Cambridge University Press, 1989).

174   **"Of course it's personal":** Billboard, https://twitter.com/Steve
      Stoute/status/194829317048512512/photo/1. (4/24/2012).

174   **#HELLOBROOKLYN:** For more on the #HELLOBROOKLYN
      campaign see K. Ozkan, "Stoute's Plan to Market the Nets? Kissing
      Up to Brooklyn," http://adage.com/article/news/stoute-s-plan
      -market-nets-kissing-brooklyn/230226/ (10/6/2011); http://www
      .translationllc.com/work/brooklyn-nets/ (n.d.); A. DeSantis,
      "All Black Everything: A Brooklyn Nets Style Guide," http://www
      .nytimes.com/interactive/2012/09/27/style/brooklyn-nets-logo
      .html?_r=0 (9/27/2012).

174   **packed a rally:** Calder, R. http://nypost.com/2012/07/14/2000

-screaming-fans-pack-plaza-outside-bklyn-borough-hall-for-nets/
(7/14/2012).

175 **"this is not my team"**: Interview with Marcus Collins, Executive
Director, Social Engagement, Translation LLC, by Zoe Fraade-
Blanar and Aaron Glazer (2/23/2015).

175 **"First Home Game Since 1957"**: Billboard, T. Bontemps, http://
nypost.com/2012/04/25/nets-brooklyn-rollout-continues-with-bill
boards/ (4/25/2012).

175 **"building a connection between Brooklynites and the players"**:
M. Mazzeo, http://espn.go.com/new-york/nba/story/_/id/8192332/
brooklyn-nets-introducing-borough-team-core-four (7/23/2012).

175 **"Our goal is to own Brooklyn"**: M. Mazzeo, http://espn.go.com/
new-york/nba/story/_/id/8192332/brooklyn-nets-introducing
-borough-team-core-four (7/23/2012).

175 **"We're a friend to the scrappy"**: http://newyork.cbslocal.com/2012/
05/01/brooklyn-nets-neighborhood-centric-video-applauds-the
-loyal-and-scrappy/ (5/1/2012).

175 **"ritual enemy"**: V. Theodoropoulou, "The Anti-Fan within the
Fan: Awe and Envy in Sport Fandom," in Bernard Cova, Robert
Kozinets, and Avi Shankar, *Consumer Tribes* (New York: Routledge,
2007), 316–327.

176 **Mikhail Prokohorov**: http://www.bloomberg.com/news/articles/
2015-12-22/mikhail-prokhorov-completes-acquisition-of-nets
-barclays-center (12/22/2015).

176 **up 23 percent**: http://www.netsdaily.com/2013/4/29/4281532/
brooklyn-nets-attendance-up-23-1-leads-nba-in-one-season-gain
(4/29/2013).

176 **"we're soon to be diehard fans"**: C. Dell and J. Moffie, "Knicks
and Nets Rivalry Begins at Barclays," http://fort-greene.thelocal
.nytimes.com/2012/11/27/knicks-and-nets-rivalry-begins-at
-barclays/ (11/27/2012).

177 **different audience was excited**: E. Piepenburg, " 'Magic Mike' Is
Big Draw for Gay Men," http://www.nytimes.com/2012/07/05/
movies/magic-mike-with-channing-tatum-draws-gay-men.html

(7/4/2012); P. McClintock, "Moms and Gays Boost 'Magic Mike's' Box Office Chances in a Big Way," http://www.hollywoodreporter.com/news/magic-mike-stripper-channing-tatum-box-office-341507 (6/26/2012).

177   **status symbol for sports stars, hip-hop icons:** J. L. Roberts, "The Rap of Luxury," http://www.newsweek.com/rap-luxury-144731 (9/1/2002).

177   **most commonly stolen vehicle:** http://money.cnn.com/2011/08/25/autos/most_stolen_cars/ (8/25/2011).

178   **corn and wet cardboard:** https://www.beeradvocate.com/beer/profile/447/1331/?ba=itsscience (4/7/2014).

178   **an unexpected rival, Narragansett:** See T. Donnelly, "PBR is dead," *New York Post*, http://nypost.com/2015/07/16/what-cheap-beer-lovers-are-now-guzzling-instead-of-pbr/ (7/16/2015); R. Greenfield, http://www.bloomberg.com/news/articles/2015-06-12/how-narragansett-became-cool-again (6/12/2015).

179   **nearly 80,000 barrels:** Greenfield, http://www.bloomberg.com/news/articles/2015-06-12/how-narragansett-became-cool-again.

179   **fan-created meanings don't need to be based in reality:** Bernard Cova, Robert Kozinets, and Avi Shankar, "Tribes, Inc: The New World of Tribalism," in Cova, Kozinets, and Shankar, *Consumer Tribes*, 1–26.

179   **owned by a corporate partnership:** http://www.tsgconsumer.com/partner-companies/detail.php?id=35 (9/20/2016).

180   **Kickstarter houses its headquarters:** Descriptions of Kickstarter headquarters from interview with Luke Crane and visit to Kickstarter headquarters by Zoe Fraade-Blanar (6/17/2015).

181   **Max Temkin and his Cards Against Humanity colleagues approached Kickstarter:** https://www.kickstarter.com/blog/case-study-cards-against-humanity (7/26/2012).

182   **"Nobody had ever heard of us":** Ibid.

182   **"Dear horrible friends":** https://www.kickstarter.com/projects/1200751084/cards-against-humanity/posts/57993 (3/1/2011).

183   **"You don't have to have three million fans"** . . . **"We're always,**

always telling creators: make it a story": Telephone interview with Luke Crane by Zoe Fraade-Blanar and Aaron Glazer (1/28/2015).

186 **Shadowrun Returns:** Harebrained Schemes LLC., https://www .kickstarter.com/projects/webeharebrained/shadowrun-returns/ (4/4/2012).

186 **"whether I should pull the trigger"** . . . **"total high-school-nerd reunion":** Telephone interview with Eric Mersmann by Zoe Fraade-Blanar and Aaron Glazer (2/18/2015).

187 **"do a quick calculation in their head":** Telephone interview with Luke Crane.

187 **Amanda Palmer raised a huge amount of money:** See D. Wakin, "Rockers Playing for Beer: Fair Play?" *New York Times*, http://arts beat.blogs.nytimes.com/2012/09/12/rockers-playing-for-beer-fair -play/ (9/12/2012); M. Hogan, http://www.spin.com/2012/09/ amanda-palmer-steve-albini-idiot-apology-volunteers/ (9/14/2012); M. Hogan, http://www.spin.com/2012/09/steve-albini-amanda -palmer-crowdsourcing-rant/ (9/13/2012).

187 **moved her crowdfunding efforts:** https://www.patreon.com/aman dapalmer (accessed 9/21/2016).

188 **"fans shouting down":** Telephone interview with Luke Crane.

188 **Kickstarter to finance his comedy movie:** https://www.kickstarter .com/projects/1869987317/wish-i-was-here-1. (updated 7/11/14).

188 **huge fan backlash:** See B. Child, "Zach Braff Kickstarter contro-versy deepens after financier bolsters budge," *The Guardian*, https:// www.theguardian.com/film/2013/may/16/zach-braff-kickstarter -controversy-deepens (5/16/2013); M. Fernandez, "Zach Braff raises money—and ire—with Kickstarter campaign for new film," *NBC News,* http://www.nbcnews.com/pop-culture/pop-culture -news/zach-braff-raises-money-ire-kickstarter-campaign-new-film -f6C10026213 (5/22/2013); L. Marks, "Is it OK for multimillionaires like Zach Braff to panhandle for money on Kickstarter?" *The Guard-ian*, https://www.theguardian.com/film/filmblog/2013/apr/26/ zack-braff-panhandle-money-kickstarter (4/26/2013).

188 **many speculated that his net worth:** M. Fleischer, "Zach Braff on

needing Kickstarter: 'I don't have Oprah Winfrey money,'" *Los Angeles Times*, http://articles.latimes.com/2013/apr/25/entertainment/la-et-ct-zach-braff-oprah-winfrey-money-kickstarter-20130425 (4/25/2013).

189 **"adversarial relationship with the 'hard core' fans":** Telephone interview with Max Temkin.

189 **new flavor of potato chip:** S. P. Wood, http://www.adweek.com/prnewser/why-lays-wants-to-quit-social-media-and-hates-america/85826 (2/7/2014).

190 **seven different Guinness World Records:** K. Lynch, http://www.guinnessworldrecords.com/news/2013/10/confirmed-grand-theft-auto-breaks-six-sales-world-records-51900 (10/8/2013).

191 **"appreciated the creative efforts of the PC modding community":** http://www.rockstargames.com/newswire/article/52429/asked-answered-the-rockstar-editor-gta-online-updates (5/7/2015).

191 **fan-created mods make GTA more valuable:** See J. Balakar, http://www.cnet.com/news/the-bizarre-and-often-hilarious-world-of-grand-theft-auto-v-mods/ (5/23/2015); C. Livingston, http://www.pcgamer.com/the-best-gta-5-mods/ (9/16/2015).

191 **"Paid Skyrim Mod Turns Into":** B. Ashcraft, http://kotaku.com/paid-skyrim-mod-turns-into-a-clusterfuck-1699913114 (4/24/2015).

191 **Mods more easily . . . for a fee:** E. Makuch, http://www.gamespot.com/articles/you-can-now-sell-skyrim-mods-on-steam/1100-642 6844/ (4/23/2015).

191 **filled with anti-Valve vitriol:** See, for example, https://www.reddit.com/r/skyrimmods/comments/33m6a9/steam_to_start_charge_money_for_certain_mods/ (4/23/2015).

192 **been shut down:** A. Kroll, "Removing Payment Feature from Skyrim Workshop," https://steamcommunity.com/games/SteamWorkshop/announcements/detail/208632365253244218 (4/27/2015).

192 **in the monetization:** B. Reed, "Bethesda's experiment with paid Skyrim mods has been an epic disaster – is there any way to fix it?" *BGR*, http://bgr.com/2015/04/27/bethesda-valve-skyrim-paid-mods/ (4/27/2015).

192 **"Bethesda should have done":** https://www.reddit.com/r/skyrim

mods/comments/33m6a9/steam_to_start_charge_money_for_
certain_mods/cqmllcq (4/23/2015).

Chapter 7: Authenticity

195   **Carrying On Like Mortal Enemies:** The details of the Iron Sheik
and Hacksaw Jim Duggan's arrest in New Jersey remain disputed.
After so many years and different motivations, versions of the incident have diverged widely. We've reconstructed the events based on
details from the following sources: H. J. Duggan and S. E. Williams,
Hacksaw: The Jim Duggan Story (Chicago: Triumph Books, 2012);
M. Huguenin, "Miscellaneous: Wrestlers Arrested," *Orlando
Sentinel*, http://articles.orlandosentinel.com/1987-05-28/
sports/0130230005_1_duggan-sumo-iron-sheik (5/28/1987);
Jash! "Iron Sheik: Very Animated People," https://www.you
tube.com/watch?v=QeXnLeMZ8S4 (3/27/2013); B. Hart, *Hitman: My Real Life in the Cartoon World of Wrestling* (New York:
Grand Central Publishing, 2008); and W. Keller, "EXCLUSIVE:
Former semi-main event WWE wrestler says if not for drug arrest,
he thinks he would have been World Champion, talks of backstage
dispute with Austin," http://pwtorch.com/artman2/publish/spot
lightarticleboxcenter/article_61210.shtml (5/8/2012).

195   **afternoon of May 26:** This and the rest of the details in the paragraph are from Duggan and Williams, *Hacksaw*.

195   **"Hands on the hood":** Quote and details in this paragraph from
Duggan and Williams, *Hacksaw*, 102.

195   **in separate cars:** Ibid.

196   **Iron Sheik had pressured him:** Ibid.

196   **Not so:** This and remaining details from this paragraph are from
Jash!, "Iron Sheik: Very Animated People," https://www.youtube
.com/watch?v=QeXnLeMZ8S4 (3/27/2013); jashnetwork, "The
Iron Sheik sat down with Buh to talk about wrestling, drugs and
women," http://jashnetwork.tumblr.com/post/46476921987/the
-iron-sheik-sat-down-with-buh-to-talk-about (3/27/2013).

197   **attendance and revenue records:** http://www.wwe.com/videos/

wrestlemania-iii-breaks-wwe-s-all-time-attendance-record-wrestle
mania-iii (accessed 9/26/2016).

197 **"Honey, we got busted"** ... **"what have you** *done* **to us?":** Duggan
and Williams, *Hacksaw,* 103–4.

198 **"won't be hitting each other":** M. Sneed, "Michael Sneed," *Chicago
Sun-Times* (7/1/1987).

198 **"bigger than a six-pack and a blow job":** Duggan and Williams,
Hacksaw, 108.

198 **shares its roots with early traveling-circus sideshows:** L. McBride
and S. Bird, "From Smart Fan to Backyard Wrestler," in Jonathan
Gray, Cornel Sandvoss, , and C. Lee Harrington, *Fandom: Identities and Communities in a Mediated World* (New York: NYU Press,
2007), 165–76.

199 **"Yeah, but that's not the point":** Telephone interview with Lawrence
McBride by Zoe Fraade-Blanar and Aaron Glazer (12/16/2014).

199 **Pretending that the action in the wrestling ring:** L. McBride and
S. Bird, "From Smart Fan to Backyard Wrestler," in Gray, Sandvoss,
and Harrington, *Fandom,* 165–76.

200 **"They want the good guy to win":** Telephone interview with Lawrence McBride.

200 **"has fun saying that":** Ibid.

200 **broke character to go comfort:** B. Owings and S. Rahmanzadeh,
"WWE Star Triple H Breaks Character to Console Young Fan,"
http://abcnews.go.com/Entertainment/wwe-star-triple-breaks
-character-console-young-fan/story?id=28398608 (1/22/2015).

200 **Smart Fans:** See McBride and Bird, "From Smart Fan to Backyard
Wrestler," 165–76.

200 **"his gimmick was being an evil dentist":** Telephone interview with
Lawrence McBride.

201 **"Spanish Announcers Table":** R. Dilbert, http://bleacherreport
.com/articles/1242501-tribute-to-the-wwe-spanish-announce-table
(7/10/2012); http://tvtropes.org/pmwiki/pmwiki.php/Main/
SpanishAnnouncersTable (9/22/2016).

201 **important outlet for storytelling and emotional release:** H. Jenkins,

"'Never Trust a Snake': WWF Wrestling as Masculine Melodrama," in A. Baker and T. Boyd, *Out of Bounds: Sports, Media and the Politics of Identity* (Bloomington: Indiana University Press, 1997), 48–80.

201 **"masculine melodrama":** Ibid., 50.

201 **Bar Nine isn't quite full:** All description and quotes that follow are from visit to Bar Nine, New York City, for a Wrestlemania 32 viewing party, by Zoe Fraade-Blanar and Aaron Glazer (4/3/2016).

202 **"Shane, what are you doing?":** *Wrestlemania 32*, pay-per-view Broadcast (4/3/2016).

202 **"You can't do this!":** Ibid.

202 **"Dammit, Shane":** Ibid.

203 **"protect my opponent":** Hart, *Hitman*.

203 **"love for the guys who are willing to injure themselves":** Interview with Lawrence McBride.

205 **being stalked by the spirit of Count Dracula:** L. Siegel, *City of Dreadful Night: A Tale of Horror and the Macabre in India* (Chicago: University of Chicago Press, 1995).

205 **As long as they are getting something important out of the relationship:** Bernard Cova, Robert Kozinets, and Avi Shankar, "Tribes, Inc: The New World of Tribalism," in Cova, Kozinets, and Shankar, *Consumer Tribes* (New York: Routledge, 2007), 1–26.

205 **Chris and Cliff, Together at Last:** Background information, unless otherwise cited, from interview with Marcus Collins, Executive Director, Social Engagement, Translation LLC, by Zoe Fraade-Blanar and Aaron Glazer (2/23/2015).

205 **two long-lost twin brothers:** K. Shivley, *How State Farm and Social Media Breathed Life Into Cliff Paul,* http://simplymeasured.com/blog/how-state-farm-and-social-media-breathed-life-into-cliff-paul/ (7/29/2014); Interview with Marcus Collins.

205 **"When assisting is in your blood":** State Farm Insurance, State Farm Commercial Born to Assist Cliff Paul, https://www.youtube.com/watch?v=tqBj3P13ABA (12/27/2012).

205 **Fans tweeted:** Shivley, *How State Farm and Social Media Breathed Life Into Cliff Paul.*

206 **Sports website and public forum:** See "Ok so is Cliff Paul a real person?" https://answers.yahoo.com/question/index?qid=201302191804 32AAPcJac (2/19/2013); "Is Cliff Paul real?" http://www.insidehoops .com/forum/showthread.php?t=294891 (3/31/2013).

206 **"year of #twinsanity":** Studio@Gawker, "Chris Paul's Possibly Real Secret Twin Brother, Cliff, Is Now On Twitter (SPONSORED CONTENT)," http://deadspin.com/chris-paul-s-possibly-real-secret -twin-brother-cliff-5974174 (1/15/2013).

206 **Cliff himself appeared:** B. Fowler, http://www.eonline.com/news/ 511528/5-things-we-learned-from-nba-all-star-saturday (2/16/2014).

206 **appeared together teaching their sons:** T. Nudd, "How Chris Paul Became the NBA's Most Gifted Endorser(s)," http://www.adweek .com/news/advertising-branding/how-chris-and-cliff-paul-became -nbas-most-gifted-endorsers-157343 (4/29/2014).

206 **"have the last name 'Paul'?":** B. Simmons, *The B.S. Report with Bill Simmons,* http://espn.go.com/espnradio/play?id=10629752 (3/18/2014).

206 **"wouldn't Cliff's birth mother":** D. Guerrero, "What The Hell Is Going On In The State Farm Cliff Paul Commercials?" http://up roxx.com/tv/state-farm-cliff-paul-commercials/ (5/6/2015).

206 **brothers could play one-on-one:** GamingWithOva, "PS4 NBA 2K14 - *How To Get Cliff Paul,*" https://www.youtube.com/watch?v=IkrU sKZVqTA (11/18/2013).

207 **whether or not Cliff Paul was real:** Interview with Marcus Collins.

207 **No one ever hid the fact:** A. A. Newman, "A Basketball Star and His 'Twin' Sell Insurance," *New York Times* (12/18/2012), B3, http:// www.nytimes.com/2012/12/19/business/media/chris-paul-to-star -in-state-farm-insurance-ads.html?_r=0.

207 **purpose of play:** M. Hills, *Fan Cultures* (New York: Routledge, 2002), 111.

207 **frees both objects from their "adult status":** Cova, Kozinets, and Shankar, "Tribes, Inc.", 1–26.

207 **an unexpected change in a familiar pattern:** T. Luna and L. Renninger, *Surprise: Embrace the Unpredictable and Engineer the Unexpected* (New York: Tarcher/Perigee, 2015).

207 **spike in dopamine:** T. Hillin, "Science explains why surprise brings

us pleasure," http://fusion.net/story/112615/why-surprise-is-so-good-for-your-brain-and-body/ (4/1/2015); Luna and Renninger, *Surprise*.

208 **fans mounted an intense lobbying campaign:** M. Woerner, http://io9.gizmodo.com/5875356/fan-campaigns-throughout-history-that-saved-scifi-and-fantasy-tv-shows (1/12/12).

209 **sold out within twenty-four hours:** "'Firefly' to become movie," http://www.cnn.com/2003/SHOWBIZ/Movies/09/04/film.firefly.reut/ (9/4/2003).

209 **$39 million gross:** http://www.boxofficemojo.com/movies/?id=serenity.htm (1/18/2016).

209 **"Martyrdom has only enhanced":** Entertainment Weekly Staff, http://www.ew.com/gallery/26-best-cult-tv-shows-ever/568019_12-firefly (3/17/2014).

209 **silly hand-knitted hat:** "The Message," *Firefly*. TV show (7/15/2003).

209 **"people can make it themselves":** L. Grady, http://www.bigpicturebigsound.com/Expanded-Coverage-of-the-Firefly-Comic-Con-Panel.shtml (7/22/2012).

210 **Fox licensed the hat design:** E. Hall, https://www.buzzfeed.com/ellievhall/firefly-hat-triggers-corporate-crackdown (4/10/2013); M. Woerner, http://io9.gizmodo.com/fox-bans-the-sale-of-unlicensed-jayne-hats-from-firefly-471820413 (4/9/2013).

210 **nicer and, for the most part, less expensive:** "Jayne's Hat," *ThinkGeek*, https://www.thinkgeek.com/product/f108/ (9/22/2016).

210 **demanded the removal of their products:** J. Pantozzi, "UPDATED: Are You A Firefly Fan Who Makes Jayne Hats? Watch Out, Fox Is Coming For You," http://www.themarysue.com/jayne-hats-fox/ (4/9/2013).

210 **"Fox Is Coming For You":** Ibid.

210 **"proud of yourselves," . . . "personally think you suck," . . . "stink to high heaven":** E. Hall, https://www.buzzfeed.com/ellievhall/firefly-hat-triggers-corporate-crackdown (4/10/2013).

211 **"All Your 'Jayne' Hats Are Belong To Us!":** Ibid.

211 **"See Spot Run With Not Jane Hat":** Ibid.

211 **"ThinkGeek had nothing to do with the C&D notices":** ThinkGeek, "Nice Hat, Jayne," http://www.thinkgeek.com/blog/2013/04/nice-hat-jayne.html (4/9/2013).

211   **"Browncoats, we hear your concerns":** ThinkGeek, "Jayne Hat Proceeds to Can't Stop the Serenity," http://www.thinkgeek.com/blog/2013/04/jayne-hat-proceeds-to-cant-sto.html (4/10/2013).

212   **as long as it serves their needs:** Cova, Kozinets, and Shankar, "Tribes, Inc.," 1–26.

212   **concepts the object represents:** Ibid.

214   **brand badly in need of popular support:** McDonald's has faced pressure both on the financial side of its business as well as in how customers view the brand. See, for example, B. Kowitt, "Fallen Archers: Can McDonald's get its mojo back?" *Fortune*, http://fortune.com/2014/11/12/can-mcdonalds-get-its-mojo-back/ (11/12/14); T. DiChristopher, "McDonald's outlook is negative, but wage hike helps: Analyst," *CNBC*, http://www.cnbc.com/2015/04/02/mcdonalds-outlook-is-negative-but-wage-hike-helps-analyst.html (4/2/2015); T. Hsu, "Five Guys voted favorite burger chain, McDonald's near bottom," *Los Angeles Times*, http://www.latimes.com/business/la-fi-mo-five-guys-burger-mcdonalds-20120918-story.html (9/19/2012).

215   **seemed to want to share unhappy McDonald's stories:** K. Hill, "#McDStories: When A Hashtag Becomes a Bashtag," http://www.forbes.com/sites/kashmirhill/2012/01/24/mcdstories-when-a-hashtag-becomes-a-bashtag/ (1/24/12).

215   **"#McDStories I could tell would raise your hair":** https://twitter.com/alexroth3/status/161873590881497088 (1/24/2012).

215   **"could smell Type 2 diabetes":** https://twitter.com/SkipSullivan/status/159734503508688897 (1/18/2012).

215   **"most sensitive B.S. meter":** C. Tice, http://www.forbes.com/sites/caroltice/2014/10/30/why-ronald-mcdonald-failed-on-twitter-branding-lessons/#2715e4857a0b6bbfb12d29ee (10/30/2014).

215   **taking pictures of the NYPD:** A. Beaujon, http://www.poynter.org/2012/new-york-times-photographer-arrested-while-covering-arrest/184074/ (8/6/2013).

216   **motivations of its fans:** C. Shirky, *Cognitive Surplus: Creativity and Generoisty in a Connected Age* (New York: Penguin Press, 2010), 95.

216   **Sarita Ekya:** Information on S'MAC and Ekya quotes from tele-

phone interview with Sarita Ekya by Zoe Fraade-Blanar and Aaron Glazer (1/14/2015).

217 **Spencer Rubin:** Information on Melt Shop and Rubin quotes from telephone interview with Spencer Rubin by Zoe Fraade-Blanar and Aaron Glazer (1/13/2015).

217 **relive a pleasurable memory:** Hills, *Fan Cultures*, 42.

218 **"providing entertainment to spectators":** P. Kerr, http://www .nytimes.com/1989/02/10/nyregion/now-it-can-be-told-those-pro -wrestlers-are-just-having-fun.html (2/10/1989).

219 **freed from many of the regulations:** Ibid.; R. Hoy-Browne, http:// www.independent.co.uk/sport/general/wwe-mma-wrestling/ historic-moments-in-wrestling-part-6-vince-mcmahon-admits -wrestling-is-predetermined-9461429.html (5/30/2014).

219 **fully four more years:** D. O'Sullivan, https://sports.vice.com/en_ us/article/the-forgotten-steroid-trial-that-almost-brought-down -vince-mcmahon (7/10/2015); http://www.huffingtonpost.com/2012/ 10/06/linda-mcmahon-lobbying-wwe-wrestling_n_1944341.html; http://www.motherjones.com/politics/2012/03/rick-santorum -wwf-pro-wresting; http://usatoday30.usatoday.com/sports/2004 -03-12-pro-wrestling_x.htm.

219 **process of leaving the WWF:** This incident has since been dubbed the Curtain Call. See N. Paglino, "The Kliq Members Scott Hall, Kevin Nash, Sean Waltman and HBK Discuss the MSG Curtain Call Incident," *WrestleZone*, http://www.wrestlezone.com/news/ 470069-the-kliq-talks-curtain-call-incident (4/17/2014); http:// bleacherreport.com/articles/986789-wwe-a-look-back-at-the -infamous-curtain-call-the-msg-incident (12/17/2011). The video is available to view at http://www.dailymotion.com/video/x6v3as_ the-kliq-curtain-call-incident_music.

Chapter 8: When Fandom Goes Wrong

222 **heavily-debated US–Korea Free Trade Agreement:** US–Korea Free Trade Agreement (3/15/2012).

223 **"American's Native Spirit":** R. Mitenbuler, "How Bourbon Became

'America's Native Spirit,'" *Slate*, http://www.slate.com/articles/life/drink/2015/05/bourbon_empire_lewis_rosenstiel_and_how_bourbon_became_america_s_native.html (5/12/2015); S. Res 294, "Designating September 2007 as "National Bourbon Heritage Month," https://www.govtrack.us/congress/bills/110/sres294/text (8/2/2007).

223   **millions of dollars lobbying:** H. Abdullah, "Bourbon distillers focus on South Korea free trade debate," http://www.mcclatchydc.com/news/nation-world/national/economy/article24699760.html (9/26/2011).

223   **carried a 20 percent tax:** Ibid.

223   **rise in the fortunes:** A. Rappeport, "Exports of US spirits reach record high," *Financial Times*, http://www.ft.com/cms/s/0/58c55c8c-4b93-11e1-b980-00144feabdco.html#axzz3iiox1lwx (1/31/2012).

223   **Hong Kong:** C. Lanyon, *48 Hours* magazine, http://www.scmp.com/magazines/48hrs/article/1541763/its-boom-time-bourbon (7/3/2014).

223   **"super-expensive Kentucky bourbon":** J. Bachman, "Bourbon Sells, and Pricey Bourbon Sells Even Better," http://www.bloomberg.com/bw/articles/2013-11-26/bourbon-sells-and-pricey-bourbon-sells-even-better (11/26/2013).

224   **Brand lore:** G. Kleinman, "The Story of Maker's Mark Whiskey," http://www.drinkspirits.com/bourbon/story-makers-mark-whiskey/ (3/15/2012).

224   **more than half a decade:** Z. M. Seward, "Maker's Mark answers your questions about why it's watering down its bourbon," http://qz.com/52807/makers-mark-watering-down-bourbon-questions/ (2/11/2013).

224   **surprise front-page article:** Kleinman, "The Story of Maker's Mark Whiskey."

225   **reduce the alcohol content:** Z. Seward, "Maker's Mark waters down its bourbon to meet rising demand," *Quartz*, http://qz.com/52478/makers-mark-waters-down-its-bourbon-to-meet-rising-demand/ (2/9/2013).

225   **extra four years:** Seward, "Maker's Mark answers your questions about why it's watering down its bourbon."

225   **the demand for Maker's Mark:** R. Samuels, and B. Samuels, Jr., *Letter to Maker's Mark Ambassadors*, cited in Seward, "Maker's Mark waters down its bourbon to meet rising demand."

225   **"we didn't screw up your whisky":** Ibid.

225   *Quartz* **ran a short piece:** Ibid.

226   **broke upon Maker's Mark with outrage:** All quotes are from commenters on a post on Maker's Mark Facebook page, "Maker's Mark updated their cover photo," https://www.facebook.com/makers mark/photos/a.10150662954248334.413743.6355923333/1015141470 2078334/?type=3 (2/9/2013).

227   **"water it down!":** Maker's Mark, "Maker's Mark updated their cover photo."

227   **Facebook page spiraled:** Maker's Mark, https://www.facebook .com/makersmark/photos/a.10150662954248334.413743 .6355923333/10151414702078334/?type=3 (2/9/2013).

227   **twitterverse was in revolt:** M. A. Lindenberger, http://nation.time .com/2013/02/12/makers-mark-waters-down-its-whisky-and-anger -rises/ (2/12/2013).

227   **"Less Potent":** G. Bullard, "Less Potent Maker's Mark Not Going Down Smoothly in Kentucky," http://www.npr.org/sections/ thesalt/2013/02/11/171732213/less-potent-makers-mark-not-going -down-smooth-in-kentucky (2/11/2013).

227   **"they didn't hold back":** Z. M. Seward, http://qz.com/54762/makers -mark-learns-a-painful-social-media-lesson-wont-dilute-its-bourbon/ (2/17/2013).

227   **"Enjoy your bankruptcy":** Maker's Mark, "Maker's Mark updated their cover photo."

227   **Bewildered by the unexpected pushback:** Seward, "Maker's Mark answers your questions about why it's watering down its bourbon."

228   **capitulating to fan demands:** Ibid.

228   **Godwin's Law:** Godwin's Law, formulated by lawyer Mike Godwin, states "As an online discussion grows longer, the probability of a comparison involving Nazis or Hitler approaches 1," D. Amira, "Mike Godwin on Godwin's Law, Whether Nazi Comparisons Have Gotten Worse, and Being Compared to Hitler by His Daughter,"

New York, http://nymag.com/daily/intelligencer/2013/03/godwins
-law-mike-godwin-hitler-nazi-comparisons.html (3/8/2013).

229 **Jack Daniel's lowered the proof:** A. Press, "Drinkers object to Jack
Daniel's watering whiskey down," http://usatoday30.usatoday.com/
money/industries/food/2004-09-29-jack-daniels_x.htm (9/29/2004).

229 **sales were higher than ever:** J. B. Arndorfer, "Weaker Jack Daniel's Becomes Spirits Strongman," http://adage.com/article/news/
weaker-jack-daniel-s-spirits-strongman/103213/ (5/16/2005).

230 **already been significantly watered down:** J. Wilson, https://www
.washingtonpost.com/lifestyle/food/makers-mark-debacle-the
-proof-is-in-the-overreaction/2013/02/25/0aba8564-7c32-11e2-9a75
-dab0201670da_story.html (2/26/2013).

230 **"customer is always right wing":** S. Brown, "Harry Potter and the
Fandom Menace," in Bernard Cova, Robert Kozinets, and Avi Shankar, *Consumer Tribes* (New York: Routledge, 2007), 177–92.

231 **"under-reacted to social media":** J. Rosen, https://twitter.com/
jayrosen_nyu/status/303222018281721856 (2/17/2013).

231 **highest grossing quarter ever:** Z. M. Seward, http://qz.com/80855/
fear-of-watered-down-bourbon-gave-makers-mark-its-best-quarter
-ever/ (5/2/2013).

231 **scrambled to buy out:** C. Subramanian, http://business.time.
com/2013/05/03/proof-positive-makers-mark-blunder-results-in
-surprise-profit/ (5/3/2013); A. Dan, http://www.forbes.com/sites/
avidan/2013/05/06/makers-marks-plain-dumb-move-proved-to
-be-pure-marketing-genius/#1fa6dc8f1e61 (5/6/2013).

232 **the Majority Illusion:** K. Lerman, X. Yan, and X.-Z. Wu, "The
Majority Illusion in Social Networks," http://arxiv.org/pdf/1506
.03022v1.pdf (2015); Emerging Technology from the arXiv, *MIT Technology Review*, https://www.technologyreview.com/s/538866/the
-social-network-illusion-that-tricks-your-mind/ (6/30/2015); Lerman, Yan, and Wu, The "Majority Illusion in Social Networks,"
PLoS ONE, 11(2), 1–13 (2/17/2016).

232 **"majority active neighbors":** Emerging Technology from the arXiv,
MIT Technology Review.

233   **writing in the *MIT Sloan Management Review:*** W. W. Moe, D. A. Schweidel, and M. Trusov, "What Influences Customers' Online Comments," *MIT Sloan Management Review* (Fall 2011): 14–16.

233   **"skew their ratings":** Ibid.

234   **"give them what they need":** T. Robinson, *Interview: Joss Whedon,* http://www.avclub.com/article/joss-whedon-13730 (9/5/2001).

235   **required traits for Peter Parker:** S. Biddle, "Spider-Man Can't Be Gay or Black," *Gawker,* http://gawker.com/spider-man-cant-be-gay -or-black-1712401879 (6/19/2015).

236   **"boring at parties":** K. Opam, "Spider-Man is contractually obligated to be boring at parties," http://www.theverge.com/2015/6/ 19/8813099/spider-man-movies-sony-marvel-boring (6/19/2015).

236   **straight white male characters:** M. Stern, http://www.thedailybeast .com/articles/2014/08/07/fear-of-a-minority-superhero-marvel-s -obsession-with-white-guys-saving-the-world.html (8/7/2014).

236   **"Black dude dies first":** TvTropes is a great resource for these types of plot devices. See http://tvtropes.org/pmwiki/pmwiki.php/ Main/BlackDudeDiesFirst (accessed 9/23/2016).

236   **fridging:** http://tvtropes.org/pmwiki/pmwiki.php/Main/Stuffed IntoTheFridge (accessed 9/23/2016).

236   **"*ten* movies headlined by blond white men":** A. Wheeler, "Why Marvel Studios Succeeds (And How It Will Fail If It Doesn't Diversify)," http://comicsalliance.com/marvel-studios-success-marvel -movies-diversity/ (8/6/2014).

237   **90 percent of American adolescents:** S. Vanderbilt, "The Comics," *Yank: The Army Weekly* (11/23/1945), https://ia601305.us.archive.org/ 28/items/1945-11-23YankMagazine/1945-11-23YankMagazine.pdf.

237   **Fredric Wertham:** For more on Wertham, see J. Sergi, "1948: The Year Comics Met Their Match," http://cbldf.org/2012/06/1948-the -year-comics-met-their-match/ (6/8/2012); and J. Heer, http://www .slate.com/articles/arts/culturebox/2008/04/the_caped_crusader .html (4/4/2008).

237   **"Hitler was a beginner":** Sergi, "1948."

237   **Comics Code Authority:** See A. K. Nyberg, *Seal of Approval: The*

History of the Comics Code (Jackson: University Press of Mississippi, 1998).

237 **terrified publishers were already defending:** Heer, http://www
.slate.com/articles/arts/culturebox/2008/04/the_caped_crusader
.html (4/4/2008).

238 **"stores were in the minority":** Telephone interview with Kelly Sue
DeConnick by Zoe Fraade-Blanar and Aaron Glazer (12/23/2014).

238 **"not drawn to things that are actively insulting":** Ibid.

238 **"Women and girls started buying manga":** Ibid.

239 **the Internet allowed women:** Telephone interview with Daniel
Amrhein by Zoe Fraade-Blanar and Aaron Glazer (2/6/2015).

239 **"The answer, in a nutshell, is NO":** S. Brown, "Harry Potter and the
Fandom Menace," in Cova, Kozinets, and Shankar, *Consumer Tribes*,
177–92.

240 **"wait, women spend money too?":** Telephone interview with Kelly
Sue DeConnick.

240 **Japanese manga market:** "Japanese Manga Book Market Rises to
Record 282 Billion Yen," Anime News Network, http://www.anime
newsnetwork.com/news/2015-01-23/japanese-manga-book-market
-rises-to-record-282-billion-yen/.83614 (1/23/2015).

240 **United States and Canada:** H. Macdonald, "ICv2 and Comichron
release 2014 sales report: comics now a $935 million business," http://
www.comicsbeat.com/icv2-and-comichron-release-2014-sales
-report-comics-now-a-935-million-business/ (7/1/2015).

240 **Miles Morales:** See, for example, E. Hayden, "The Backlash to the
Backlash of a Multiracial Spider-Man," *The Wire*, http://www.thewire
.com/entertainment/2011/08/backlash-backlash-multiracial-spider
-man/40901/ (8/5/2011).

242 **victim of her own success:** Z. Crockett, http://priceonomics.com/
how-esurance-lost-its-mascot-to-the-internet/ (12/18/2015).

242 **many of them X-rated:** J. Edwards, http://www.cbsnews.com/
news/esurance-axes-erin-after-the-secret-agent-took-on-an-x-rated
-life-of-her-own/ (6/15/2010).

242 **adopted by the working-class youth population:** C. Bothwell,

"Burberry versus The Chavs," http://news.bbc.co.uk/2/hi/business/4381140.stm (10/28/2005).

242 **"worn by the person who mugged them":** Ibid.

242 **decade to reclaim ownership:** C. Ostler, http://www.dailymail.co.uk/femail/article-2822546/As-Romeo-Beckham-stars-new-ad-Burberry-went-chic-chav-chic-again.html (11/5/2014).

243 **sent a cease-and-desist:** O. Fleming, http://www.dailymail.co.uk/femail/article-2661504/Ikea-threatens-legal-action-against-popular-fansite-allows-customers-cleverly-modify-furniture.html (6/18/2014).

243 **demanded that Yap hand over the URL:** J. Yap, "Big changes coming to IKEAHackers," http://www.ikeahackers.net/2014/06/big-changes-coming-to-ikeahackers.html (6/14/2014).

243 **"blogger who obviously is on their side":** G. Sullivan, "IKEAhackers.net in trademark flap with store it pays tribute to," https://www.washingtonpost.com/news/morning-mix/wp/2014/06/16/ikeahackers-net-is-getting-shut-down-by-the-store-it-pays-tribute-to/ (6/16/2014).

243 **without on-site advertising:** J. Mullin, http://arstechnica.com/tech-policy/2014/06/ikea-waits-8-years-then-shuts-down-ikea-hackers-site-with-trademark-claim/ (6/15/2014).

243 **fans of the site exploded:** K. Campbell-Dollaghan, "Why Ikea Shutting Down Its Most Popular Fan Site Is a Giant Mistake," http://gizmodo.com/why-ikea-shutting-down-its-most-popular-fan-site-is-a-g-1591401344 (6/16/2014).

243 **"steaming bullshit":** C. Doctorow, http://boingboing.net/2014/06/15/ikea-bullies-ikeahackers-with.html (6/15/2014).

244 **"we deeply regret":** J. Karmon, "After global outcry, IKEA softens stance against superfan (updated story)," https://www.yahoo.com/news/blogs/spaces/ikea-threatens-legal-action-against-ikea-fan-s-8-year-old-site-230646533.html?ref=gs (6/18/2014).

244 **invited to visit the company's home offices:** J. Yap, http://www.ikeahackers.net/2014/08/trademark-talks-lets-settle-this-face-to-face.html (8/2/2014).

244 **"Pop the lingonberry juice":** J. Yap, "Trip update Part 1: Museums and meatballs," http://www.ikeahackers.net/2014/09/ikeahackers -to-go-on-part-1.html (9/25/2014).

244 **"routine procedure in defense of trademarks:** R. Tepper, "World Nutella Day Saved After Ferrero Drops Cease-And-Desist Complaint," http://www.huffingtonpost.com/2013/05/21/world -nutella-day-saved_n_3314815.html (5/21/2013).

244 **Nutella's American Facebook page:** https://www.facebook.com/ nutellausa/ (accessed 9/23/2016).

244 **Sara Rosso, a Nutella superfan:** For Rosso's recounting of the creation and rise of World Nutella Day see her blog post: "World Nutella Day: From My Crazy Idea to a Worldwide Movement," https://when ihavetime.com/2016/02/05/world-nutella-day-from-my-crazy-idea -to-a-worldwide-movement/ (2/5/2016).

244 **"Why weren't they eating":** Ibid.

245 **"This is something I did as a fan":** R. Tepper, "Sara Rosso, Nutella Superfan, Gets Cease-And-Desist Letter From Ferrero Over 'World Nutella Day,'" http://www.huffingtonpost.com/2013/05/17/sara -rosso-nutella-cease-and-desist_n_3294733.html (5/17/2013).

245 **"desist buying Ferrero products?!?":** "World Nutella Day," https:// www.facebook.com/WorldNutellaDay/posts/10151663010986873? comment_id=28391408&offset=0&total_comments=121 (5/16/2013).

245 **"not the first person":** Ibid.

245 **"offering a royalty-free license":** C. Doctorow, http://boingboing .net/2014/06/15/ikea-bullies-ikeahackers-with.html (6/15/2014).

246 **make it clear:** For an interesting discussion on the legal use of trademarks, see a discussion of Clipper Darrell, a superfan of the Los Angeles Clippers who got into a battle over his nickname with the team: S. Stradley, http://www.stradleylaw.com/clipper-darrell-and -the-legal-issues-of-super-fandom/ (3/5/2012).

246 **Rosso willingly—and happily—transferred ownership:** World Nutella Day Transfer, http://www.nutelladay.com/transfer/ (1/15/2015); https://www.youtube.com/watch?v=U6SR903MTfY (1/21/2015).

247 **"If you trust your customers"**: D. Tapscott and A. D. Williams,
     Wikinomics: How Mass Collaboration Changes Everything (New
     York: Portfolio, 2010).

248 **"I never tho't I would do that!"**: Drake, Alice. *Travel Diary of Alice
     Drake* (1896–1900). Handwritten ms. at Gilmore Music Library, Yale
     University.

Afterword

249 **"how Crabby saved my life"**: Email from Squishable Customer
     (6/18/2015).

INDEX